Deeper Still and In bet

The Year of the Lord's Return Revealed

By Grover Garman

Copyright © 2016 by Grover Garman

All rights reserved.

No part of this book may be reproduced, stored in a retrieval system, or transmitted by any means, electronic, mechanical, photocopying, recording, or otherwise, without written permission from the author.

ISBN-13: 978-1539400745

ISBN-10: 1539400743

Bible Translations

Unless otherwise noted, all scripture quotations are taken from the *Holy Bible*, King James Version, Cambridge, 1769. Used by permission. All rights reserved.

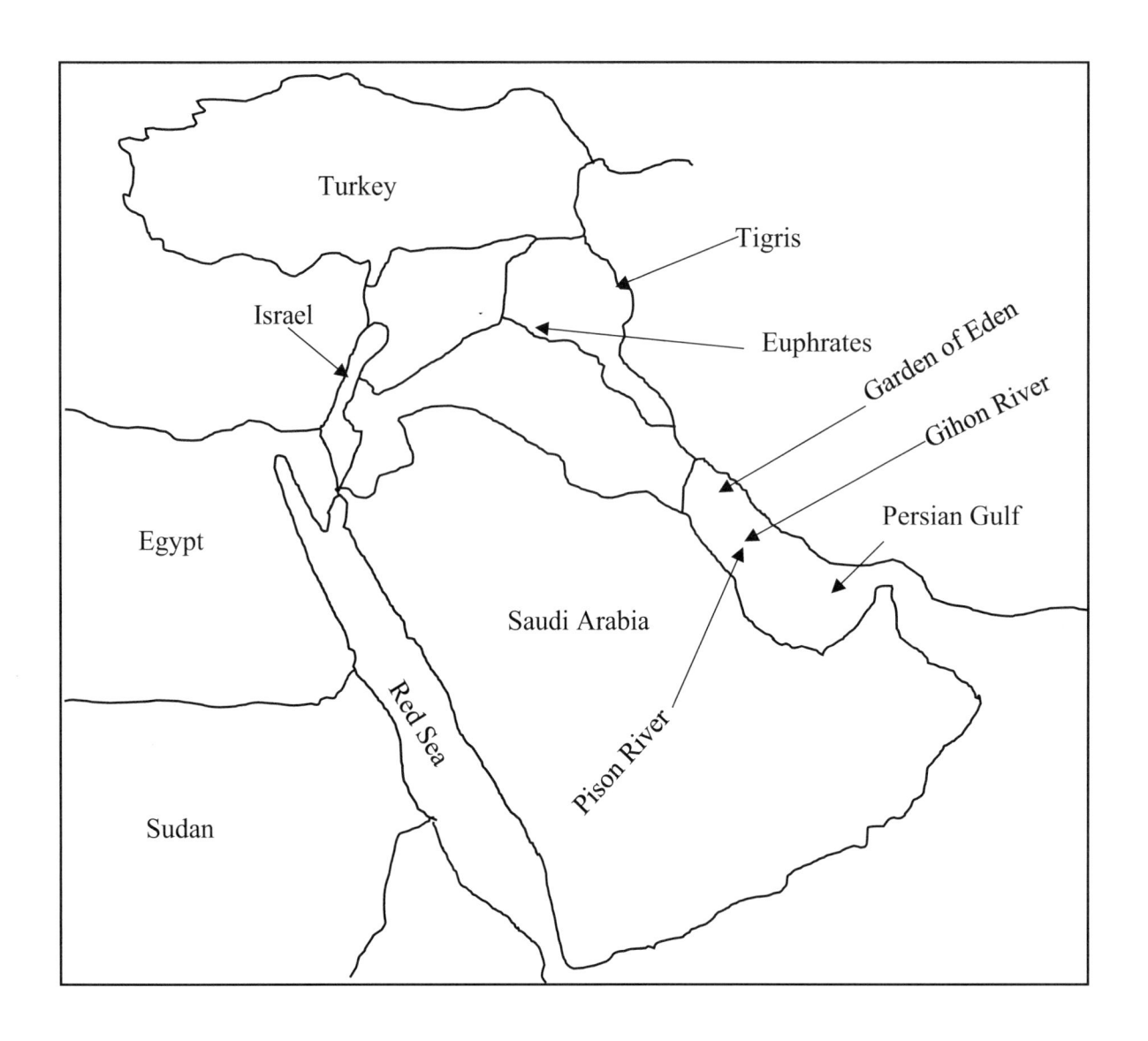

Table of Contents

Introduction	1
The Explanation	3
The Secret	11
Adam and Eve	17
The River	43
How to Catch and Hold the Truth	93
My Two Birds	107
The Threads of Similarities	129
Water Baptism	135
God Is Chapter 9	177
Speaking in Tongues	201
Many Roads to Choose	219
Riding the Rails of Truth	237
Miracles	263
The Prodigal Son's Return	275
Now You're Ready to Solve the Confusion	287
The Exact Year Jesus Returns	303
Tables and Drawings	327

Introduction

Understanding – deeper Insight into GOD'S mind – Laughter – closer relationships – and peace of mind are your rewards for reading this book from **FRONT** to **BACK.**

Why front to back, you ask? This inspired work of GOD has a positive progressive rhythm to it. Like a RIVER flows from the mountain top to the valley below, gaining depth and width; this book flows from little to no understanding to complete understanding. If you skip thru it, you may miss a piece of the puzzle in regard to a particular subject. This book simplifies many subjects deemed by the church world too complicated to understand: Such as, the relationship between GOD-father-son-holy ghost. You will see undiscovered thoughts of GOD that will cause one to say: Wow! "This is so simple, why didn't I see it?"

The greatest secret; **the year Jesus returns**, is also revealed in this book. Remember, Jesus said, "**no man knows the hour or day**" MATTHEW 24:36: But he said nothing in regard to the **Year**.

Daniel gave Israel the exact year Jesus would make his first appearance; this being 453 years from the day they started to rebuild the temple in Jerusalem. This 453 is the result of separating 30 years and 7 years from the 490 years given in Daniel. The 30 years was the age a priest had to be before he began his ministry, and the 7 was the length Christ ministry should have been. However, according to the scriptures, it had to be cut to 3 ½ years. The KEY to finding that special time, when the messiah would first appear, was knowing the exact year Israel was given the "okay" by their captors to rebuild.

The "KEY" to finding that special year when Jesus makes his second appearance on earth, is knowing the year Israel was recognized by GOD as becoming a nation: And it wasn't 1948.

God cannot lie; which is the reason he stopped at, *"no man knows the **hour** or the **day***. HE didn't say year, that would have been a lie: Because it is there, hidden within the scriptures.

The **WISE** men in MATTHEW knew when and where to find the Messiah. REV. 13:18a said: *Here is **wisdom**, let him that hath understanding count the number*. Or in other words, take into consideration the NUMBER.

Could GOD have given those men in MATTHEW the title, WISE Men, because they were experience in the "**HANDLING**" of numbers? I wonder if it helped in finding the star that led them to the "first coming" of the Messiah?

The Explanation

What is DEEPER STILL and IN BETWEEN THE LINES? Well, it is a journey, an expedition between two points of interest. The first point is (A) humanity's thoughts, and the second point is (B) God's thoughts. The reason for putting humanity's thoughts first is this: When we came into this world, we began to grow and develop our own way of thinking due to our surroundings, the teaching of others, or by everyday occurrences. We are not interested in GOD'S thoughts or his character. This is why we put GOD'S thoughts as point (B). Unless GOD somehow excites our mind into looking up and investigating his way of thinking, we would never take an interest in him, especially someone we could not see or hear. The Bible says in Romans, *I revealed myself to those who did not ask for me.* Rom. 10:20b (NIV), and in John, *No one can come to me unless the Father who sent me draws them...* John 6:44a (NIV). Spiritually speaking, the pressures of everyday life forces us to look in all directions for help. While searching for assistance, GOD catches our attention through created objects, which includes people. Now, we're going to give you a brief explanation on the two parts of the title of this book.

DEEPER STILL is a hunger, a thirst, a craving to know everything about GOD, to understand his emotions, individual identity, and his very heartbeat. It is also about realizing there is no limit to the unasked questions inspired by reading GOD'S Holy Word, the Bible. For though these words were written by men, and later translated and passed down through time by other men, they were chosen and preserved by GOD. Hidden within that **treasure-filled** book is a directory on how to find and have a close, very close, active relationship with GOD. So close in fact, he calls us his children. Now for GOD to place you in that group, his children, you will have to receive God's own nature at some point in your life. Then, once you receive his nature, you will spend the rest of your life searching and finding out the likes and dislikes of GOD. This book is dedicated to going deeper into the mind of GOD.

With this book comes some guarantees. You "will see" new thoughts never exposed before, and you "will be" given a "deeper understanding" on subjects that you thought you already knew. DEEPER STILL is about inspiring you to dive into the Word in search of those thoughts considered insignificant to pursue, or just simply overlooked. The Bible throws a question our way in the first half of Zechariah. *¹⁰For who hath despised the day of small things? for they shall rejoice, and shall see the plummet (plumb line) in the hand of Zerubbabel...*Zechariah 4:10a. "Small things," in this passage means insignificant things.

DEEPER STILL asks, "What builds a strong relationship between two people, a few big things, or a thousand little things?" My answer up until a few years ago was, "LORD, I want a deeper experience. I want to see limbs restored, the blind given new eyes, and diseases removed." At that time, I associated the performance of a few big miracles to having a closer relationship with him. However, in 2005 GOD changed my mind through a question. HE asked, "If you found yourself surrounded by professional pickpockets, which would be more difficult for them to steal from you: a single 100 dollar bill, or a single bag filled with 10,000 pennies?"

Well, after a bit, I responded with, "I believe the 'bag' is more difficult to steal." God asked, "Why?" My answer was, "The 10,000 **individual** pennies together in that bag, adds more weight to the relationship between me and my money. Therefore, it would be more difficult for a thief to **separate** me from the relationship I have with my money."

Then, I began to see GOD'S point. It is not a few big things learned about each other through "casual" contact, but strong unbreakable relationships are founded on the knowledge of hundreds, or even thousands of likes and dislikes of our partners in life. It is this multitude of little things that makes our partners who they are. As we learn them, we should put that knowledge to work each day by catering to those likes and dislikes. For example, a couple's marriage is having trouble, forcing the two farther apart. So, they go and buy BIG expensive gifts for each other. But that does not repair, nor does it build a relationship. They should start seeking to discover their partner's likes, and cater to those little discoveries. They should sit down and take the time to talk to one another.

In learning to like some of the things your partner likes, the bottom line is to try winning your partner's affection every day as you did before you got married. Hey! Rub her feet, make her breakfast, entertain her little whims, and forget about being right all the time. Also, do things together, such as, watch Football (OH YEA), or watch three hours of home repair (yuck), I mean, (oh yea)!

DEEPER STILL is all about helping us accumulate more of those little things we never heard of before. But, when crammed into a small bag such as your heart, it builds a stronger relationship between you and GOD. It is this constant gathering of <u>little things</u> that keeps this relationship strong and unbreakable because it is founded on <u>intimate</u> knowledge and understanding of HIS nature. This in turn will lead to more confidence and trust. We are going to repeat our guarantee. In this book, "you will see" more of those undiscovered thoughts.

What inspired this book was a statement from people who have been around church all their lives, who say, "<u>There's nothing preached or taught that I have not heard before.</u>" DEEPER STILL and IN BETWEEN THE LINES challenges all to go on a journey where no man has gone before, to a place of undiscovered thoughts. First, we need a confidence builder before we start, such as scriptures to confirm there are undiscovered thoughts still yet in the Bible. *[17] How precious also are thy thoughts unto me, O God! how great is the sum of them! [18] If I should count them, they are more in number than the sand: when I awake, I am still with thee.* Psalm 139:17-18.

HEY! I do not know what inspiration came into your mind after reading these two scriptures, but I can tell you what came into mine—no limit. Take a close look at how that scripture is worded, where it says, "*they are more in number than the sand...*" If it had said they would outnumber the grains by the sea, I would have been limited in my train of thought, even though sands by the sea still represents a great number. However, because it says, "thy thoughts...*are more in number than the sand...,*" I am now forced to "**broaden** my thinking" to include all areas. Thus we find ourselves arriving at this conclusion: There is **NO LIMIT** to the undiscovered thoughts of GOD hidden in the Bible, and they are just waiting for us spiritual explorers to discover them. Some will say, "How can that many thoughts be in the Bible as compared with the number of grains of sand, because the Book is not that big?" You know, I like that question because it leads us into a brief explanation of the second part of the title of this book.

IN BETWEEN THE LINES brings an understanding of the many ways and means GOD uses to bring us into a closer relationship with him. Now, let's repeat that question. "How can that many thoughts be in the Bible as compared with the number of grains of sand, because the Book is not that big?" Answer: GOD inspired the writing of the Bible. It is a collection of words, sentences, paragraphs, events, stories, and personal experiences of people. All of which, GOD uses to reveal his thoughts pertaining to this life and the life to come after death. GOD brilliantly takes different parts of the Bible and brings them together in your mind to reveal all things. One example is Water Baptism. Now, we will not go into Water Baptism at this time, because we have devoted an entire chapter to that subject. However, I will say this: In the Old Testament, there is a place where it refers to the two ways we verbally apply that experience. These being, in the name of the FATHER-SON-HOLY GHOST, and in the name of JESUS.

IN BETWEEN THE LINES is all about reminding us of the many tools and avenues GOD uses to bring understanding, direction, and strength into our lives. Here are but a few: a song, a TV program, a news article, a book, a pat on the back, a good word from somebody, a situation experienced by your or somebody you know, and the greatest tool of all, the Bible.

I was lifted out of the muck of doubt one day. It was February 8, 2006 when I awoke with this question overwhelming my soul: "GOD, do you love me—me? This was the result of things going terribly wrong in my life at that time. Fortunately, I believe in communicating with GOD, so I sat on the couch, lifted up my hands, and began singing praises to HIM. After a few songs of worship, I thanked HIM for the many times he came to my rescue. Then, finding myself "consumed" by HIS presence, I prayed, "Lord, I know the Bible says you love us all—however, I need something from you on a more personal level, like 'I love you' from another source other than the Bible."

Before I tell you how GOD answered, I want to draw your attention to the 23rd chapter of Psalm. At the end of my prayers, I sat in "quiet meditation" waiting for some response, and as always, HE did reply: *³He restoreth my soul: he leadeth me in the paths of righteousness for his name's sake. ⁵Thou preparest a table before me in the presence of mine enemies: thou anointest my head with oil; my cup runneth over.* Psalm 23: 3, 5. Still, these two verses by themselves did not solve my problem. Not that the Word had no power, but it was the fact that I refused to accept it and believe it.

Without faith, I could not conquer this issue I was wrestling with, which was, "Does GOD love me—me? Now, little did I know that the remembrance of these two verses was the first step in God's plan toward answering my prayer. HIS next step came that evening when the time to go to church drew near. As that time approached, my wife fell ill, and she chose to stay home. She told me to go on to church without her. We were in the habit of going out to eat after church service, but this Wednesday would be different. Because of my wife's illness, I decided to eat before church so I could get home immediately after service. While I pondered on where to go, there came a **sudden urge** to check out a new Thai restaurant that had just opened up. After arriving at the restaurant and being seated by the host, I noticed that someone had left a local newspaper, called the Up-Town on my table. After giving the server my order, I picked up the paper with the intention of browsing through it.

However, as I opened it up, I was **inwardly compelled** to look at the back of the paper. There, I found the astrological chart with those twelve signs representing the months of the year. I said to myself, "Even though they are a joke, just for the fun of it, I am going to look up the sign that my birthday falls under and see what it says." I was born on March 5th, which I found under the sign of Pisces. Here is what is said: "I love you, I love you, as the plant that has not bloomed yet, and carries hidden within itself the light."

Oh my—I was floored. I began to weep with delight. Then, I got tickled and began to laugh. "Why laugh?" you ask. Because at that very instant, I remembered the passage in Psalms. *5 Thou preparest a table before me in the presence of mine enemies: thou anointest my head with oil; my cup runneth over.* Psalm 23:5. Some will say that event was merely a coincidence, or that the other eleven astrological signs had "I love you" written down also. At first, that is what I thought, so I looked. I did not find a single one, "I love you" anywhere else. I did not find anything close to what Pisces had to say. WOW! Do you want to know how this affected my life? I have never doubted GOD'S love for me again, because I knew "GOD" had set the table.

Again, some will ask, "How can you be so sure it was GOD?"

Let's look at the request and the answer under a microscope. We're going to bag all the little details, or **pennies**, and see what their combined weight has to say. First, the requests: "GOD, do you love me—me," and, "I need a personal 'I love you' not from the Bible." GOD made the answer personal to me only, because there were twelve astrological signs, and I love you" was found only under the sign of my birthday. In addition, GOD gave me an "I love you" twice. Then, remember the scripture GOD put into my mind before I got to the restaurant: *"He prepared a table for me."* That local paper, the **UP-TOWN**, was on my table waiting for me.

In addition, GOD threw in an explanation why I was going through these tuff times. You can see this where the newspaper said: "You are a plant that has not bloomed yet, and carries hidden within itself the light." The Bible said, *[14] Ye are the light of the world...* Matt. 5:14a. However, to see this hidden light, my vessel had to be broken up before it could benefit anyone. This breaking up of my life would come through the natural occurrences life hits you with. The story of GIDEON in the **seventh** chapter of **Judges** is a good example of this. There GOD told Gideon, *"Take 300 men with trumpets in one hand, and empty pitchers with lit lamps inside in the other hand."* Then, GOD said, *"Take three groups of 100 men each, and surround the enemy in the valley below (on three sides)."* Then, God said, *"Blow the trumpets and **break** those pitchers."*

When the enemy heard those trumpets and saw the light burst forth, fear and pandemonium gripped their camp, causing them to fight and destroy each other. HEY! Here is another penny's worth to put into your BAG. Our enemies, **fear** and **doubt**, lay in wait in the valleys of our lives. We are the pitchers that need to be broken, and the victory—is that light. I can now help someone else. I learned how to let GOD bring me victoriously through those valleys. Now, I've got light to give. This BOOK is that **LIGHT**.

Do you see how GOD'S skillful use of tools, situations, and the Bible brought me safely through the valley? IN BETWEEN THE LINES is about helping us to understand the many avenues and tools GOD uses to bridge that gulf between point A, "**humanity** thoughts," and point B, "GOD'S thoughts."

Oh, by the way, I still do not believe in such foolishness as the Zodiac. It was just a tool used by GOD to help re-establish "my" faith in his Word. GOD knows us better than we know ourselves. If GOD thought there was a chance I would somehow end up placing my faith in such garbage, HE would have never used that newspaper to help me.

The Secret

I want to give you a sentence that GOD gave me, because it changed my life forever in regards to studying HIS Word. HE said—do not study to prove your point, but study to give HIM a chance to disprove, prove, or improve your point of interest. In other words—do not study with a predetermined answer in mind—because you will find yourself twisting scriptures in order to confirm the answer you have already chosen before you started studying that subject—in addition, you will simply disregard pertinent information pointing to an answer different from the one you started with.

I was doing this very thing and did not realize it. After much prayer and listening to GOD through quiet meditation, HE exposed something about me that I did not like. I was a borrower and not an owner. I was living off the hard labor of others, such as preachers and teachers, and stories told to me by people, and from books which took someone much time and effort to write. GOD reminded me that nobody likes people who borrow things. There was a man who borrowed from me all the time. I remember thinking, "Why will he not put in the time and labor so he can buy that item so that he could have it as his own?" However, I was doing the same thing when it involved GOD'S Word and the truths I held so dear. I rarely took time to research the subjects I heard preached or taught. Instead, I simply took their interpretations as my own. I am not saying we should disregard preaching or teaching. I am saying they should be the "catalyst," or the "inspiration" that launches you on your <u>own in-depth study into those subjects</u>.

There is a currency used to purchase spiritual understanding, and it is called TIME. Have you heard that old saying—TIME SPENT? The only way you can call a spiritual truth your own is when you "fully" understand it. This can only come from spending your own time and labor in researching that subject. You cannot fully understand any subject by simply hearing it preached or taught. It takes both hearing and study to bring understanding. *[17] So then faith cometh by hearing, and hearing by the word of God.* Romans 10:17. Notice that it did not say liberty or freedom comes by hearing. LIBERTY and FREEDOM comes from understanding. The Book of John says, *[32] And ye shall **know** the truth, and the truth shall **make** you free.* John 8:32. To know, means to understand that subject. So GOD is saying, "Your understanding of that truth is what 'leads' you to LIBERTY and FREEDOM." Once that is understood, you will be more able to let GOD apply that truth to your life.

Faith cometh by hearing, and hearing by the word of GOD, is the same as someone saying, "There is a weapon that can save you, and that weapon is the rifle." *Know the truth and the truth shall set you free,* is like someone saying, "You must now load, aim, and fire the rifle before its power can save you. Paul said, *[15] Study to shew **thyself** approved unto God, a workman that needeth not to be ashamed, rightly dividing the word of truth.* 2 Tim. 2:15. Notice again that Paul said, "…rightly dividing the Word..." Thus, we know there is a right way in studying GOD'S Word. Question: What is the right way? Answer: *[13] Howbeit when **he**, the Spirit of truth, is come, **he will guide** you into all truth: for **he** shall not speak of himself; but whatsoever **he** shall hear, that shall **he** speak: and **he** will shew you things to come.* John 16:13. GOD helps us collect all the tidbits of information, and **HE** skillfully weaves them together in our minds. From this process comes understanding.

However, some will say, "I do not care what the information said. My father, mother, preacher, and church believes it differently, and that is what I am going to believe. We are not saying these people are right or wrong. We are saying this attitude is wrong. Consider this attitude as a "wall" built by you. Since you put it there to protect yourself, you will not cross it. How will **you** expand your borders? How will you grow in **your** relationship with GOD? If Columbus had not questioned what the brilliant men of his day were saying (the sea will swallow you, and you will never return, and you will die), he would have never sailed past the wall of information and doubt surrounding him. He would have missed finding that beautiful land called the New World. Columbus went on a fact-finding search of his own to see what truth he could find.

There is a story about a scientist and an airplane. This guy's specialty was in mathematics—he was a numbers cruncher. Most of the 10,000 people at the aircraft factory did not know this man. You would probably never find his eight by eight foot office without someone's help. To a lot of people, he was an **insignificant fly on the wall**. However, there came a day when he read the crash report on one of their new planes. That plane had less than 1500 hours of flying time. In this report was a statement that caught his attention. It said, "The tail section of the plane was found several hundred feet away from the crash site." The tail section of the airplane was torn off, and separated from the rest of the airplane due to its "impact" in the rough mountainous area.

Because of reading about a similar crash and ruling which took place a month earlier in a different part of the world, our little insignificant scientist "began" to ponder this question: "I wonder if the tail section fell off in flight, thereby causing the crash? If so, this would explain the separation of the tail from the rest of the crash site." Therefore, he launched his own investigation to answer his question. He "began to accumulate" all the information possible, which in the early fifties, was not easy. He examined the metals and the stress put on those metals due to the extreme climate changes. "After crunching the numbers," on the data collected, this is what his report to the company said: "Ground that new plane, because the tail section is not adequately supported, and it will fall off. There is an untested factor aiding in the failure of the tail—vibration. It is the constant **shaking** transferred down the body of the aircraft to the tail section from the four propeller-driven engines.

Well, the company was outraged. No way were they going to accept the findings of one little insignificant numbers-crunching scientist and lose millions of dollars. Therefore, they ignored his report. However, that did not stop him. He knew what truth the "*facts*" pointed to. That plane, **under the right conditions**, would crash, and people would be lost. He went public with his findings. His report found its way into the ears of the "law makers." So, the government grounded all those new planes. They said, "We want you to shake one of those planes for 3,000 hours, and then check to see if there is any stress damage." At about 1,500 hours into the test, the tail section fell off. The little insignificant man saved lives because he had the courage to question someone's answer, and put IT to the test by his own research.

*[26] Whose voice then shook the earth: but now he hath promised, saying, Yet once more **I shake** not the earth only, but also heaven. [27] And this word, Yet once more, signifieth the removing of those things that are **shaken**, as of things that are made, that those things which **cannot** be **shaken** may remain.* Hebrews 12:26-27.

SHAKEN in this scripture means, things and opinions created by man. People are separated—they crash and burn in their relationship with GOD—because that which they believed in, failed them. For this reason, Adam and Eve failed in their relationship with GOD, which is why we are going to look at their lives in the next chapter. Be sure not to miss that chapter, because we guarantee that you will see things never seen before.

Remember—do not study to prove your point, but rather, study to give GOD a chance to disprove, prove, or improve your point. A good forensic scientist is not afraid to search for clues, because he knows they will lead to the answer. GOD wants you to never be afraid to ask a question, but be afraid not to.

If a preacher or a teacher gets mad when you call into question a subject they have taught, or if they respond like a politician, circumnavigating the question with no real answer or insight, then they probably do not have the understanding necessary to take you below the surface of that subject in question. Do not be afraid to ask. Hey! It is your life and eternal soul. You deserve an answer. GOD'S will is for you to understand without the shadow of a doubt lingering over you.

Adam and Eve

Adam and Eve's relationship with GOD crashed and burned because the tail of their spiritual airplane broke off in flight. It could not handle the **"shaking"** it received at the hands of the devil in the Garden of Eden. The tail of their spiritual airplane, the tail of truth which kept alive their relationship with GOD, was—*do not eat the fruit from the tree of knowledge of good and evil, or you will* <u>*surely die*</u>.

Adam and Eve fell because they lacked understanding of that truth. This was the result of a poor relationship with GOD. They thought the death GOD was talking about is when you stop breathing, and there is no life left in the body. This belief probably evolved from influences surrounding their everyday lives, such as animals, birds and other creatures falling to the ground and ceasing to have any life left in them. You see, they never experienced death before. They only had two ways to learn about this experience. One, we just mentioned, and the other—was to ask GOD. When Adam saw Eve eat that fruit, <u>and she did not die</u>, confusion suddenly gripped his heart. Adam thought God had lied. So, he "accepted the devil's explanation of benefits" he would receive as soon as he ate that fruit—<u>you surely will **not** die</u> and <u>you will be like GOD</u>, knowing good and evil.

Eve probably lost her faith in GOD'S Word the same way. She likely witnessed the serpent eating, or at least touching the forbidden fruit, when suddenly this thought filled her mind—he—did—not—DIE. The <u>tail of truth</u> she believed in, broke apart and fell away in her heart and mind. This caused her relationship with GOD to crash and burn. Now, you are probably thinking, "The Bible did not say the serpent ate or touched the fruit. It only said he spoke to the woman." Do you remember the old saying—One picture "speaks louder" than a thousand words? The devil is a spirit and cannot be seen with the naked eye. However, he does have a voice. We hear the devil's voice in two ways. First, through actions witness, and Second, through thoughts that enter into our minds. The source of these negative thoughts might even be from the mouths of family and friends, entering into our world by way of "their" tongues. This is like what Peter did in Matthew 16:21-23, where he rebuked Jesus for saying he must die at Jerusalem. Remember the Lord's response to Peter's rebuke *"…Get thee behind me, Satan…"* Matt. 16:23a.

In the fall of Adam, I believe we have an example of both actions witnessed, plus thoughts entering into the mind. Satan chose the serpent because he possessed all the characteristics that paralleled his own personality. The serpent was crafty, clever, cunning, and an experienced ambusher of unsuspecting prey—all of which were qualities the devil loved and admired.

Now, there is one "absolute" and indisputable" truth. Somebody or something proved to Eve, by example, the fruit was good to eat, and it would not kill her. This is confirmed in the Word of God. *⁶ And when the woman **saw** that the tree was good for food, and that it was pleasant to the eyes, and a tree to be desired to make one wise, she took of the fruit thereof, and did eat, and gave also unto her husband with her; and he did eat.* Gen. 3:6. Remember, kings of old had servants who would test their food before they ate it. That way, they **could see** if death was in that food. The devil needed the action of something seen. He provided an example to help sell Eve on his version of what would happen if she ate that fruit, which was—*you will **surely not die***. Question—who is using you as an example, God, or the devil?

We know Adam and Eve did not have a good relationship with GOD because of clues left for us in their story. The first one exposes Eve as the weakest link in the chain. It shows that her relationship with GOD was slightly less than Adam's. The devil, who is very observant, chose to **shake** Eve a little to test her resolve. He wanted to see what she believed in, and how much she understood her beliefs. Therefore, the devil beat on that truth and shook it until it broke away out of her life. There was a void left once the devil removed GOD'S Word from her heart, an empty space which he quickly filled with his distorted truth.

Let's look at that first clue. In a paraphrase of Gen. 3:1-5, we see Satan interacting with Eve. *"Did GOD say you cannot eat from every tree of the garden?* Eve responded with, *"Yes we can—we just cannot eat from the tree in the midst of the garden, <u>lest ye die</u>.* Look at verse three, where it said, *"<u>lest ye die</u>."* Eve left out one word in her response to the serpent—**<u>surely</u>**. However, we see GOD using this very word in the command to Adam. *¹⁷...in the day that thou eatest thereof thou shalt **<u>surely</u>** die.* Gen. 2:17b. Look again at a paraphrase of Gen. 3:4. *The devil said to Eve, you will not **<u>surely</u>** die.*

This tells us that even the devil knew exactly what GOD had said. By omitting the word, **surely**, and along with the fact that there is no recorded conversation between GOD and Eve, we can conclude that Eve got her information from Adam, and not GOD. Therefore, we can see that the important truth that bolstered Adam's strength, was of less importance in Eve's heart and mind. We call this experience—<u>lost in translation.</u> We all have been guilty of accepting second hand information at one time or another, rather than taking the time to get it from the original source. Gossip is another example of secondhand information changing a story, but enough said about that.

I had an embarrassing experience in high school concerning second hand information. One day my teacher said, "Get a book, any book, and in two weeks, I want an in-depth written book report." Well, I did my report on a book, but my source information came from a movie about the book, and not from the book itself. My teacher was a bookworm, a fact I did not know at that time. Now, I think my teacher had to have read every book that humankind has ever written. In addition, we did not know she planned to call upon certain students to give an oral report, and we did not know she planned to ask that student questions about the book in front of the whole class. She revealed her plan just one day before the day of reckoning, by telling us that a few souls were going to be put to the test. By the way, when I say a "few," I mean four students out of thirty-five.

The night before the big day, I thought, "What are the odds of my teacher making me give a verbal report?" "A thousand to one," I said to myself. "Even if called, I am okay, because she would have never taken the time to search and find that 'obscure' book about the Old West. She will have to rely on my interpretation of that book. She will have to get her questions from my book report. YES! I am good to go." However, this was no ordinary teacher. She knew me far too well. Man! I did not realize how closely she watched me. Somehow, she knew I would take the easy route and copy someone else's translation of a book, or that I would get my INFORMATION from a movie about the book.

There I was in class with my—tail section—comfortably seated in my chair, when all of a sudden, silence in the classroom was broken with these three words. "GROVER COME FORTH." Oh my! Fear suddenly gripped my heart. However, as I walked toward the front of the class, I was able to shake it off and regain my composure, because my faith hung on one point. She did not have the book, so she would not know what was in the book. Therefore, she could only get her questions from my written book report.

Let me tell you, I was full of confidence again. It was flowing in me like a mighty river. My thoughts were, "Ha-Ha—I am the man—I am Mister Cool—I am the one—I came, I saw, and I conquered." All of this was going on in my head as I approached the front of the class. Once I reached the front and slowly began to turn around to face my fellow students, I noticed out of the corner of my eye, that my teacher had moved to a seat in the middle front of the class. Upon completing the turn, and having the class in full view of both eyes, my attention came to rest on my teacher. In her hand lay an unfamiliar sight. It was a book.

All of the sudden, I said to myself, "Please, please, not the book I am supposed to give a report on." She was holding it upright, just under her chin. She had a smile that went from ear to ear. Those big pearly white teeth were reflecting beams of glistening light, kind of like when the full moon "reflects light" into darkness, which in my case, wound up being my soul.

Oh yes! I did say that in her hands was an unfamiliar sight. Well, I meant just that, because I had never read the book. As a matter of fact, I was not sure that book even existed. Hey! The movie said it got all its information out of a book, and that was good enough for me. However, here it was—THE BOOK—and in the hands of a very skilled and cunning teacher who now began to show forth "serpent-like" qualities.

Yep! This teacher was crafty, clever, cunning, smart, and an experienced ambusher of unsuspecting prey—ME. Suddenly, the turbulence that was already **shaking** my airplane (my life), got worse, because I heard these words leave her mouth. "I love movies about the Old West, and that was a good one." Then, the questions came that I had no answers to. The questions seemed to last an entire hour, but in real time, it was only about ten minutes. During this time, the shaking and the vibration kept increasing, until I lost—**MY TAIL**. Yep! My plane crashed that day. My faith rested on second hand information. I just could not answer the questions my teacher was shooting my way.

Eve should have gone straight to GOD from whom that command originated, and asked for more understanding in regard to the fruits of life and death which hung from that tree.

The second clue exposing Adam and Eve's poor relationship with GOD is in Genesis 3:8. *⁸And they heard the voice of the LORD God walking in the garden in the cool of the day: and Adam and his wife hid themselves from the presence of the LORD God amongst the trees of the garden.* Here, **cool** of the day is not referring to the weather, but to the relationship between them and GOD. I myself thought it had to do with the weather until GOD spoke to my heart. As soon as I read the word, "cool," GOD brought forward into my mind some scriptures. *¹⁴And unto the angel of the church of the Laodiceans write; These things saith the Amen, the faithful and true witness, the beginning of the creation of God; ¹⁵I know thy works, that thou art neither <u>COLD</u> nor <u>HOT</u>: I would thou wert cold or hot. ¹⁶So then because thou art <u>lukewarm</u>, and neither <u>cold nor hot</u>, I will spue thee out of my mouth.* Rev. 3:14-16.

I love how GOD presents one word and a few scriptures together into our minds, and causes our thought processes to go in an all new direction. GOD'S hatred of lukewarm relationships is in many scriptures throughout the Bible. Here is another penny's worth to put into your bag. **Cool,** which refers to lukewarm, is in GENESIS, chapter **three**, the first book. Lukewarm, which refers to **Cool**, is in REVELATION, chapter **three**, the last book of the Bible. WOW! GOD's hate for such relationships was the first and the last thing HE revealed to the Church. A coincidence? I do not think so. I think GOD just wanted to make it easier to remember, because of the importance HE places on having a close relationship with his children.

After the creation of Adam and Eve, the only recorded conversation between those two and GOD came after their failure. Do you remember this old saying? "If you do not have anything good to say about someone, then do not say anything at all." Think about this for a minute. The making of man was one of GOD'S greatest creative endeavors. He said in the Bible that *we are the apple of his eye.* However, there is not one good comment from GOD on the lives of Adam and Eve. The Lord only left us the story of how he created them, plus their failure in the garden. Consider another man GOD loves. The Bible, in the second book of SAMUEL, chapter eleven, tells how King David sleeps with another man's wife and gets her pregnant. Then, he sets the wife's husband up to be murdered just to cover up his indiscretion. However, what did GOD say about David?

*He is a man **"after"** my own heart.* (Paraphrase of portions of **I Samuel 13:14**). Question—what made David so special in the eyes of GOD? Answer—David <u>sought</u> GOD, not only in his failures, but also in his victories. By victories, I mean when things were going good. David did not hide himself from GOD amongst the trees as Adam and Eve did.

Amongst the trees represents where and how Adam and Eve made their living. Remember what GOD said to Adam in **GENESIS 2:16b**. *Of every tree of the garden thou mayest freely <u>eat</u>.* Those trees they could eat from represented how we go about the business of making a living. As Adam and Eve hid from GOD in their everyday labors, or **amongst their trees**, so we also hide from GOD by becoming busy in our everyday lives.

Remember the story about two sisters in the New Testament in the Book of Luke. *[38] Now it came to pass, as they went, that he entered into a certain village: and a certain woman named Martha received him into her house. [39] And she had a sister called Mary, which also sat at Jesus' feet, and heard his word. [40] But Martha was cumbered about much serving, and came to him, and said, Lord, dost thou not care that my sister hath left me to serve alone? bid her therefore that she help me. [41] And Jesus answered and said unto her, Martha, Martha, thou art careful and troubled about many things: [42] But one thing is needful: and Mary hath chosen that good part, which shall not be taken away from her.* Luke 10:38-42.

It is not a relationship when the only time you talk to someone is because you need something, or when trouble comes your way. A good relationship evolves when two parties respond to one another from the heart, <u>listening</u> to what each other has to say on a daily basis. I don't know about you, but I wonder why Adam and Eve did not ask GOD any questions, especially since all things were new. What questions do you have? Will you ask GOD for the answers?

Here is one I asked GOD concerning the fall of Adam and Eve. "Lord, would you describe the flaming sword used to drive Adam and Eve out of the Garden of Eden, which was spoken of in **Genesis 3:24**? Immediately, **Revelation 3:16** came to mind. *[16] So then because thou art lukewarm, and neither cold nor hot, I will spue thee out of my mouth.* Suddenly, the word, **"spue"** caught my attention. This word means to **spit**, and as we all know, spit consists mostly of water. We spit to clear out of our mouths that which is undesirable.

The next piece to the puzzle came from the Discovery Channel on TV. They showed secret satellite photos released in 2008 by the U.S. Government. They covered all the area around the Persian Gulf. The photos revealed two ancient riverbeds that went into the Persian Gulf out of Saudi Arabia on one side, and out of Iran from the other side. Then, I remembered Genesis where it told us of a river that flowed **OUT of the Garden** of Eden, and how it split apart and came to be four rivers. The names of these rivers are **Pison, Gihon, Hiddekel, and Euphrates.** *[10] And a river went out of Eden to water the garden; and from thence it was parted, and became into four heads. [11] The name of the first is Pison: that is it which compasseth the whole land of Havilah, where there is gold; [12] And the gold of that land is good: there is bdellium and the onyx stone. [13] And the name of the second river is Gihon: the same is it that compasseth the whole land of Ethiopia. [14] And the name of the third river is Hiddekel: that is it which goeth toward the east of Assyria. And the fourth river is Euphrates.* Gen. 2:10-14.

Throughout history, bible scholars and historians have long sought to identify the location of the Pison and Gihon? However, they were unable to because they simply disappeared. We know the Euphrates and the Hiddekel, now called the Tigris, flow from the mountains down through present day Iraq. These two rivers join together to form one mighty river that empties into the Persian Gulf. I wondered—could these recently discovered dried-up rivers be the Pison and Gihon, because that is exactly where the

Bible said they should be? This means, the Garden of Eden would have been in the area that is now covered by the Persian Gulf. As I was pondering this new information on the Gulf area, I happened onto the History channel. Guess what subject they were discussing? You got it, the Persian Gulf. The program revealed that most Geologists believe the Persian Gulf was at one time, a rich fertile valley, and it was void of the salt-water sea that now covers it. The Geologists said, "Thousands of years ago, this lush valley suddenly filled with water due to the rise of the earth's temperature which melted the glaciers and some of the polar ice caps.

Then, while looking at a large picture of the Persian Gulf, I notice that it looked a lot like a sword. It had the shape of a sickle sword I had seen while studying battles of ancient times. Now I got excited, and said to myself, "Could it be that simple? Could it be that the water of the Persian Gulf is the sword used by the angel of GOD to force Adam and Eve out of that Garden?" Now before I could come to accept this new discovery, I first had to answer two more questions related to the two clues recorded in reference to the description of this sword.

24 So he drove out the man; and he placed at the east of the garden of Eden Cherubims, and a flaming sword which turned every way, to keep the way of the tree of life. Gen. 3:24.

I had to answer these two questions. What was the flame of the sword? And what did it mean when it said "I*t turned in every way,"* (or in other words), in every direction? Well, I am an out-door person who loves to camp, fish, lay on the beach and sit around the fire. One day while I looked out across the choppy water, GOD began to pull my mind in an unusual direction. HE said, "The **flaming** sword that **turned** in every direction is represented by the waters of the Persian Gulf in two ways. First, both the flame of a fire and the salt in the water has the power to consume and destroy an object.

Second, both the flame and the waves display the same motion. The flickering flame of a fire and the waves of the Persian Gulf move in every direction."

So then, the actual sword that forced man out of the Garden of Eden was the **waters** of the Persian Gulf. WOW! Water drove the natural man out of the Garden. And as we would find out later, GOD would use Water baptism to bring man back to him—GOD being that spiritual Garden.

Water represents the Word throughout the Bible. Disobedience to GOD'S Word, this spiritual water, forced Adam and Eve out of the Garden—out of a relationship with GOD. Through the obedience to the Word, this spiritual water, mankind can again enter the Garden. We can renew that relationship. GOD used nature's geographic formations to help confirm historical and spiritual events. For instance, GOD stenciled a huge picture pictorial on the face of earth in reference to the fall of man.

Get a map that has these three geological formations: the Red Sea, Saudi Arabian Peninsula, and the Persian Gulf. The Red Sea represented the devil. Notice how it looks like a serpent with its mouth open, ready to devour Israel, who also represented all of GOD'S people. The Bible constantly reminds us that the devil wants to devour GOD'S people. The Saudi Arabian Peninsula looks like a boot. This signifies that someone or something, forced Adam and Eve out of the garden. They would have stayed, had they been given the choice. In short, they got the boot. The sword that drove man out of the Garden was the waters of the Persian Gulf. Disobedience to the Word of GOD drove mankind out of the garden. GOD gave boundaries to the Persian Gulf waters, forming it into the shape of a sword. I know there are people that will not accept this. Mainly because it is just too simple, or too obvious. Think about this: if you were an anthropologist, and you saw these pictures inscribed on the wall of an ancient cave, you would probably arrive at the same basic interpretation. A serpent chased, or helped in booting out somebody from that area around the Persian Gulf. We have to remember, GOD'S wall is any part of HIS creation. HE sometimes does things so big and obvious that we simply overlook them.

*²⁰ For the <u>invisible</u> things of him from the creation of the world are clearly seen, being **understood** by the <u>things that are made</u>, even his eternal power and Godhead; so that they are without excuse:* Rom. 1:20.

All things created have a voice. All natural things created have the power to confirm GOD'S existence, praise his glory, and speak of his wisdom. Again, <u>one-picture speaks louder than a thousand words</u>. The Bible said Jesus entered Jerusalem riding a colt of a donkey. It also said the Pharisees attempted to stop people from worshipping him. Read what Jesus had to say to those Pharisees.

*⁴⁰ And he answered and said unto them, I tell you that, if these should hold their peace, the **stones** would immediately cry out.* Luke 19:40.

This is exactly what the Red Sea, Saudi Arabia Peninsula, and the Persian Gulf are doing. They are crying out that the devil helped in getting man booted out, and the waters of the Persian Gulf kept mankind out of that PERFECT land.

I think most people want a closer relationship with GOD. However, most feel that they can never understand GOD because of his greatness and complexity. But that is not true, we can understand the mind of GOD. All we have to do is <u>track</u> each new thought from its very inception. With total trust in GOD'S help, track that new thought from GENESIS through REVELATION, and I guarantee that you will understand.

For instance, look again at that big giant sword. GOD is using the Persian Gulf to establish the Sword as a TOOL with the POWER to bring change in mankind's life style. Hey! Take the "S" from SWORD and what have you got? – WORD! Throughout the BIBLE you will discover GOD comparing the natural sword to a spiritual sword. *¹⁷ And take the helmet of salvation, and the sword of the Spirit, which is the word of God:* Eph. 6:17. GOD wants us to understand what makes a natural sword and how to use it, so we can better understand what makes a spiritual sword and how to use it.

I first became interested in the sword after I had read a passage in Luke. *³⁸ And they said, Lord, behold, here are **two** swords. And he said unto them, It is enough.* Luke 22:38. This launched me into a study of both the natural and spiritual swords. Three parts make a natural sword, the handle, blade, and the cutting edge. Three parts make a spiritual sword: **FAITH** is the handle—the **BLADE** is GOD'S Word—and the **CUTTING EDGE of the sword** is the understanding of GOD'S Word.

Any natural or spiritual sword that is missing any one of those three parts will not serve you well in battle. For instance, if you were facing an adversary in battle, and all you had was the handle with no blade, you would lose the fight. If in a spiritual battle with the devil, and all you had was faith, with no Word to cling to—no set of directions to follow—no spiritual blade—you would eventually lose the battle.

Consider yourself in another fierce battle. However, you are holding that razor sharp blade in your bare hands, because the sword has no handle to hold on to. You will get a few good blows in, and you might even cut and damage your opponent. However, every time you would strike and cut your adversary, you would also cut your own hands due to the pressure "your bare hands" were applying to that razor-sharp cutting edge. Eventually, you would drop the blade because it would be cutting you worse than you were cutting your adversary. Then, having nothing with which to defend yourself, you will lose the battle.

Likewise, if while battling the devil, you might be able to recite the Word of GOD from memory. But, if you have no **faith**—no "handle" with which to hold the blade, you would have no way to grip the promises revealed from within the Word. You will lose that fight with the devil because you do not have the faith necessary to hold onto the promise of victory to come. The Word would fall away out of your life as it did in Adam's life.

Let's look at one more battle. This one has occurred without the use of the third part of the sword, the **sharp cutting edge** of the blade, which spiritually speaking, is the understanding of GOD'S Word. Look at our adversary for a moment. He has a helmet, good armor, and he is very skilled in the use of his weapons. On top of that, he cheats. He is one tuff dude.

Okay—here we go—the fight is on—me with my club and my opponent with his weapons. Oh! Wait a minute, did I say, "CLUB?" Wow! I did not take the time to put a razor sharp EDGE on the blade of my sword. Without that cutting edge, it is just a *shiny* CLUB. Well, let's get on with the fight. I swung my club and hit him—down he went, "The fight is over," I thought to myself. "Hey, I won." I walked away as my adversary was crumpled up on the ground. Suddenly I heard a noise behind me. I turned just in time to see my enemy coming at me swinging his weapon. Again I knocked him to the ground with my club. However, he just kept getting up and attacking me. This went on all day and through the night. Finally, I just ran out of strength. I couldn't raise my club to defend myself any longer, so I surrendered.

Spiritually specking, this is exactly what happens to many Christians. They never seem to "understand" what it takes to get the victory. They keep fighting the same problem over and over until they just wear down and give up. They can never deliver a killing blow that would silence their persistent adversary for good.

What if you had to share living quarters with a super-natural snake for your entire natural born life? However, you would never be able to end that serpent's life. How can you stop the serpent from biting you and injecting its poison into you? The only safe way to protect yourself is to cut his head off with a sword, like David did to the giant named Goliath.

Since we are on the subject of King David. Let us "go back" and quickly review that story, which is found in the 17th chapter of 1st **SAMUEL**. Here, we find the army of Israel facing off against the army of the Philistines, with Goliath in between the two armies challenging Israel's champion to come out and fight. However, the Israelites were afraid to fight because of the size of Goliath. Young David happened to come into the Israelite's camp about the time Goliath was again issuing his "daily verbal" challenge. David heard Goliath, but he didn't see any of the Israelite soldiers step forward to fight.

He said to Saul who was King of Israel, "I will fight this giant." Saul basically said to David, "You are a kid with no fighting experience, and Goliath is a professional killer." David said to Saul, "I was watching over my father's flock of sheep, and a bear and a lion took one of the lambs. I went and caught them by their beards and slew them. The Lord that delivered me out of the paws, or the grip of the bear and lion, will deliver me out of the hands of this Philistine." Saul said, "Go for it kid, and take my armor and sword." David response was, "These are not mine, and I have not proved them in battle, I have no **confidence** or **skill** in handling the sword.

David went off to fight Goliath with the weapons he had proved in battle—his staff, five smooth stones, and his sling. We all know how David slung the stone and hit the giant. Then, David cut off his head with the giant's sword.

However, we are going to look at this story through spiritual eyes to help us understand what it has to teach us. But, I first want to remind you that GOD, in order to reveal other spiritual truths or applications, will use the very same words in this Bible story. We will only look at one spiritual application—the sword.

Look at King Saul and his spiritual sword. Saul's knowledge of GOD'S Word represented the **blade.** Saul also understood the Word. He knew GOD gave him the authority to defeat all enemies of Israel. This understanding of GOD'S Word represented the **sharp cutting edge** of the spiritual sword. Let me remind you that Saul only had two parts of the spiritual sword. His "knowledge" of GOD'S word is the blade, and his "understanding" of that Word is the sharp cutting edge. However, Saul did not have FAITH, the third part of the sword. Saul had no spiritual "handle" to hold the sword with. Therefore, he was ready to turn loose of his sword and give it to David. Saul wanted David to fight his battle. Saul could not fight, because he had "no" faith—no handle to hold onto the promise of victory to come. Without faith, knowledge and understanding of the Word does you no good. Actually, it could lead you further away from GOD. Saul eventually lost his relationship with GOD. He did not have all three parts of the sword—Faith—knowledge—and—understanding. Let's look at David's confrontation with Goliath. Consider the three problems young David first encountered in his Christian walk—the bear, the lion, and Goliath.

Deliverance from the bear and the lion represented a physical miracle. Goliath represented a spiritual enemy. He could talk to you and get into you head. Plus, he was skilled in the use of the sword. This is symbolic of the devil's skill in using GOD'S Word to deceive us, like he did when he deceived and confused Adam and Eve.

We assume that David had no fears or doubts, but that simply is not true. The Bible said he put five stones in his bag. However, he only used one to take down the giant. David's bag represents our hearts, the place where we collect and hold our questions, doubts, fears, and all we have learned in life. Two stones in David's bag represent the Euphrates and the Hiddekel, now known as the Tigris River. The Euphrates represented creation, and the Tigris, the interaction between all creation. Doubt, confusion, fear, and defeat are by-products of this natural river system. We are shaped into the person we become due to the interaction we experience in our daily lives.

Two other stones in his bag represented the Gihon and Pison, two spiritual rivers from which comes understanding, power, and victory. Gihon represented GOD'S Word, and the Pison, HIS spirit. We will reveal and explain these four rivers in the next chapter.

The fifth stone used to kill the giant is Jesus, who represented spiritual victory. Jesus Christ is the product of the Word and spirit of GOD. These two spiritual rivers bring victory to all who have them flowing in their heart. David had confusion and doubts to deal with like the rest of us, which is confirmed by his rejection of the sword as the weapon of choice. In David's story, we want to read BETWEEN THE LINES to establish comparisons between then and now, so we can better understand how his battle can be applied to our lives.

First, consider King Saul as representing the ministry in our day—he is the preacher. Second, consider the sword that Saul tried to give David as representing the written Word of GOD, the solution to the problem at hand. Third, are those four unused stones in David's bag: two stones are natural rivers that represent GOD'S creation and the interaction between that creation. The product of these natural rivers is confusion, fear, doubt, and defeat. The other two stones in his bag are spiritual rivers. Gihon is the Word, and Pison is GOD'S spirit who actively brings the Word to pass. All four stones represent four rivers, the Euphrates, Tigris, Gihon, and Pison.

Again, these will be explained in the next chapter.

The fifth stone which gave David the victory is Jesus Christ. This stone "FLOWED" from amid those other four stones. The life of Jesus Christ flowed from both the natural and spiritual rivers. Out of the chaos of everyday life, flows the "**inherited**" over-coming power of GOD in all those who carry the two spiritual stones in their bags (their hearts).

If you do not know what you have **"inherited,"** then how can you put it to use? Is that not the story of the poor old beggar? He failed to go to the reading of his rich father's will and remained poor, because he did not know what he had inherited? **Imagination** is the ability to form images and ideas in the mind, especially those things never seen or experienced directly. *[15] Verily I say unto you, Whosoever shall not receive the kingdom of God as a little child, he shall not enter therein.* Mark 10:15.

Now then, the definition of **Meditation** is the emptying of the mind of thoughts, or the concentration of the mind on one thing in order to aid mental or spiritual development. From here on out, we want you to use both the childlike quality of "imagination," and the adult quality of "meditation." Because as busy adults trying to make a living in this world, we sometimes lose the ability to use our imagination. For instance, as an adult, I look into the sky and I see a cloud. If someone were to ask, "Hey, what are you looking at?" I would respond, "I am looking at a cloud." However, childlike imagination would have said, "I see a whale, an elephant, a lion, or a spaceship." We need to find the time and the place where our minds are at peace, ready to receive from GOD, rather than what the "natural eye" sees.

For example, in first KINGS the eightieth chapter, there is the story of Elijah praying for rain on Mount Carmel. It was to bring an end to the drought that plagued Israel. During prayer, Elijah sent his servant seven times to the top of the mountain to look out toward the sea. After viewing a cloudless sky on his six previous attempts, the servant had this to say to Elijah at the end of his seventh trip. "Master, I see a **cloud the size of a man's hand.**" Because of this report, Elijah knew GOD was involved, and that HE was going to bring rain to the area in answer to his prayer.

Let's look a little deeper into this story of Elijah praying for rain. It is a good example of how GOD can use our imagination through prayer and meditation. Elijah's "natural eye" did not see the cloud. Elijah saw the cloud through his servant's eyes. Our brain is our servant. GOD shows this servant many things during prayer and meditation as our **imagination** ponders over the stories in the bible. Question: Why did Elijah have his servant repeatedly look to the Sea to find the solution? Answer: It is GOD'S way of telling us, "Keep your mind, (your servant), in the Word (the Sea), for your answer "will come" through persistent effort.

Okay, let's put those powers of meditation and imagination to use, and go through this battle. David suddenly realizes that he has a Goliath of a problem in his life. He goes to church where he hears preacher Saul, who, under the inspiration of GOD, places the Sword in David's hands. This sword, being the Word of GOD, the "solution" to the Goliath of a problem confronting David's heart and mind. However, he cannot use this sword because he does not have the experience in handling such a weapon. He does not **understand** how he will be able to apply this Word, this Sword to the problem. David has faith because he remembers how GOD delivered him from the bear and lion, so he carries this praise and worshipping attitude down into the valley, (or home in our case).

He is going to face this Goliath of a problem with the help of GOD. But first, he has to have the complete sword in his hand. Spiritually, David carried in his heart and mind two parts of the sword as he went to face Goliath. He had faith, which is the handle, and the Word, which is the blade, the solution to the problem at hand. But he did not have the third part, the sharp cutting edge, which is the understanding of how to apply the Word, this being confirmed by the rejection of Saul's sword.

David studies the problem that is standing before him. He sees the shield, armor, helmet, spear, and the sword Goliath has brought to the fight. At some point in time, in between the studying and meditating, GOD began to show David how that Sword will be applied to silence Goliath forever. This, we see in 1ˢᵗ Samuel 17:45-46. Where David said to Goliath, "*You come to me with your weapons, I come to you in the name of the Lord. He will* deliver you into my hands, *and I* ***will take your head off.***

David began to realize, faith alone could not silence that Goliath of a problem from specking into his life. David now knew that he had to **cut the head** of the problem off. However, David had rejected the power of the Sword due to his inexperience. After worship, prayer, and meditation, David suddenly realized that doubt and fear was no longer an issue. They were gone, however, the feeling of no direction and no understanding were still with him. With the **absence** of doubt and fear, he drew close to Goliath, closer to victory. David loaded his sling during meditation, (he filled his mind with the Word), and whirled the sling that held that stone, around his head. Spiritually speaking, the Word was rolling around in his head. David is waiting on GOD to give the direction on the way to proceed. "Let the stone go," whispered GOD, "And I will guide it to the target." After the stone buried itself in the head of Goliath, David ran and picked up Goliath's Sword. He then brought the Sword down hard across the neck of Goliath, severing the head from the body.

When David held that head up high for all the public to see, the enemy fled. GOD'S people, who were facing the same Goliath of a problem, were inspired to get back into the fight. Now, David fully understood how to apply that Word, the "Sword" that preacher Saul had tried to give him.

David never faced Goliath again. However, **1st CHRONICLES, Chapter Twenty,** tells us that some of King David's men did face and defeat giants that were of the same family Goliath came from. His men had to eventually face and defeat their own Goliaths.

When I first came to GOD, my situation was similar to David's start with the Lord. I had three addictive problems to deal with which RULED my LIFE: alcohol, smoking, and cussing. I could not say two words in a row without using profanity. The addiction to alcohol and cigarettes immediately left me while being in the presence of GOD for approximately thirty minutes. According to the medical field, that is impossible. However, the cussing remained with me for several weeks until I heard the teaching of an old minister. He said, "Many Christians cannot get rid of a problem simply because they keep worrying about that problem. They keep that problem in their minds and heart due to their worry." Therefore, I went to the old preacher and asked him for help.

Here is what he said to me. "**You cannot receive** if you **do not believe.**" Then he gave me two scriptures, like a doctor gives a patient medication, and told me to take them and go home and worship and praise GOD for delivering me out of the "grip" of the bear, which was alcohol, and the "grip" of the lion, which was cigarettes. Then, he said, "Once you feel the presence of GOD, begin to pray and ask GOD for understanding on how to defeat this Goliath of a cussing problem. Then sit quietly in meditation and wait for GOD'S response."

The two scriptures the old preacher gave me were from Matthew and Mark. *[7] Ask, and it shall be given you; seek, and ye shall find; knock, and it shall be opened unto you:* **Matt. 7:7**, and *[11] But when* **they** *shall* **lead** *you, and* <u>deliver you up</u>, **take no thought** <u>beforehand what ye shall</u> **speak**, <u>neither do ye</u> **premeditate**: *but whatsoever shall be given you in that hour, that speak ye: <u>for it is not ye that speak</u>, but the <u>Holy Ghost</u>.* **Mark 13:11**.

Well, after I brought my cussing problem to GOD through prayer, I sat in quiet meditation waiting on GOD to answer. It did not take long for HIM to <u>**"whisper"**</u> these words in my mind. "<u>TRUST in ME</u>", <u>I will bring new words into your heart and mind that you will speak</u> **"when they lead"** <u>you</u> into times of <u>great stress.</u> WOW! All of a sudden, I understood that I had been fighting this battle alone. What I should have done was let GOD do the fighting for me. I am not going to worry about what words will come out of my mouth. I am going to trust in GOD'S ability to bring fourth the proper words when the world leads me into those over-whelming situations. Did not GOD create the mind and mouth of man to begin with? Hey! Check this out—I now had in my hand the complete **S-Word** of the LORD. <u>Faith</u> the (handle), <u>GOD'S Word</u> (the blade), and the <u>understanding of the Word</u> (the sharp cutting edge of the blade).

The proof came the next day at the turkey packing plant where I worked. I was the one who had the most difficult job on that packaging line. I ran a ten-foot, and very old packing machine. It folded and glued the top flaps of the boxes, each holding four very big turkeys. In front of me on the line were six people. Their job was to fill each box with four turkeys, and then *"shove"* those boxes my way. At the start of the day, I did not know the world would <u>lead me into</u> and <u>deliver me up</u> to a <u>terrible situation</u>. My test came when **one,** who was a **troublemaker** to begin with, said, "Let's see if we can send those boxes down the line faster than the operator can put them through the packing machine." Well, needless to say, it was not long before those turkeys overwhelmed the packaging machine and me. I had turkeys flying everywhere, because of a big boot that came down and folded the last flap of the lid. This boot also had enough power to move those heavy boxes through the machine. You see, when the first box got wedged in the machine, that caused the other boxes to bunch up where that big boot came down. Instead of the boot coming down on the top of the boxes, it was coming through those boxes, getting under those turkeys and lifting them into the air.

If we had shotguns that day, we would have bagged a bunch because there were turkeys flying everywhere. In addition, glue was squirting out, people were hollering, and the boss was screaming. On top of that, the emergency kill switch that was supposed to shut the machine off did not work. What does Murphy's Law tell us? What can go wrong will go wrong. Well, it did on that day.

Now to my favorite part, which was when the grace and the miracle of GOD exposed itself. The volcano was about to erupt, OH YEA. I wanted to scream out—and I did. "PRAISE THE LORD-PRAISE THE LORD-PRAISE THE LORD." I couldn't say anything else. All words that left my mouth were clean and beautiful praises to my GOD. In addition, while I was dancing around praising GOD, and while everyone had stopped working to watch me, the packaging machine shut off on its own. The only noise that anybody heard in that part of the plant, was my voice praising GOD. As David did, I also learned that you need to cut the head off, <u>so that particular problem will have</u> **no voice** <u>in your life</u> **ever again.**

Remember this, Adam and Eve had faith and GOD'S Word. However, they did not understand the Word. They did not have the third part of the sword, <u>the sharp cutting edge,</u> and that is why they failed. King Saul had GOD'S Word, and he had understanding of that Word. However, he did not have <u>faith,</u> the handle of the sword, and he failed. Men like Abraham, David, the prophets and apostles **understood** the importance of possessing all three parts of the sword.

Here is another penny's worth of information to put in our bag. GOD must have placed a lot of importance on understanding the concept of the sword, for him to carve such a big example into the earth right after the fall of man. Can you see the resemblance between the Red Sea and a serpent? Does it not look like a serpent with its mouth open, ready to devour GOD'S people? Does not the Saudi Arabia peninsula look like a boot? Does the Persian Gulf not look like a sickle sword, with the blade facing toward the serpent?

Let's read the Romans passage again. *²⁰For the invisible things of him from the creation of the world <u>are clearly seen</u>, being **understood** by the **things that are made**, even his eternal power and Godhead; so that they are without excuse:* Rom. 1:20. This book will revolve around this spiritual sword and all the voices that exist In Between the Lines.

Spiritually speaking, there are two ways in which to hold and carry the cross. Most of the church world carries it over their shoulder as a weight dragging along the ground.

This is why they stagger from side to side and continually trip and fall. We hope that this book will help you to properly grip this cross, which, is how one would grip a sword, by the handle. We have to let GOD change how we look at the cross. When we first come to GOD, it is on our knees <u>begging</u> forgiveness, and many never get past that. They continue to crawl and beg throughout their relationship with GOD. I should know—that used to be me.

One day as I was meditating, I saw the cross stuck in the ground with the Hand of GOD on the HANDLE. The handle being that part of the cross extending just above the head of Christ. Yes, I said HANDLE, because that was the word that filled my mind as soon as I saw this vision in my head. Think about this for a moment. Take a miniature cross about four foot long with a point at the end, then stick it into the ground. Get down on you tummy and look up at it, what does it look like? It looks like a cross. Then, stand up next to the same cross and look straight down at it. What does it look like now? It is a **sword** stuck in the ground. That is how GOD views the cross. As a sword, the spiritual weapon of his choice. GOD wants his people to see the cross as a weapon of deliverance. The Word became the Sword of deliverance because Jesus, who was the Word made flesh, was nailed to that cross.

The only way to learn how to handle this spiritual sword with BOLD authority, is to fall in love with IT. *[15] Study to shew thyself approved unto God, a workman that needeth not to be ashamed, rightly dividing the word of truth.* 2 Tim. 2:15. Notice that GOD said a workman, and not a child. The difference between a spiritual MAN verses a spiritual child is, the man knows and **understands** the Word, and a child does not. I no longer rely on men when it comes to my relationship with GOD. This does not mean that I do not learn from the Word as it is preached or taught by men. On the contrary, I am much more flexible now than I have ever been before when it comes to my ability to learn. I used to rely on men to give and "establish" what I should believe. I now <u>rely on GOD</u>

to "establish" what things I should believe from what I read, and the Word that I hear from the teaching of men. I do not beg GOD'S forgiveness every day, I thank GOD for his forgiveness every day. I have great confidence and boldness and I can sit and talk to the greatest preachers of our time. I am a nobody who barely got through high school, only because I did not take that experience seriously, which I highly regret. Spiritually though, you do not have to be brilliant when you know the most brilliant one of all. This book is dedicated to better connecting you to that brilliance.

From now on, view the cross as GOD sees it, from above, looking down. Picture in your mind, GOD as your bright and shinning knight who is "Forcing" the cross into the "ground" like a sword. Picture HIM standing by that sword saying. "This I give to my children. No longer shall they be subject to the power of sin or that fallen nature they were born with—they shall win the war."

This does not mean the **S-WORD** will not become weighty at times. But what you have to understand, is how to let GOD keep that sword out of its sheath and off your back. How to let HIM put it in your hands as a weapon instead of just a weight to carry around.

QUESTION -- Why are there only TWO geological formations on earth that clearly resemble a boot? QUESTION -- Why is ROME, who represented evil, found within the little boot, and Israel who represented all of GOD'S people, found as part of the BIGGER boot? QUESTION -- Are these two more accidents of nature? Come on! Think about it.

Deeper Still and In Between the Lines · 41

The Three Crosses Represented in the Old Tabernacle

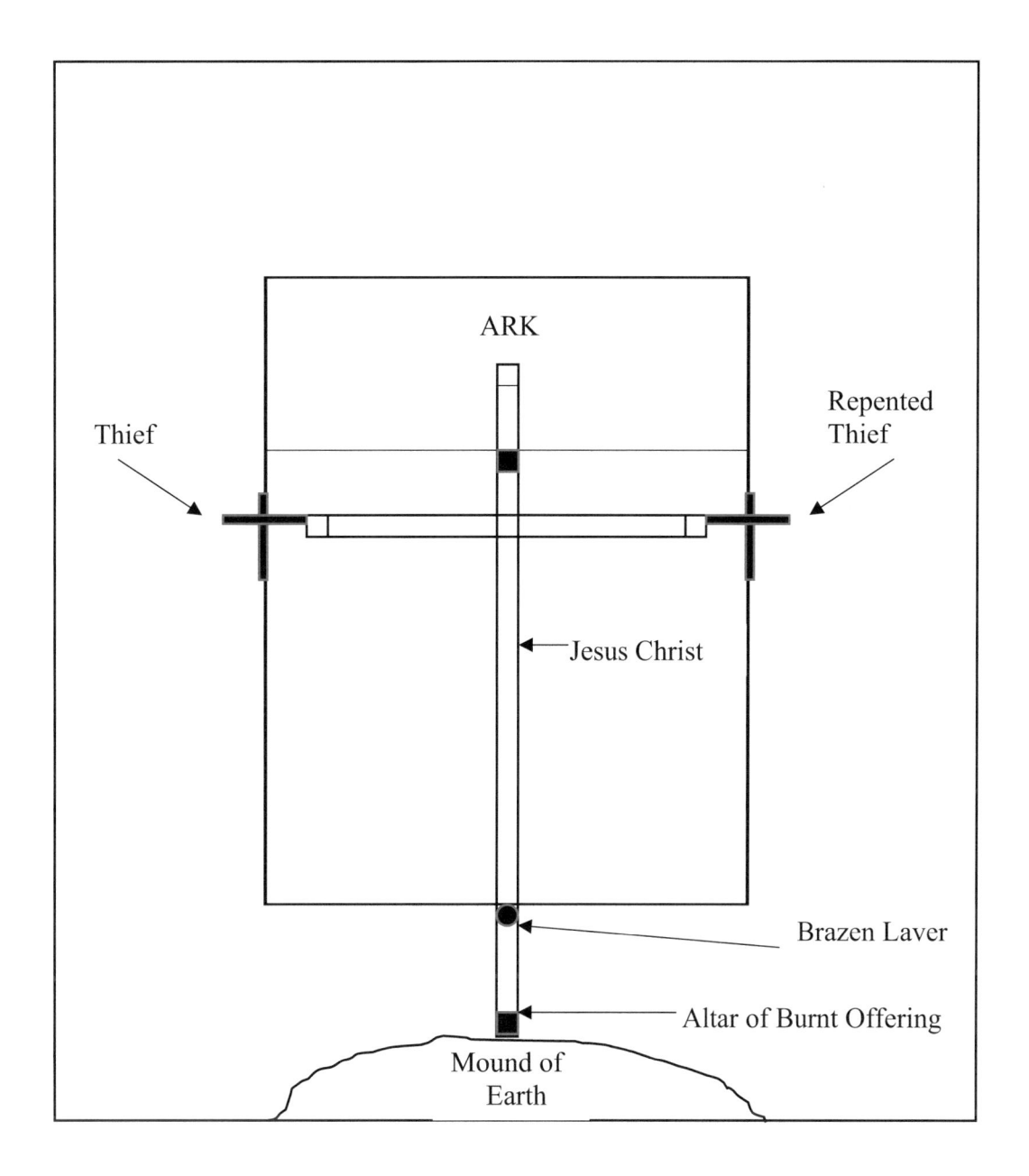

The River

I asked GOD, "What about the river that flowed out of the Garden of Eden, that paradise, the happy place you had given Adam and Eve?" HE said, "Come follow me out of the Garden and "back up river" to where it originates, high up in the mountain."

This was GOD confirming through scripture what he spoke in my mind. *[10] I was in the Spirit on the Lord's day, and heard behind me a great voice, as of a trumpet.* Rev. 1:10.

This means, to understand the present one must study the past. If you want to walk with GOD in the present you must take a walk with HIM through the PAST.

Not far out of the Garden we crossed two rivers. I asked, "What about these two?" HE said, "The Pison and the Gihon represent two spiritual rivers that give eternal life to all that find them. *[38] He that believeth on me, as the scripture hath said, out of his belly shall flow rivers of living water.* John 7:38. HE said, "However, we will discuss them later.

We continued "up the river" where the Hiddekel, now called the Tigris, joined up with the main river. Finally, we arrived **high up** in the mountain where it all originated. The Euphrates is the main river because it came first and covered more distance than the Tigris. Then God said, "Let us proceed back down river. So we followed the Euphrates as it left from on high and traveled down toward the Garden of Eden.

Before we take you on this journey, we want to draw your attention to these words: **high up in the mountain.** Spiritually, you need to see this river system, consisting of the Euphrates, Tigris, Gihon and Pison, as representing the River of Life which came into existence by the will of GOD, from on high. Included in this river are all the natural things created which the eye can see, and all spiritual creation the natural eye cannot see. We will also learn the Tigris is used to illustrate how the interactions between all of creation brings change into our lives. *⁵Behold, I was shapen in iniquity; and in sin did my mother conceive me.* Psalm 51:5. This river system will open up doors of understanding you have never entered through before.

The upper Euphrates River that meanders through the mountains "resembles" a bow. I know you are probably thinking, "Why is this important?" Well, the arrow the bow delivers has the power to destroy or to save a life, depending on if you are on the receiving end of the arrow, or you are in control of the bow, and you sent the arrow. Understanding the dynamics of the bow and arrow will help us gain control over this river of daily life that fires those killer arrows.

Before you consider this comparison foolish, and you close your mind to it. I want you to remember this. GOD does not waste words or time. If it is in the Bible, then HE preserved it for a reason. So it is with these four rivers. GOD put them there to attract the attention of some spiritual explorers who happened to be wading barefoot through the water soaked sandy beach, when all of the sudden, they stepped on four little stones buried in the sand. The sand represents the unlimited number of GOD'S thoughts. The water, GOD'S Word, penetrates throughout the sand. It touches and reveals those thoughts buried in the Bible. The stones represents those four rivers. Barefoot in the sand represents no preconceived ideas as to where the four rivers will take us.

I want to explain more clearly, walking barefoot through the water soaked sand, and, those four stones found in the sand represents four rivers. Have you ever walked along a water-soaked sandy beach with your shoes on? If so, then you probably agree that the experience was tiring and cumbersome. Your brain cannot receive that wonderful feeling of the sand messaging your feet due to the tough leather of the shoe between the sand and your feet. It is the same with <u>predetermined</u> answers. They, like the leather of your shoe, keep that wonderful experience of understanding GOD'S Word from ever reaching into your life.

Now for the phrase, "<u>The four stones represents those four rivers.</u>" This means— every word, geological formation, situation, and personal experience recorded in the Bible represent a stone. GOD uses these to catch our attention in hope we might **<u>ask</u>** these questions. "Why are these here, and what do you Lord have to say in regards to them? We see GOD using stones in this manner in the fourth chapter of the book of JOSHUA. HE parted the Jordan River, thus allowing the Israelites to enter the promise land and defeat the city of Jericho. GOD told Joshua, while they crossed, "Have one person from each tribe carry a stone out of the river and <u>pile them up</u> on shore." His purpose for using these stones is stated in Joshua. *⁶That this may be a sign among you, that when your children ask their **fathers** in time to come, saying, <u>What mean ye by these stones?</u> ⁷ Then ye shall answer them, That the waters of Jordan were cut off before the ark of the covenant of the LORD; when it passed over Jordan, the waters of Jordan were cut off: and <u>these stones</u> shall be for a <u>memorial</u> unto the children of Israel for ever.* Joshua 4:6-7.

Every Word in the Bible is a stone, and with the help of GOD has the power to lead us in many directions. Look, we do not become spiritual brain-e-acts overnight just because we accept GOD and his plan into our lives. On the contrary, it takes time and effort from both GOD and us to become spiritual thinkers. Through Christ, HE used many natural examples to teach his apostles spiritual truths. By studying these rivers, we will see the stones crying out. Through this natural source some spiritual understanding will be gained.

What spawned this study was a foolish question I heard Christians ask, and the foolish answer to that question given by others. The question was, "Why did GOD bring trouble upon me?" The foolish answer was, "GOD brings trouble into our lives to show his power and glory by delivering us out of that trouble." Alternatively, the goal in this lesson is to change both the question and the answer. The wise question is, "From where did this trouble originate that is now confronting me?" The wise answer is, "It did not come from GOD. Instead, it came from the river because God is not a troublemaker but a trouble solver.

28 And we know that all things work together for good to them that love God, to them who are the called according to his purpose. Rom. 8:28. This means that if you trust GOD, he will make every situation that touches your life, a positive life-changing experience in the end. *3 Thou wilt keep him in perfect peace, whose mind is stayed on thee: because he trusteth in thee.* Isaiah 26:3.

Many people think GOD brings difficult situations into our lives so HE can solve them, but that is not true. We hope you come away with a new slogan or battle cry by the end of this study of the natural and spiritual—BLAME IT ON THE RIVER. We hope the face on the target of your frustrations and revenge will no longer be GOD or Mankind. Instead, we hope you see only the RIVER. Every time trouble inters your life by way of natural situations, such as my septic tank lid collapsed, two-inch hail fell from the clouds and broke my truck windows, my roof sprang a leak, or both toilet bowl lids broke in the same day. I will not go into great de -"tail"—ha ha—on the natural forces that worked together to bring about the failure of those two lids. However, I will tell you my new battle cry—BLAME IT ON THE RIVER. When people hurt you through word or deed, it is painful. However, when people you trusted and loved hurt you—it kills. So what do you do when that happens? We hope you will blame it not on the individual.

Instead, we hope you blame it on sin. BLAME IT ON THE RIVER, because mistakes are simply a natural by-product of this River System.

7 Woe unto the world because of offences! for it must needs be that offences come; but *woe to <u>that man</u> by whom the offence cometh!* Matt. 18:7. Look again at what verse seven said—*woe unto the world because of offences.* Remember, we want you to view the world as the River of life, in which all GOD'S creation exist and flourish <u>as they so choose</u>. From these created wonders comes offences. This includes all of nature and every living creature, from mankind down to bacteria. All have been given the right to carve out their own place in this world.

GOD does not play football, bungee jump, hit a baseball, or ride a 2000 pound bull—men choose this life style. GOD does not <u>willfully</u> pick-up a deadly snake—men choose this life style. GOD does not use his head for a battering-ram to stop a running-back carrying the football—men choose this life style.

Before we focus our attention on these four rivers. We want you to forget that life exists outside the area of these rivers. This will allow us to better glean the little penny's worth of understanding hidden beneath the surface.

First, most historians agree that human civilization got its start in Mesopotamia, the area where the Euphrates Tigris Gihon and the Pison are to be found. The word Mesopotamia means, between the rivers. Next, the comparison between the Euphrates River system and an archer's bow did not originate with me. I got this out of a book GOD inspired me to read titled, "WHO'S WHO and WHERE'S WHERE in the BIBLE."

I live in-between where <u>two rivers</u> meet and I fish in them during spring and summer. Question—Is it a coincidence that I live in between two rivers, and I am writing about two river systems coming together to form one big river? Answer—NO—and here is why. Several years ago GOD spoke to me while crossing over the Spring River bridge just outside of Joplin, Missouri.

Before I tell you what HE said. I need to expose my thoughts leading up to that day. You see, every time I crossed that River, I would say to myself, "Oh, if I only lived on the bank of 'that' River, I could fish and hunt off my porch any day I wanted. Man that would be the life."

One day GOD spoke these words while crossing "that" River. "Grover, I have placed you in between two rivers that you can use at any time." I was shocked, and I said to myself, "WOW! I never really thought of that before." I realized I had taken that fact for granted. All of a sudden, I felt like the cow who ignores the good grass in his pasture, and <u>forces</u> his head through the sharp-barbed wire fence to eat the same grass from someone else's pasture. To help you understand how I overlooked the fact that I had it better where I now lived, I will give you a description of where my house is in relation to these two rivers. I have the best of two worlds, city and country living. My house is on two acres in the middle of a densely wooded two hundred acre plateau, surrounded on three sides by three hundred foot canyons. I am only ten minutes from the city and major shopping centers. The largest River is a half- mile east of my house at the base of one canyon, and the smaller lies a half-mile North at the base of another canyon. These rivers come together one mile northeast of my house, which puts me in between.

However, this distance from each is the reason I took my place of residence and situation for granted. I could not see the rivers from my back porch due to the trees and canyons blocking my view. I forgot these rivers were mine to be enjoyed at any time. When GOD reminded me, I was suddenly able to see HIS blessings in regard to where I now live.

Here are more, almost over looked, little blessings in reference to where I live. I am not wealthy, I own my house and the two acres like most home owners, month by month. This wonderful couple, who happened to be my good friends, purchased all the land that lies between my house and those rivers. He used his heavy equipment and cut a path through the wilderness that lies between my house and both rivers. Due to his generosity, I have unrestricted access to those rivers. I have ridden my four-wheeler into the river and fished from it.

One day I got so comfortable I fell off, only to be awakened by the water rushing over my body. If my wife needs me, she calls my cell phone and I am home in five minutes, if I do not have a fish on my line. If I want to hunt rabbits quail turkey pig and deer, I step out my door and start hunting. Oh! By the way, I have hunted from my front and back porch while holding a cup of coffee. Remember, all this is just ten minutes from the city and major shopping. Now I ask you—do you think it has been a good life for me in regard to where I now live? Herein lies the problem, we cannot see the blessings of GOD because we are looking only at the forest and the canyons that lay between.

Next point to remember, is the "Euphrates" in Hebrew simply means the River, which is a delivery system and a place where God gives creatures the right to flourish. So it is with our world in which we live. It is a place where all GOD'S creation lives <u>as they so choose</u>. On occasion, these deliver into our lives unpleasant situations. In addition, being that the Euphrates River system has the <u>basic shape of a bow, that</u> in turn *points* our attention to this fact. The bow is a delivery system for an arrow, which happens to be the definition of the Tigris River in the Hebrew language.

Here is the summary thought on these two rivers. The Euphrates represents all GOD'S creation, including the devil, who by his own choice went from good to evil. The Tigris represents the "interaction" between all creation. The Euphrates and the Tigris rivers together represent the natural river system.

The next river flowing into the Euphrates is the Gihon. The definition of Gihon is gusher. Water is the liquid used to represent GOD'S Word. Water washes an object clean and the Word washes our hearts clean. Jesus said, *[3] Now ye are clean through the word which I have spoken unto you.* John 15:3. Spiritually, the Gihon represented GOD'S Word. The Bible confirms this comparison in Genesis. *¹³ And the name of the second river is Gihon: the same is it that compasseth the whole land of Ethiopia.* Gen. 2:13. The words, *"whole land,"* is referring to the everyday lives of mankind. *(You) know that man doth not live by bread only, but by every word that proceedeth out of the mouth of the LORD doth man live.* Deut. 8:3b.

Finally, the last of the four rivers flowing into the Euphrates is the Pison. Question—What gushed forth from the Word? Answer—Jesus Christ, who was the Word made flesh. Here are two interesting definitions of the word gusher. First, a well from which oil flows freely, and an Effusive Person. This is someone unrestrained in expressing feelings; giving or involving an extravagant and sometimes excessive expression of feelings in speech or writing. This person is Jesus Christ, GOD'S extended hand to mankind. In addition, the use of oil in the Bible refers to spiritual anointing. The Bible says, *¹⁴ And the Word was made flesh, and dwelt among us, (and we beheld his glory, the glory as of the only begotten of the Father,) full of grace and truth.* John 1:14. So then, the Pison River represented the active presence of GOD who always makes his Word come to pass. Christ is the Effusive person through which this spiritual oil gushed.

The rivers Gihon and Pison together form the spiritual river. All humanity lives and dies within the boundaries of these four rivers. About now you are probably wondering, "Where are we going from here, and what is the next stop in this study of the four rivers?" Well, as the train conductors in the old days would bellow out, "NEXT STOP—THE OLD WILDERNESS TABERNACLE."

Every wall, measurement, and piece of furniture held one or more meanings. However, we are going to focus our attention on these four rivers. First, let us look at the outer wall of the first Tabernacle. The 100-cubit long by 50-cubit wide surrounding walls represented the Euphrates River. All of creation, including mankind is represented within its boundary. Earlier we said, you were to forget about life existing outside of this compound, because GOD alone inhabited eternity. The area inside represents life and death, the short time the <u>natural</u> man has been given to exist in GOD'S creation.

Hidden treasure will be found as we travel with GOD through the one entrance, and onward through the Holy Tent located in the center of the courtyard. The open area surrounding the Tent represented the Tigris River, from where all those nasty arrows are shot from due to the interaction between all GOD'S creation.

The 30 cubit long 10-cubit wide Holy Tent inside the compound, also called the **Tent of Meeting,** is divided within into two sections by a heavy curtain. Spiritually, the first room is the Gihon River (the Word of GOD)—and the second room, the Pison River (The Most Holy Place), the active presence of GOD. The entire tent, including the heavy dividing curtain represented Flesh, a temporary dwelling place.

Why did GOD name these two rooms The Holy Place and The Most Holy Place? Answer—The Holy Place symbolized one thing held in a common bond between both GOD and man—the flesh—we by birth, and GOD by CHOICE. This we begin to see in Exodos 3:1-15, when Moses met with God at the burning bush. GOD said, *Take off your shoes for this is a* **Holy Place***.* Both Moses and the bush was in contact with the <u>**natural dust of the earth**</u>. The flesh being the only common bond shared by GOD and mankind at that time. However, the spirit of mankind and GOD were totally separate, having no bond whatsoever. This shared common bond of the flesh was the very thing that separated us.

These two rooms divided by the curtain, paralleled GOD fellowshipping Moses through the burning bush, and later, the world through the body of Christ. The Most Holy Place was where the spirit of GOD gave the High Priest the Word to give to the people. GOD alone inhabited that room.

The curtain was removed when Christ died, spiritually making that tent into one room. Through this sacrifice, all mankind can have a relationship with GOD. Now we can have a common bond in spirit as well. To have this relationship, all mankind will have to follow the footsteps of the High Priest, from the altar to the Basin Laver and on into the Holy Tent.

We first enter the Tabernacle through a twenty cubit long curtain. This area being the open courtyard between the Holy Tent and the four surrounding walls. The Tabernacle was always set up so the high priest entered from the East and walk West toward The Most Holy Place, which paralleled the path our SUN travels.

Briefly we need to discuss the Sun and Moon, two celestial bodies that exert the most influence over earth, <u>our home</u>. Two creations GOD uses to point out his deity and HIS relationship to the life of Christ. The Sun is the <u>source</u> of <u>light</u> and <u>life</u> to our planet. The Moon is the body that reveals the light of the Sun in darkness, by <u>reflecting</u> that light. The Sun represented GOD, who is the source of all spiritual light and life. The Moon represented the body of Christ, from whom reflected all GOD'S spiritual light into the darkness of our world. Symbolically, you are following the path, or the "process" GOD laid out concerning salvation when you entered the Tabernacle from the East and followed the Sun's path to the West.

Here is the basic structure of the Tabernacle. The inner color of the walls surrounding the courtyard was white, a color representing mankind. The entry into the Tabernacle courtyard was at the East end through a twenty cubit wide curtain door. This door consisted of four layers of blue purple scarlet and white fabric sewed together to form one curtain. Three COLORS represented Divine nature and the white curtain, under the three, represented human nature. This curtain represented <u>Jesus Christ</u> entering the world as both divine and human. The four posts the entrance curtain was fastened to represented the entry point into the area which brings one under the authority of the four rivers. Going past those four posts and entering the courtyard is the same as being born into this world. When you are born you become part of creation, the Euphrates River. That in turn subjects you to the actions of all creation, the Tigris River. All creation is subject to the Word, the Gihon River. This Word is in force and brought to life by GOD, the Pison River. The open area of the courtyard represented mankind's attempt to live without GOD'S assistance.

Upon entering the compound, you first encountered an Altar of sacrifice followed by a highly polished water filled Brazen Laver, placed just before the entrance to the Tent. The priest could see his reflection as he washed in compliance to GOD'S command. The priest had to sacrifice an animal at the altar and wash before he could enter The Holy Place. These, being in line, pointed the strait and narrow way one must take to connect spiritually with GOD, which "spiritual" connection is represented **_"inside"_** the Tent. *[14] Because strait is the gate, and narrow is the **way**, which leadeth unto life, and few there be that find it.* Matt. 7:14.

The Tent took-up nearly ten percent of the compound, because GOD wanted the courtyard area around it to look small. HE wanted a visual example to help mankind understand how close we all are to having a relationship with HIM. No matter how sinful you are, no one is far from having a relationship with HIM. Look at what GOD has to say about how easy it is to find him. *[27] That they should **seek** the Lord, if haply they might feel after him, and find him, though he be not far from every one of us*: Acts 17:27.

Here is my favorite scripture concerning the closeness of GOD'S presence. *[17] And it shall come to pass in the last days, saith God, I will pour out of my Spirit upon **all** flesh: and your sons and your daughters shall prophesy, and your young men shall see visions, and your old men shall dream dreams:* Acts 2:17. WOW! All we have to do is—_LOOK UP_—and DRINK.

Why is it that all mankind does not have a relationship with GOD, or the spirit in them as some claim? You must first believe the Word, because faith is the key which unlocks the door to your heart. It gives GOD an open door into your mind and allows HIS active presence into your life. *²⁰ Behold, I stand at the door, and knock: if any man hear my voice, and open the door, I will come in to him, and will sup with him, and he with me.* Rev. 3:20. Many people hear GOD'S Word preached in church, "but few" open their hearts to that voice. "We" have to *open the door*. Believing, allows GOD to use his Word to establish a relationship through knowledge and understanding.

The Bible confirms this in John 7:38. *³⁸ He that believeth on me, **as the scripture hath said**, out of his belly shall flow rivers of living water.* It is a relationship that will put you over and not under the river of life. In Matthew 14:22-32, Jesus gave us an example of how one can gain this power to tread upon these waters. HE sent his disciples by boat to the other side of the lake while HE prayed. Shortly after their departure, we find the disciples in troubled waters. Suddenly, Jesus appeared out of nowhere walking on the water. When Peter saw the Lord, he cried out, *"Jesus if that be you, tell me to come to you."* Jesus said to Peter, "Come." With eyes fixed, that fisherman "stepped" out of the boat and began to walk on water toward the Lord. However, he started to look at the big waves and the hard blowing wind that buffeted him. Looking at his **situation** instead of the Lord caused him to sink down under the water. That is when Peter cried out, "S*ave me Lord."* Jesus reached out his hand and pulled Peter up. Then walked with him on the water back to the boat. Our power to walk these waters, or the power to overcome all life's problems, comes by keeping our eyes on the Lord.

Again, the first object you see upon entering the Tabernacle courtyard is the Altar of Burnt Offering. It represented the first spiritual step all mankind "must make" in establishing a relationship with GOD. It was **"made of wood"** covered in Bronze with four horns on top of its four corners. It set upon a mound of earth in the courtyard. Symbolically, the mound of earth represented all humanity. The **wood** under the metal represented the **individual** who rises out of humanity. GOD gives us the right to compare man to wood in many scriptures, such as, Psalm 1:3a. *³And he shall be like a tree planted by the rivers of water.*

The four horns represented authority. The heavy metal covering the wood, is the weight applied to all mankind by the natural and spiritual forces. The Bronze which covered the altar, is made by combining two metals, Tin and Copper. Tin is the natural, and Copper is the spiritual, because it ***IMPROVES*** any metal it is combined with, and its worth was almost equal to that of Gold at the time the Tabernacle was built.

We want to focus on the two river systems flowing together to form one heavy cover, which all humanity is subject to upon entering this world at birth. This heavy metal is life. It is the natural and spiritual forces of life that weight us down, drowning us in fear and despair. The Bible confirms there are two forces at work. *⁴⁴There is a natural body, and there is a spiritual body.* 1 Cor. 15:44b. When an animal was to be sacrificed on the altar, the priest had to lay his hand on the animal. The sin and guilt, (or condemnation), was moved from humanity to the creature. Then the priest would slaughter the animal. He would dab blood on each of the four horns of the altar from the animal that was without blemish. This sacrifice bought "temporary" forgiveness of sin and freedom from guilt for the people of Israel. We know this creature without blemish is symbolic of Jesus Christ. His death bought permanent forgiveness of sin and freedom from guilt for all that "continually" believe. His blood has been dabbed on the four horns of the altar. He has power and authority over these rivers, and this power HE passes on to all who accept HIM.

To become a child of GOD, you must understand the two doors involved. The first is your heart, and the key to unlock it is your faith. The second is GOD'S heart, and that key is obedience. We call these, the two touches to salvation. The first is outward. It is when we hear of the power of the cross and come to church to see what is going on. The second is when we obey what we hear, this is an inward touch because it is an active response of true faith.

⁵Jesus answered, Verily, verily, I say unto thee, Except a man be born of <u>water</u> and of the <u>Spirit</u>, he cannot enter into the kingdom of God. John 3:5. This kingdom is HIS thoughts exposed by His Word, and HIS nature by the actions of HIS spirit. It is how GOD thinks and reacts to any given situation. HE will <u>help us</u> to think like HIM and to act like HIM. *¹³For it is God which **worketh** in you both to **will** and to **do** of his good pleasure.* Phil. 2:13. Water represented the Word, and these two scriptures confirms you must have this spiritual river at work in your heart—GOD'S WORD (the Gihon River), and the **SPIRIT of GOD** (the Pison River), the active presence of GOD. The fire that consumed the altar sacrifice represented GOD'S consuming wrath against the sins of mankind. Isa. 9:18a says, *¹⁸For <u>wickedness burneth as the fire</u>,* and Isa. 9:19a says *¹⁹Through the wrath of the LORD of hosts is the land darkened, and the <u>people shall be as the fuel of the **fire**</u>*.

What if you were disabled, having only one arm and this super-natural creature came to you and said, "I will give you happiness and eternal life if you allow me to make you whole by giving you my super-natural arm?" I will tell you what I would do. I would take his arm and <u>claim the "gifts"</u> offered by the creature.

Salvation is the spiritual grafting of GOD'S arm into our lives. This arm is the Word of GOD (the Gihon River), and GOD'S active presence (the Pison River). Salvation is about becoming one with GOD. It is impossible for Humanity to please GOD with its one **natural** arm. It is impossible to find peace and contentment, nor can we overcome all arrows that life fires at us without HIS arm of deliverance.

Without GOD, our lives run parallel to this one day in the life of the "one armed" man in New York City. Suddenly he awakes, only to realize he is late for his interview to a huge job offer paying five times what he is currently making. He jumps into his clothes at a breakneck speed. As he races the three blocks to the interview, he noticed his new pants kept wanting to slide down toward his ankles. He had forgotten to put on his belt. There he was, running while holding up his pants with his ONE ARM. Suddenly, he turns a corner and runs smack into a "guy" who is having a very bad day. The **"blazing hot"** coffee in this stranger's hand "spilled" all over the two of them. The stranger "vented his rage" by throwing a punch. The ONE ARMED man tried to block it while backing quickly away. That is when his pants dropped down around his ankles, causing him to fall backwards off the curb in front of a fast moving cab. Later, when he came too, he looked up from the Hospital's emergency bed and said to the doctor, "Man, I sure needed two arms today."

Again, let's look at those stones King David put in his bag. *[40] And he took his staff in his hand, and chose him five smooth stones out of the brook, and put them in a shepherd's bag...* 1 Sam. 17:40.b These stones were made smooth by the sand and grit the water carried as it flowed over them. GOD gave us the right to use these stones to represent those four rivers because they came from the brook. David's bag is our heart. Two stones in David's bag represent the natural river system, the one arm mankind is born with. Two other stones were the spiritual river system, the arm of GOD found only at work in people who took GOD'S offer. The fifth stone David used to defeat the giant is the victory rock. This stone represents the righteous thoughts and actions produced by GOD, seen operating in the everyday life of Christ. This victory in David's life came from having the arm of GOD, that spiritual river system, the Gihon and Pison flowing in his life. David put that Goliath of a problem under his feet. He walked on water that day. The two spiritual rivers produced knowledge and understanding of GOD'S Word, and faith in GOD'S ability to bring HIS Word to pass.

Spiritually, all humanity is born into this world, GOD'S creation having one arm only. Without GOD'S ARM, we all must deal with life's arrows by ourselves. This is what the open area of the Tabernacle courtyard surrounding the Holy Tent represented, people without GOD'S help struggling to live in the River of Life.

An arm is made up of two sections. The first part is from the shoulder to the elbow, and the second part is from the elbow to the wrist. At the end of the arm we find the hand. The arm is what extends the hand outward to be grasped in friendship, and to establish a new relationship with another party. The first part of GOD'S arm, from the shoulder to the elbow, is HIS Word. The second part of HIS arm, from the elbow to the wrist, is GOD'S Spirit. This is HIS active involvement in bringing that Word to life. The spiritual hand, which the arm of GOD extends, is the "life" of Christ.

I must ask you to be patient. Because by the end of this lesson on these rivers, there will be hidden treasure revealed in the story of Gideon. However, in order to see it, we must transition the two spiritual rivers into representing GOD'S Arm.

Here are some scriptures to help us make this transition. *[9] Hast thou an arm like God? or canst thou thunder with a voice like him?* Job 40:9; and *[15] Thou hast with thine arm redeemed thy people, the sons of Jacob and Joseph. Selah.* Psalm 77:15; and *[1] Who hath believed our report? and to whom is the arm of the LORD revealed?* Isa. 53:1; and *[21] And hast brought forth thy people Israel out of the land of Egypt with signs, and with wonders, and with a strong hand, and with a stretched out arm, and with great terror;* Jer. 32:21.

Let us look again at the Altar of Burnt Offering. The whole fourth chapter of **LEVITICUS** is dedicated to GOD forgiving sin through the act of the sinner putting his hand, (not hands), on the animal on the altar while confessing his sins, and then slaying the animal and dabbing the blood on the four horns. Note again, the Bible throughout the fourth chapter of LEVITICUS repeatedly said, "*Put your "hand" on the animal to be sacrificed.*" GOD did not say, "Put your hands on the animal," because in the eyes of

GOD, mankind has only one arm. GOD sees **all mankind** as handicapped and in need of his strong arm. This alter ritual represented what GOD expected from the Israelites and all mankind when it came to establishing a relationship with HIM. They were to admit through the word out of their mouths, and hopefully from their hearts, that they are sinners. Then they were to take action by following GOD'S Word, all the while believing GOD has forgiven them and that HE will be an active part of their everyday life from then on. It was a ritual established by GOD to give the Israelites the opportunity to extend their arm out and embrace GOD'S hand with their hand. There is only one way to embrace HIM in fellowship, and that is by extending your arm out and grasping HIS hand with your hand. *[18] That by two immutable things, in which it was impossible for God to lie, we might have a strong consolation, who have fled for refuge to **lay hold upon the hope set before us**:* Heb. 6:18.

We want you to consider the two parts of your arm, the shoulder to the elbow and the elbow to the wrist, as representing your word and you bringing that word to life through your action. This parallels GOD'S arm, which is HIS Word brought to life through HIS action. The arm of GOD has extended HIS hand, (Christ). We must embrace GOD'S hand with our hand. That being our faith, by extending our arm which is our word of confession, and confirming that confession of faith through action. This is why the church uses the ritual of Water Baptism in "establishing" a relationship with GOD. It is the only ritual confirmed by GOD to **help** mankind in **establishing a strong foundation**. Faith in the Word is the concrete footing on which this relationship is built.

Water baptism **helps** to **establish** this rock solid footing because it removes condemnation. Without which, you can come to GOD not as a fearful sinner, but as a child of GOD full of "joyful" anticipation regardless of your many failures or short comings. Remember, condemnation caused Adam and Eve to hide.

The Basin Laver was the next spiritual piece of furniture the priest had to stop at. He "had" to wash and "prepare" himself before he entered The Holy Place, the Tent of Meeting. The Altar was where the Israelites died to themselves by admitting that they were sinners. The highly polished water filled Basin was where the priest could see his reflection through the water, which is what the Word does in our hearts as we look through it. The priest was washing away fear and condemnation, thus allowing him to enter The Holy Place. The "Altar" and the "Washing" was the foundation that the priest had to establish before he could go any farther in his relationship with GOD. People who begin to seek GOD give up and fall away because they do not build a strong foundation to start with. You must believe the Word. If the high priest had failed to wash both hands and feet as the LORD commanded, he would have eventually died in The Most Holy Place where he met with GOD, because that would have confirmed his doubt in the Word of GOD.

After experiencing the sacrifice at the Altar and washing in the Basin Laver, the priest entered The Holy Place. Inside the tent was a curtain made of many layers of fabric. This curtain divided the tent into two compartments, which symbolically became one room upon the death of Christ. The curtain dividing the tent into two rooms represented the sinful nature of our flesh, the natural desires that separated mankind from GOD. The first room was The Holy Place and the second was The Most Holy Place. The first compartment contained three pieces of furniture. A solid gold one piece Candlestick, a wood table covered in gold two cubits long one cubit wide and one and one-half cubits high, and a gold covered alter where incense was burned. The altar of incense was in the middle and against the curtain that divided the tent into two compartments. The Candlestick was always placed next to the South wall, to the priest's left as he entered through the only entrance into the tent. The Table, which was called the Table of Shew Bread, was always placed next to the North wall to the priest's right upon entry into the

Tent. We are not going into all the design and beautiful detail of the Candlestick, that you can read about in **EXODUS 25: 31-40.** However, we do want to discuss the basic design of the Candlestick. The pure gold Candlestick had a main shaft and six shafts coming off the main shaft. Three on one side and three on the opposite side, and all running upward **parallel** to the main shaft. No one knows how high the Candlestick stood, because it is one of two pieces in the Old Testament Tabernacle that had no measurements given. There is a reason for GOD not giving any measurements for the Basin Laver and the Golden Candlestick. Both are used to represent GOD'S Word, and there is no measuring GOD'S Word because it is limitless.

[7] Deep calleth unto deep at the noise of thy waterspouts: all thy waves and thy billows are gone over me. Psalm 42:7. This simply means—As you fellowship GOD through his word, regardless if it is for pleasure during good times, or during bad times when seeking an answer to a problem—GOD, through his word, will inspire you onward. *Deep calling unto Deep* reminds me of how a professional cave explorer must feel when he discovers a new opening—(I've got to see where that takes me). GOD'S Word is a cave with more than one outlet. And each outlet leads to another room which also has multiple outlets and so on and so on. There is not one question humanity can ask, that GOD through his Word cannot answer, if we patiently seek and ask.

Now back to the Candlestick **against** the South wall. This wall we associate with the Gihon River. Because GOD placed the Candlestick, which represented HIS Word, up against that south wall. It was the only source of light in that tent. It was fueled by oil at the top of those seven shafts. Without the light, the priests could not serve GOD, they could not find their way, and they would have tripped and fallen because of the total darkness. [105] *Thy word is a lamp unto my feet, and a light unto my path.* Psalm 119:105.

The Gold that the Candlestick was made from represented the Word. The flame represented the visual outward change brought about by the spirit of GOD, which in turn reveals the path to a relationship with GOD to the world.

Straight across from the Candlestick **against** the North wall was the Table of Shew Bread. This wall we associate with the Pison River, GOD'S spirit, his active presence bringing HIS Word to life. This table was always to the right of the priest as he entered the tent. That Table held the bread of life, the Manna GOD sent from Heaven and fed the Israelites when they were hungry. This spiritual Manna is Jesus Christ, the Word of GOD brought to life by the actions of GOD. *¹⁴ And the Word was made flesh, and dwelt among us, (and we beheld his glory, the glory as of the only begotten of the Father,) full of grace and truth.* John 1:14.

We are not going to explain all the things the Candlestick and the Table of Show Bread represented, because those are well documented and can be found on the internet. We will reveal some things overlooked. Unseen treasure, that can only be revealed through the understanding of what the four rivers represented.

Here we are in the first big room of the Cave, GOD'S word, pondering a new thought. Wait—listen—did you here that—it was a voice calling out—Deeper-Deeper-Deeper.

If you were standing in the center of the room called The Holy Place, symbolically, you would be standing on the main beam of the CROSS. If you were to stand directly between the Candlestick and the Table of Shew Bread in that same room, you would be standing on the beam that held Jesus Christ "Hands" in place. If you were to draw a line from the Altar in the courtyard through both rooms up to the Ark of the Covenant in The Most Holy Place, and a line connecting the Candlestick and The Table of Shew Bread, the two lines would form a CROSS. The main beam that held the body of Jesus points upward toward Heaven when placed in the ground. This beam points toward GOD'S thoughts and his actions. The cross beam that held the hands of Jesus runs horizontal. This beam running parallel to the earth points toward mankind's thoughts and actions. Notice, we did not say the wood of the cross represented both GOD'S and mankind's thoughts and actions. We said, they pointed toward, they direct our attention to the thoughts and actions of GOD and mankind.

The "area" inside the first chamber of the Tent of Meeting, (The <u>Holy Place),</u> represented the <u>area of the cross</u> the **BODY** of Jesus Christ covered. The head of Christ being the Altar of Incense and his feet being the entry curtain into The Holy Place, because it said in **JOHN 1:14** Jesus Christ was the Word made flesh. The uncovered part of the cross, above the head of Jesus, represented that compartment of the tent called The <u>Most Holy Place</u>, the official dwelling place of GOD through which HE would speak to HIS people.

<u>The Holy Place,</u> the first compartment, is where the priest "<u>begins</u>" to connect SPIRITUALLY with GOD ***through*** the <u>Word</u>. Symbolically, when he entered the Holy Place he was touching the body of Jesus Christ. He was **<u>grasping</u>** the Word. To grasp means to understand and to hold on firmly to something. The Holy Place, paralleled the SPACE on the cross that ran from the **<u>feet</u>** to the **<u>head</u>** of Jesus. The LIFELESS body of Christ represented the WRITTEN Word which mankind is responsible to fulfill, but could not. The <u>uncovered</u> area of the cross, **<u>Below</u>** the feet of Jesus to its entry into the ground, is paralleled <u>OUTSIDE</u> the Tent <u>by the short distance</u> from the Altar of Burnt Offering to the entry curtain of the Holy Place just past the Basin Laver.

Question! Why did GOD put two of the three steps to salvation, **outside the Holy Tent** in the open courtyard where those that do not know GOD are also represented? Answer—To show us that it takes MORE than saying I BELIEVE, and that it takes certain steps to build a ROCK solid FOOTING of Faith. Because, due to our stubborn pride, our hearts are not that easy to change.

Repentance is the Altar of Burnt Offering experience and **Water Baptism** is the Brazen Alter experience. Both were <u>outside</u> the Holy Tent of Meeting. <u>Understanding</u> the importance and the <u>spiritual mechanics</u> involved in these two steps helps inspirer you to properly apply them to your life. These go a long way in establishing the FAITH necessary to make that Spiritual connection represented in the second room, where the priest talked with GOD.

To build a house, you first dig the footing and you put in steel-rebar for added strength, and then the concrete. Now you can build on that footing. Repentance, is "digging the hole" for the footing. GOD'S Word is the steel-rebar **"you put in"** the hole, (your heart) for added strength. GOD'S Spirit is the concrete that ties it all together as one solid mass. It is not easy to place your Faith in someone else's ability to change your thoughts, speech, desires, and habits. GOD put these two steps to salvation outside the Tent to inspire us to search for the answer as to why He did it. While in pursuit of why, we would learn both the importance of each step and the proper way in which to apply them to our lives.

The priest entering the Holy Place symbolizes a spiritual grasping of the Word of GOD. The priest, through his **active** faith, was connecting inwardly with the Lord. He was **beginning** to connect Spiritually, becoming one with GOD. When we connect with GOD through our active faith, the cross becomes our cross to bear with GOD. This fulfills HIS command to all found in Matthew 16:24, *[24] Then said Jesus unto his disciples, If any man will come after me, let him deny himself, and take up his cross, and follow me.* Do not let the words, take up his cross and deny one's-self, scare you. They simply mean you will SAY and DO the RIGHT thing because of the inspiration of GOD in your mind and heart. Granted, saying and doing the right thing will at times bring you pain. Oh yes! You will have to endure the pain of forgiving someone who has done you wrong.

That comes with the cross. Most people who say they believe in GOD, have never touched the body or life of Jesus inwardly. They have never TRULY possessed that wonderful gift GOD gave us. Remember, the priest had to grasp with his hand the sacrifice. To "grasp" the Word means, one "UNDERSTANDS" and HOLDS FIRMLY his belief in the Word.

GOD commanded the Israelites to set the Altar on a mounded up pile of earth every time they moved and resettled. Spiritually, the Altar is the place where the Cross made contact and entered the ground. The mound of earth that the Altar sat upon represented all humanity reaching upward toward GOD, because mankind came from the dust of the earth. This mound of earth is also the group of people who could never quit reach high enough to make a spiritual connection with GOD. *⁷Ever learning, and never able to come to the knowledge of the truth.* 2 Tim. 3:7. This group are those who make the first touch, which is outward only. The wood, under the metal that covered the Altar, is the individual who comes out of the mass of humanity and spiritually climbs up the cross from the earth to the feet of Jesus. This being the same distance between the Altar of Burnt Offering to the Tent. This barren part of the cross "visually" shows the extra effort needed to reach above and connect with GOD. This distance is where a new Christian **establishes** the foundation of faith. The individual, who really wants GOD, will make the climb higher up the tree and make that spiritual connection. This individual is of the group that makes the second touch.

There are two touches one must make in establishing an ongoing relationship with GOD. We, like the Israelites, first start our climb at the Altar. In this group, will be some people who come to church because they heard of the goodness of the Lord. They, in a sense, touch the wood of the cross. Yet, they never seem to find the second touch. They never spiritually connect with GOD, their humanity gets in the way. GOD is using that distance from the Alter onward past the Basin Laver to the Holy Tent, to help us understand how to bridge this gap between the first and second touch. This distance is hard to cross due to human nature and our self-reliance. This gap is bridged by active faith. By obeying, one is **strengthening** his faith and **setting** in his heart a devotion to GOD'S Word. This faith, once established, will continually excite the heart to search and learn. Repentance and Water Baptism are the steps we use in order to climb the cross upward from the mound of earth. We all have to touch GOD twice.

Let us give you the spiritual definition of touch. There is an outward touch one does simply because he was told to do it, or one touches an object because he saw someone else do it. However, there is an inward touch that says, "I believe this will make a difference when I do it, because I believe in the ONE who said it."

MARK 5: 25-34, tells the story about a woman that had a disease of the blood for twelve years. Upon hearing that Jesus had the power to heal, "she sought him out." She found Jesus surrounded by a huge crowd of people, which is what that mound of earth under the Altar represented. As she **"PUSHED"** her way through the crowd, she said to herself, *"If I may touch but his garment, I shall be whole."* When she touched Jesus, the Lord turned and asked, "Who touched me?" HIS disciples pretty much said, "Are you kidding us Lord? Who can tell? Just look at the multitude of people thronging you?" *⁵Jesus answered, Verily, verily, I say unto thee, Except a man be born of water and of the Spirit, he cannot enter into the kingdom of God.* John 3:5.

Look at the story of Zacchaeus in the 19 chapter of LUKE. He was a short man who could not see over the mass of people surrounding Jesus. (He could not see over that mound of earth) in order to make contact with Jesus. Zacchaeus **climbed up above** the mass of people in a sycamore-tree. When Jesus saw "him up the tree," HE said, "Zacchaeus, come down out of that tree, I **want** to come into your house today." After Jesus entered the house, or should I say the heart of Zacchaeus, that little man's life changed. Zacchaeus had been accused of cheating people out of their money because he was a rich tax collector. Zacchaeus said to Jesus, "I will give half of my wealth to the poor, and I will pay back four fold if I have cheated anybody." When Jesus heard "that", he said, **"Today,** salvation has come to this house." Zacchaeus attempted to touch the Lord twice. The first attempt was outward, it was when he heard of the fame of Jesus and came to see what was going on. This is what all the other people surrounding Jesus came to do. The second attempt began when he <u>climbed up the tree to **reach** higher,</u> and was completed when he <u>obeyed</u> the command of the Lord to come down out of the tree. After he <u>obeyed,</u> we find the Lord in the house of Zacchaeus, (the Lord is now in his heart). There is one small point about the sycamore tree, it has a very short trunk. This points to the short distance of the cross, between the mass of people thronging the Lord, and the individual that makes the spiritual 'CLIMB" to connect with GOD.

The reason people are unhappy, though they attend church, is they have never touched the Lord the second time. They wonder why there is confusion, fear, and depression in their lives. *²⁶For as the body without the spirit is dead, so faith without works is dead also.* James 2:26. Here is a sad fact—most people who go to church have no ongoing, every day personal relationship with GOD. HE is the greatest, kindest, most thoughtful, powerful, brilliant, pleasurable and fun individual I have ever encountered.

Yes, I did say individual, and yes, I did say fun. The hardest and the longest laugh I ever experienced came when I was engulfed in the spirit of the LORD. *...the joy of the LORD is your strength.* Neh. 8:10b.

Well, get ready, because we are about to go through another hole in GOD'S cave. The one piece Golden Candlestick had a center shaft and six shafts coming out of the main shaft. Three on one side and three on the other. At the top of the seven shafts, and on the same plane, were the flames that brought light to the area. The six shafts of the Candlestick represented mankind, because GENESIS 1:25-31said GOD made man on the sixth day. The Gold the Candlestick was made from represented the Word of GOD. The Oil that fueled the flame is GOD Himself. The flame itself atop the seven shafts represented Victory, the outward change that all the world could see, a product of the Word and the active presence of GOD. The entire Candlestick, as a single unit, represented the church through which GOD brings LIGHT and VICTORY to the world.

GOD would build this church at LOCATIONS in time; providing us with **Three Windows** though which to view, represented by three bowls shaped like almonds on each of the six shafts; each bowl having, knops (buds), and a flower. The center shaft had four bowls, each containing knops and flowers. This gave each of the six shafts the appearance of a golden almond-tree budding with fruits in three stages. This was like Aaron's rod, which is recorded in **NUMBERS 17:8** as having budded, blossomed, and bore almonds all in one night. In addition, the total number of bowls knops and flowers on each of the six shafts was nine. Their total number on the six shafts equal fifty four, and the center shaft had twelve; added together, you get 66 which is the exact number of books that make up the Bible. The base and the foundation of the Bible is its first five books. GENESIS is the supporting base of the Candlestick. The base touches the earth, it gives us the basic history of mankind and our fall from grace.

EXODUS, LEVITICUS, NUMBERS, and DEUTERONOMY, are represented by the four almond-bowl clusters on the main shaft. They begin to teach us what sin is and why we should leave it behind. They lay the foundation for mankind's restoration to grace.

The three groups LOCATED on each of the six shafts represented *__three__* WINDOWS, or VANTAGE points through which the CHURCH will view and judge all things. All truth is "captured" and all "understanding" received as we __gaze through__ the Father-Son-Holy Ghost. Three WINDOWS in the House, (the church), established by GOD that his children can SEE the WORLD through. GOD gives us a Father's perspective view in the Old Testament and a Son's perspective view in the New Testament. Then, <u>from within,</u> we receive the Spirit's perspective view, which is GOD himself translating the Old and New Testament. This view is represented in the second room of the Tent called The Most Holy Place. GOD established ***three*** angles from which to SEE in order to judge, teach, and to restore mankind back to grace. Each LOCATION, with its bowl bud and flower, is taking us higher up the Candlestick to the point where the light is produced.

The first WINDOW located in time is marked by the period the Old Testament covered. The second WINDOW location is marked by the period the New Testament covered. The third WINDOW location is marked by the out pouring of the Spirit of GOD on the Day of Pentecost.

The first almond-bowl represented GOD our creator, the Father of us all, giving us our first drink from HIS Word. It is our Heavenly Father revealing HIS expectations to his children, and the reality of our situation. Revealing his likes and dislikes, and exposing the areas in our lives that haft to be changed. It is from this view, or vantage point of a **FATHER,** GOD would begin to teach from. This first level is the Old Testament. From this LOCATION, GOD is preparing us for the next WINDOW of opportunity to SEE through, the New Testament, where we meet the **Son.** This second almond-bowl would be through a Son's relationship to his father. It again would be from the view or vantage point of a Son. This vantage point prepared us to receive the last WINDOW from which to get a view from. This third location would be through the spirit, (the **Holy Ghost**) which became available to all on the day of Pentecost. Through the Spirit means, GOD'S active presence working in you and with you to become more like HIM each day. This third location point is GOD using the first two levels, the Old and the New Testaments to teach from. This is why it is so important to study the first two levels, or time periods, and to set aside some time to meditate. This gives GOD the time to tie all scriptures together in our minds. Through Christ, GOD shows us a life that fulfils all the requirements written in the Word. The third level is when GOD himself becomes an influential part of your thoughts and actions.

Here, we want to stop and discus this third level, where we become one with GOD. There is something very important we want you to remember. Just because GOD becomes an influential part of our thoughts and actions, does not mean HE gets to choose our final decision or the course of action taken concerning each situation. We can overrule and we can push aside HIS influence of thought and reject HIS strength. This rejection is more likely to happen when we fail to have the complete SWORD of GOD in our hand, which is—Faith—the Word—and Understanding of the Word. *^{32}And the spirits of the prophets are subject to the prophets.* 1 Cor. 14:32. This means, we have the final say.

*^{5}**Let** this mind be in you, which was also in Christ Jesus:* Phil. 2:5. Question—what was in the mind of Christ? Answer—faith—the Word—and the understanding of the Word.

^{16}Let the word of Christ dwell in you richly in all wisdom. Col. 3:16a. This three letter word is BIG, because it says—to get something, "you first must see it is there" and then be "convinced" it is freely yours for the taking. The Tabernacle gives us a visual on how to "spiritually" connect to GOD, by following the high priest—from the entrance into the courtyard—through the Alter—the Brazen Laver—The Holy Place—and finely, into The Most Holy Place. There are deep rooted "spiritual stumbling blocks" which can ONLY be removed by following GOD'S chosen path. The doing of these steps (ALONE) does not save you. Salvation comes through **understanding the why, (**COUPLED WITH), **the doing of those steps.** Again, you must SEE it before you can grab it.

Notice, this scripture said, *let* the Word dwell in you *richly.* The definition of Richly is; beautiful and elaborate; something with a DEEP fully saturated color; completely and plentifully filled. This can only happen if we take a few minutes each day and poke a few pennies worth of information out of GOD'S Word into our bags, (our hearts).

Let me tell you what a minister with twenty years' experience said to me. "People do not want to go deeper, they just want a basic salvation." Basic means elementary, a starting point, something **without extra** and somebody that shows no increase. The Bible clearly teaches this attitude runs parallel to mankind's way of thinking, and not GOD'S. **MATTHEW** 25:**14-30,** tells the story of the master who gave three servants talents before he left on a long journey. One servant received five, the second, two, and the third, one. Upon his return, the master received an **increase** from the first two servants. However, the third with only one talent, had no extra or increase to give. The master said to the servant with one talent, *"You are lazy and unprofitable, and therefore you will be cast out into utter darkness.* Amos 3:3 says, *³ Can two walk together, except they be agreed?* How can we please GOD if we do not know what the agreement between us says? *³⁰ He must increase, but I must decrease.* John 3:30. John was not only talking about his ministry or his popularity decreasing, he was talking about GOD'S influence increasing in our lives. GOD draws pictures to help us understand spiritual things so we can stay **In Between The Lines.**

Well, back we go into The Holy Place. According to EXODUS 26:35, The Golden Candlestick was "always" placed to the left of the entrance inside the tent "next" to the South wall. EXODUS 40:22, said The Table of Shew Bread was always placed to the right inside the Tent "next" to the North wall. The entire tent represented, including the dividing curtain, flesh which is a temporary dwelling. Consider the area, in between the Candlestick and the Table of Shew Bread, as the narrow corridor in **MATTHEW 7:14,** *narrow is the way, which leadeth to life.* Picture yourself "reaching beyond" the small distance separating either the Candlestick or the Table from the Tent, and then touching that "fleshly" wall beyond each spiritual object. This is a picture of going beyond the influence of GOD'S Word or Spirit and falling under mankind's influence of thought and actions. It is sometimes difficult to SEE the line separating the spiritual and the natural, which is why we struggle through—prayer—study—meditation.

To stay Between the Lines one must know what the Word says, and through faith, allow GOD'S active presence to interpret and influence our response in every situation. Spiritually speaking, if you were to push beyond the boundary of GOD'S Word or HIS RESPONSE TO A SITUATION, you would find yourself in the natural river, a world governed by mankind's thoughts and actions, where fear doubt confusion and disbelief linger. This area dominated by the natural river is represented by the tent wall and beyond to the outer-wall of the Tabernacle.

What put Jesus Christ on the cross? Answer—mankind's thoughts and actions.

⁶ Their webs shall not become garments, neither shall they cover themselves with their works: their works are works of iniquity, and the act of violence is in their hands. Isa. 59:6. *⁷ Their feet run to evil, and they make haste to shed innocent blood: their thoughts are thoughts of iniquity; wasting and destruction are in their paths.* Isa. 59:7. GOD'S purpose is to bring our thoughts and actions in agreement with his. To do this, GOD used these four natural rivers to lead us into the Old Tabernacle, a place that clearly show us a distinction between the two ways to go. *¹³ Enter ye in at the strait gate: for wide is the gate, and **broad** is the way, that leadeth to destruction, and many there be which go in there at: ¹⁴ Because strait is the gate, and narrow is the way, which leadeth unto life, and few there be that find it.* Matt. 7:13-14. The "broad" way is the Euphrates and Tigris, the natural river system surrounding The Holy Tent. The narrow way is the Gihon and the Pison, the spiritual river system, the AREA WITHIN the Holy Tent.

Isa. 55:8 says, *⁸For my thoughts are not your thoughts, neither are your ways my ways, saith the LORD.* Isa. 55:9 also says, *⁹For as the heavens are higher than the earth, so are my ways higher than your ways, and my thoughts than your thoughts.* This is confirmed by the cross itself. Christ's hands was nailed to the beam that ran parallel to the earth. The NAILS that held the hands of Christ to the cross are the thoughts and actions of mankind. GOD used these four rivers to help us recognize how to stay between the two spiritual rivers. "You" have to put the Word in your heart, then through faith, allow GOD to bring it to life. *¹³Howbeit when he, the Spirit of truth, is come, he will guide you into all truth:* John 16:13a.

The second touch is the union of your spirit with GOD. This can only happen with complete trust. This strong foundation of trust, especially for new believers, can only be established by combining faith with action. This was the reason GOD represented the bottom part of the cross outside the Tent. That is the **space between** the Altar and the entry to The Holy Place. This being the "same distance" from the feet of Jesus to where the cross entered the ground. Since the day that Jesus Christ set the example. The church uses Repentance and Water Baptism to cross that distance between the Altar of Burnt Offering and the entry into the Tent. Spiritually speaking, Water Baptism **helps** new believers climb that tree, (the cross), from the ground to the feet of Jesus. This one time only Water Baptism experience is the foundation block our future relationship with GOD will be built upon, because it requires faith and action. I know some will say, "The thief hung on the cross next to Jesus was not baptized—he was saved—he went to paradise with the Lord." To them I say, "That thief had no more spiritual battles to fight. That thief had no more need of spiritual weapons. His fight was over. However, that is not the case with you and me. We still have battles to fight." By the way, have you ever gotten a good look at the biggest enemy you will ever face? If you have not seen him yet, just look in the mirror.

We are not going into much detail on Water Baptism at this time. However, I would like to give you an example of how important this _weapon_ is and how to swing it at the devil. *⁴ (For the weapons of our warfare are not carnal, but mighty through God to the pulling down of strong holds;)* 2 Cor. 10:4. For Christians, Water Baptism is the biggest condemnation killer in the spiritual arsenal. When I first came to GOD, I wanted to lift my hands to sing and praise GOD in church, but I could not do it. That devilish voice would whisper, "You fought with your wife. You got mad at your car and threw your wrench out into the woods. You kicked the dog, or should I say a person because he was in your way, keeping you from getting that promotion." Then he would hit me with, "You do not deserve, nor do you have the right to worship GOD." Condemnation separates you from GOD. It is like putting the Grand Canyon in between you two, and there is no natural way to cross such great divide. But spiritually there is a way, which is understanding how to use the first weapon given the church. *³⁸ Then Peter said unto them, Repent, and be baptized every one of you in the name of Jesus Christ for the remission of sins, and ye shall receive the gift of the Holy Ghost.* Acts 2:38. Remission means forgiveness, which applies to past present and future sins. The gift of the Holy GHOST means we have been guaranteed "personal" access to GOD at all times, regardless.

Here is a spiritual comparison between **ACTS 2:38** and the Old Testament Tabernacle. When you repent, you are at the Altar of Burnt Offering dying to yourself. When put under the water in baptism, you are the priest washing in Basin Laver, **building your faith** to enter the Tent of Meeting. You're now in The Holy Place **under** the water. You are covered by GOD'S Word. Your heart has been **washed** clean in the Word of GOD through your act of obedience. When you rise up out of the water. You have, along with the priest, stepped inside The Most Holy Place. As the priest received the spirit of GOD, so you also have received the active presence of GOD in your life. This gives you the right to always have the fellowship of GOD regardless of your faults and short comings. I learned how to take the sharpened spiritual sword in my hand and chop the head of the serpent off. I would remind myself that I had accepted and believed GOD. This acceptance was confirmed and established through my own action of obeying ACTS 2:38, and MATTHEW 28:19. I now enjoy GOD'S presence any time and any place. The devil does not attempt such trickery on me anymore, because I cut the head of the condemnation problem off, it no longer had a voice in my life. It could no longer keep me from lifting up my hands in church to praise GOD. Learn how to use the whole sword—Faith the handle—the Word the blade—and the Understanding of the Word, which is what sharpens the cutting edge of the spiritual sword.

Do not misunderstand us on the point of GOD'S forgiveness in regards to past present and future sins. We do not want you to think this gives you the right to keep on sinning and making the same mistakes over and over, because it does not. Salvation is the process of growth. It is about a gradual change brought about by influence of the Word and Spirit of GOD. Salvation is the "process" of staying In Between the Lines more and more each day. Staying within those two spiritual rivers. This example of using Water Baptism as a weapon was to teach you how to silence one spiritual giant, whose name is—Condemnation. You can only be changed through constant fellowship with GOD. However, this fellowship cannot, and I repeat—cannot happen if you have condemnation in your heart, because DOUBT is its offspring.

Now let us again look at the question and answer which inspired this study on the four rivers. The (foolish) question—why did GOD bring this trouble upon me? The (foolish) answer—GOD brings trouble into our lives to show HIS power and glory by delivering us out of that trouble. With anger in our hearts, we have all at one time or the other looked up toward heaven while shaking our fists and said, "GOD, why did you do this to me?" We are not going into great detail with hundreds of pages of examples and stories to try and convince you to reject the above foolish question and answer. However, we will give you a couple out of the Bible to help you choose the wise question and answer. The (wise) question—from where did this trouble originate that is now confronting me? The (wise) answer—it did not come from GOD, instead, it came from the river, because GOD is not a troublemaker HE is a trouble solver.

For a moment, let us go back to the Old Tabernacle because there is something we held back. And that is, information concerning the floor of the outer courtyard and of the Holy Tent area. The floor of both areas was the same—dirt, which is a substance that spoils the cleanness of something or somebody. Spiritually, Christians have to deal with all the same arrows or problems that the natural river system fires into all mankind. However, believers can simply turn those worrisome problems over to GOD who keeps brushing the dirt off our garments.

19 So shall they fear the name of the LORD from the west, and his glory from the rising of the sun. When the enemy shall come in like a flood, the Spirit of the LORD shall lift up a standard against him. Isa. 59:19. That standard is the Word hidden in our hearts. GOD shall bring it to the surface so all can see the victory of how the dirt cannot stick to you. I never suffered depression again after I fully, and I mean 100% accepted these facts—that GOD loved me and that I was "absolutely" his child. Due to my "understanding" of scripture, doubt and fear no longer lingers because they just get chased off. Faith comes from having knowledge and understanding of the Word, which exposes the character of GOD. Knowledge, concerning the character of GOD, strengthens my faith in HIS ability to solve all problems. Here is a phrase GOD gave to me that I now live by, and I hope it will become your battle cry. IF YOU "SEE MORE" YOU WILL "BELIEVE MORE." Having more penny's worth" of information and understanding in your bag will produce more faith. Spiritually speaking, to SEE means to understand. *³ Thou wilt keep him in <u>perfect peace</u>, whose mind is stayed on thee: because he trusteth in thee. Isa. 26:3. ⁷ Casting all your care upon him; for he careth for you.* 1 Pet. 5:7.

GOD does not tempt mankind with evil to prove HE can deliver us. I know some will say, "What about GOD putting the devil in the Garden of Eden to tempt Adam and Eve?" To them, I say, "The devil was not put here to tempt mankind. On the contrary, GOD hoped the devil would be tempted to repent and ask for help after he had seen the wonderful life GOD gave Adam, who already had the tree of <u>CHOICE,</u> (the tree of life) to deal with." *¹² How art thou fallen from heaven, O Lucifer, <u>son of the morning</u>! how art thou cut down to the ground, which didst <u>weaken</u> the nations! ¹³ For thou hast said in thine heart, I will ascend into heaven, I will exalt my throne above the stars of God: I will sit also upon the mount of the congregation, in the sides of the north:* Isa. 14:12-13.

These scriptures expose the wicked heart of the devil before GOD "restricted" his movement, which is what (*cut down to the ground*) means. This was disciplinary action dealt to the devil and he did not like it. Instead of repenting and asking forgiveness and help, he rebelled yet again. Most people are under the opinion the devil was sent to test or tempt Adam and Eve. I found myself embracing the same opinion before I really got to know GOD'S character. One day while meditating on the story of creation, GOD brought to mind James 1:13. *¹³ Let no man say when he is tempted, I am tempted of God: for God cannot be tempted with evil, <u>neither tempteth he any man</u>:* Then these words came to mind. Adam, an earthly creation, was at that time the only example of a righteous life that was under the protection and blessing of GOD. Wow! GOD exposed two reasons and HIS motivation of why he restricted the devil's movement. The motivation is love for his creation. And the devil, as far as we know, was the first creation to be given freedom to choose his own way to go. 1st reason—GOD hoped the devil would be inspired to come and **ask** forgiveness and help, so he too could have the good life Adam was given. The Lord allowed the devil to participate in the building of all that was created, up until the time HE put restrictions on him. This paralleled the participation of Judas Iscariot in the ministry of Jesus Christ. GOD knew the heart of Judas was set on evil from day one. Yet, HE allowed Judas to participate in the building of his new church. GOD'S love never gave up on him. HE continually attempted to turn the heart of Judas away from evil, as HE did with the devil. However, Judas gave up on GOD and took his own life. Peter, one of the greatest disciples, cursed and betrayed Jesus and then sought the Lord's forgiveness and was reunited. GOD'S patience and love is not easily discouraged. If you want to know the character of love and the value GOD places on it, read the entire 13th chapter of 1st **CORINTHIANS.** For instance, the character of love is exposed in the **seventh verse;** *charity,* **beareth** *all things,* **believeth** *all things,* **hopeth** *all things,* **endureth** *all things.* The value GOD placed on love is exposed in the **thirteenth verse;** *and now abideth faith, hope, charity, these three; but the greatest of these is charty.* Remember, the translation of charity—is **love.**

The 2nd reason GOD restricted the devil takes us back to the natural river system. All creation, both seen and unseen, has been given the right to exist and to interact until our world ceases. We all have been guilty of crediting GOD for our troubles. If we were to look deep into those troubles, we would discover they are a product of the natural flow of the River of Life. For instance, a tiny bacteria who has the right to exist comes in contact with a person—Wham—person gets sick. GOD did not bring trouble to that person. It was a chance meeting on the River of Life. Some will say, "What about Job? Look at the trouble the Lord brought to him."

Quickly, let us look a little deeper. Like a dam holds back the water, GOD was the one holding back trouble to begin with. Spiritually speaking, Job kept climbing over and "beyond" GOD'S help and continually drank from the troubled water. I mean, he did not just drink from it, he wallowed in it. *25 For the thing which* **I greatly feared** *is come upon* *me, and that which I was **afraid** of is come unto me.* Job 3:25. Job could not enjoy any of the blessings given him because he lived in fear and doubt. Job's relationship was stuck in the muddy water and going nowhere. He was already "embracing" the trouble that latter came to pass. In **JOB 1:11-12,** the devil tried to get GOD to bring the trouble down on Job's head, but the Lord refused. Instead, GOD basically said, "I will step out of the way and let the natural river take its course."

So the paths of two crossed and the lives of Job and the devil begin to interact with one another. What the devil did not know was, he would be partly responsible for bringing Job and GOD closer together. For thirty-seven chapters we read about Job's suffering, accusations against him, his wrestling with the Word, and finally, his claim that he is righteous. Then GOD speaks from chapter thirty eight to forty two, revealing Job's lack of understanding. In **JOB 42:3** he said to GOD, *³ Who is he that hideth counsel without knowledge? therefore have I uttered that I <u>understood not</u>; things too <u>wonderful</u> for me, which <u>I knew not</u>.* Then in **JOB 42:5** he said, *⁵ I have <u>heard</u> of thee by the <u>hearing</u> of the ear: but now mine **<u>eye seeth</u>** thee.*

Job finally <u>understood</u> that it was he who had stepped over and past GOD'S line of protection. It was he who brought the trouble down on his own head through his unbelief. The first part of **JOB 42:12** said, *so the Lord blessed the latter end of Job more than his beginning.* Our lives will be enriched every time we give GOD the opportunity to speak through the study of HIS word, prayer, and meditation.

Quickly, let us walk back through the Tabernacle because we left out one small angle from which to look. *³ Jesus answered and said unto him, Verily, verily, I say unto thee, Except a man be born again, <u>he cannot</u> <u>**see**</u> the kingdom of God.* John 3:3. The first entry into the Tabernacle puts you into the outer courtyard. This represented our natural birth into this world. Entry into The Holy Tent is the spiritual second birth. All mankind starts in the outer courtyard and have to deal with life's problems on their own. Those who spiritually make their way into The Holy Tent and take the Arm of GOD, have the greatest protector and trouble solver as their partner. *⁴ Yea, though I walk through the valley of the shadow of death, I will fear no evil: <u>for thou art with me</u>; thy rod and thy staff they comfort me.* Psalm 23:4. We hope you will not be quick to blame GOD for your troubles, but that you will blame it on the River, and then turn to GOD for help.

Remember we said that we would expose some things below the surface in the story of Gideon. However, before we could go to that story, we had to gain an understanding of those four rivers. Again were at the mouth of one of GOD'S caves. And the natural light, (mankind's ability to reason), is not going to be able to follow us in very far. So we have to use a supernatural light. OH—I am so excited, because I cannot wait for you to see an answer to a question I had for years. My question was, "Why GOD, did you have Gideon pick the 300 men that reached into the river with their hands, and brought the water up to their mouths to drink?"

Using your imagination, picture GOD in the form of a man standing alone outside a wooden box filled with water. The water is the situations encountered in daily life. Imagine HIM squatting down just outside the box while keeping himself **<u>upright,</u>** spiritually we mean, always compliant to HIS own Words. Have him REACH HIS <u>*arm*</u> in the water and then bring HIS <u>*hand*</u> up to his mouth to drink. Remember, the two rooms in the Holy Tent represented the Word and the spirit of GOD, which together is HIS arm actively extending HIS hand. The high priest in the Tabernacle was GOD'S hand, and in the New Testament this hand extended was Jesus Christ.

Let us follow the **<u>anointed</u>** priest as he left The Most Holy Place to deliver GOD'S Word to the people. Spiritually speaking, here is the room by room and river by river order through which, the now <u>officially</u> anointed priest walks through the world and on into eternity.

FIRST, he leaves (the Pison River) The Most Holy Place.

SECOND, he enters (the Gihon River) The Holy Place. This being the Word used by the spirit of GOD to defeat the ARROWS of the third river.

THIRD: This third river is the (Tigris River). This being the open courtyard where the priest, (like us), **interacts** with all creation. This area being the troubled waters of everyday life.

FOURTH, (through the Euphrates River). This being the curtain doorway of the fence surrounding the entire complex. Spiritually, this is the doorway of LIFE; and later, of DEATH. This was the "spiritual walking order" of Christ in relationship to the Old Tabernacle, **after** his spiritual anointing was officially revealed to the world. This anointing being confirmed by the dove after he was baptized in water by John. This order of walk was first introduced in **GENESIS 2:10-14,** where GOD put these Rivers ***"flowing out'*** of Eden to the GARDEN in this order: Pison, Gihon, Hiddekel, and Euphrates. GOD, at some early point in time changed the name of the Hiddekel to the Tigris. There is a question that arises out of this sequence. How do we get this spiritual walking order into our lives? Answer—follow GOD FROM START to FINISH through the whole walking sequence.

First—GOD needed a body born of woman. A natural born house through which to work in order to enter into the Euphrates River system, the river of everyday life. Second—Christ, through youth to adult-hood is subjected to the Tigris River, where all creation interacts with one another from which comes all the ARROWS of despair. Third—Christ enters the Gihon River—the WORD (The Holy Place) through the curtain of obedience by the act of Water Baptism. Fourth—Christ enters into the Pison (The Most Holy Place), the spiritual anointing represented by the Dove. Now he is ready to do a 180 degree turn and face the world's problems. So GOD walked that body of Christ back toward eternity. He delivered the Word to the struggling people in the Tigris river area. Then delivered that life into eternity. Throughout all eternity to come, the invisible GOD of creation will be identified and worshipped through the image of Jesus Christ.

In the New Testament, two disciples asked Jesus if they could sit on his right and left side in glory. Jesus answered them in Mark 10:38. *38 But Jesus said unto them, Ye know not what ye ask: <u>can ye **drink** of the cup that **I drink of**</u>? and be baptized with the baptism that I am baptized with?* GOD suffered through the body of Christ because of this drink. This drink being the waters of everyday life.

Here is why Gideon was told to choose the three-hundred. These represented GOD drinking from the troubled waters of life. The <u>walls</u> of the box we had you fill with water represent the Euphrates, the entry into life by way of birth. The water itself is the Tigris, GOD'S creation <u>interacting</u> with one another and each trying to satisfy its own desires. Out of this turmoil comes disease, fear, hate, jealously, envy, vengeance, pride and greed. Outside the box is eternity, that GOD alone, our heavenly FATHER inhabited.

Picture GOD on his knees, slightly bent over the box. This is GOD humbling himself through Christ as witnessed in the **New Testament.** Now have GOD Sticking HIS arm in the water and bringing his hand up to his mouth to drink. HIS hand being Jesus Christ. This is GOD **drinking** from the same Tigris River of despair, and enduring the same ARROWS of pain that all mankind experience.

Gideon's story helps us understand the mechanics involved in establishing and maintaining this spiritual relationship. The three bowls, with knops and flowers spaced at different LOCATIONS up the six shafts of the Candlestick, represent three <u>WINDOWS</u> built into ***GOD'S House,*** <u>the Church</u>. These GOD will use to reveal, confirm, define all truth, and answer all questions and to overcome all situations. This is why GOD choose and divided the 300 men into 3 groups, and why GOD placed them in <u>three **LOCATIONS**</u> surrounding the enemy. It is the view we receive <u>through</u> a <u>Father's</u> perspective, a <u>Son's</u> perspective, and the <u>Spirit's</u> perspective. The last view, is GOD working from within to bring to light all truth hidden in the Old and New Testament. HE is using both Testaments to answer all questions and to solve all problems.

The water being drank from the Hand, is GOD suffering through Christ on the same level of interaction with all of creation as we do. HE conquered sin—HE stayed upright—the waters did not drown HIM—He walked on the waters. The life of Christ is why we can fully trust in GOD. **HEBREWS 6:18,** *it is impossible for GOD to lie,* and in **JAMES 1:13,** *GOD cannot be tempted with evil.* The devil tempted, insulted, beat and cut the body of Christ with <u>no effect</u>. GOD wove this body and all the natural things it experienced into his eternal being and labeled it His Hand. Jesus, represented our eternal GOD, and HIS last name Christ, the natural man.

GOD is invisible and can occupy all space. However, in order for GOD to show you something in this story of Gideon. We ask that you imagine GOD as a man. Quickly, we will look at this story found in the "sixth" through the "eight chapter" of the book of **JUDGES.** For seven years the Midianites swarmed into Israel at harvest time. They took livestock crops and anything else they could get their hands on. GOD sent an angel to where Gideon was hiding and told him he was chosen to defeat the raiders. Naturally, Gideon like Mosses and the rest of us argued with GOD over this calling. However, GOD finally convinced him.

Gideon sent out the call to all Israel, and thirty-two thousand showed up. GOD said, "I cannot use all these people to save Israel, because they will get puffed up thinking they did this through the power of their numbers." GOD said, "Say to the people, whoever is afraid, go home," and twenty-thousand did. GOD said again, "The number of the people is still too great." HE had Gideon take them to water. GOD said, "Set aside those who brought it up to their mouths and lapped it from their "HAND" like a dog would do," and their number was three hundred. The rest of the people were sent home. Afterwards, GOD surrounded the enemy from high-up in the mountains at three locations and gave Gideon instructions on how to deal with the enemy. *⁷ And the LORD said unto Gideon, By the three hundred men that lapped will I save you.* Judges 7:7a. The 300 represented GOD, and the water lapped is the natural River which is the source of those arrows of despair. The three groups represented the three bowls with knops and flowers found on those six shafts of the Golden Candlestick.

First set is the informative group of words that make up the Old Testament. Here we have been given a **FATHER'S** perspective view regarding what is acceptable and expected of his offspring, plus, the penalty for failure. This view reveals his acceptance that we cannot in our present condition fulfill those demands, and that he is preparing a way in which we can. This being Christ, the next level up the six shafts. This *Second* set is the New Testament. This is the perspective view we get through the WINDOW of a **SON** fulfilling the Father's demands, plus, it is information helping us climb up the Candlestick to the final stage. This *Third* set of bowls with knops and flowers is the **SPIRIT'S** perspective view. This WINDOW of OPPORTUNITY being initiated when GOD "officially" poured his spirit out on the day of Pentecost. This point is reached when we fully accept GOD'S personal involvement in our thoughts and actions.

In Gideon's story, the first step in gathering the 300 is the Old Testament. Again, this is the view we get through the WINDOW of the *Father,* because it organized and prepared them for battle. Also in this story, you will read about him "secretly" taking his servant, (his right-hand-man), down in the valley to give us a "view" of what was going on in the camp below. This paralleled the New Testament, where GOD gives us a **"view"** through the WINDOW of the *Son,* a life that fulfilled all the Father's expectations. And finally you will read how the 300 took and broke pitchers with lighted lamps inside, allowing that light to pour out to all in the valley below. This paralleled the outpouring of the spirit to all on the day of Pentecost. This is the third WINDOW and last "location" up the Candlestick. It is the **"view"** seen through the WINDOW of the Holy Ghost. This is GOD'S personal involvement in explaining HIS thoughts hidden in the two Testaments, and in helping us to respond to all situations in thought and action parallel to that seen in the life of Christ.

GOD will <u>EXPOSE</u> all things as WE LOOK through **three** <u>WINDOWS of OPPORTUNITY,</u> the *Father-Son-Holy Ghost*. GOD will reveal the path to victory after the Israelites get a good look from <u>three</u> vantage points. *⁸So the people took victuals in their hand, and their trumpets: and he sent all the rest of Israel every man unto his tent, and retained those three hundred men: and the host of Midian was <u>beneath</u> him in the valley.* Judges 7:8. Gideon was <u>preparing</u> the Israelites to do battle and win their freedom. This is the **FIRST** WINDOW, the Old Testament, the perspective <u>view</u> we get through the Father. Looking through this WINDOW, we see our mistakes, weaknesses, our hopeless situation, and it prepares us to meet the next level. After preparing the 300 for battle—Gideon—(GOD), took his servant, (body of Christ), down in the valley.

This TRIP to the valley represented the **SECOND** WINDOW built into the House of GOD, the New Testament, where GOD interacted with mankind through the body of Christ. This secret visit is why most of the Israelites rejected Jesus. GOD hid <u>behind</u> the fleshly wall of Christ. They could not see that this life was given to benefit them in the long run. The Israelites expected not a servant, but GOD, passing out judgment on the Romans and restoring Israel to its former glory. *¹¹And thou shalt hear what they say; and <u>afterward</u> shall thine hands be strengthened to go down unto the host. <u>Then went he down with Phurah his servant unto the outside of the armed men that were in the host</u>*. Judges 7:11. Phurah in Hebrew means Branch. This is a messianic title related to the shoot, a descendent of King David, which is Christ Jesus. Gideon in the valley with his servant, is the view we get through a **Son's** perspective. The **THIRD** WINDOW, or "location" up the Candlestick is the view we get through the **Spirit's** perspective. This level being established when the spirit was poured out on all flesh after Christ's ascension. This pouring out of the spirit is represented when the three groups broke their lamps.

Thus allowing the light to be poured out of the pitcher on all people, <u>including those lost souls in the valley</u>. *²⁰And the three companies blew the trumpets, and brake the pitchers, and held the lamps in their left hands, and the trumpets in their right hands to blow withal: and they cried, The sword of the <u>Lord</u>, and of <u>Gideon</u>.* Judges 7:20. The pitcher is the broken body of Christ. GOD'S Word is the lamp inside the pitcher. GOD'S spirit is the oil in the lamp that produces the light. The lamp being in the left hand represented the Candlestick in the Holy Tent, which was also on the left hand side of the tent. Both, the lamp and the Candlestick represented the Word. The trumpet is Jesus Christ. The fact that it was in their right hand represented the Table of Showbread in the Holy Tent, which was also on the right side. The right side represented GOD'S active involvement bringing his word to life.

³⁸For I am persuaded, that neither death, nor life, nor angels, nor principalities, nor powers, nor things present, nor things to come, ³⁹Nor height, nor depth, nor any other creature, shall be able to separate us from the love of God, which is in Christ Jesus our Lord. Rom. 8:38-39. **<u>Learn</u>** to stay In Between The Lines. Every time you go too far to the left or to the right, you risk running off into the ditch and getting into trouble. You could get a flat, or get stuck. It could cause you to arrive late at the destination GOD has chosen for you. Such as a preacher, teacher, evangelist, or a writer of deeper things. Spiritually, everyone drives off into the ditch more than once in their ongoing relationship with GOD. Some of us who run our lives off the road and into the ditch of despair, never call for help. We never call that spiritual tow truck to come pull us back on the highway. We leave our vehicles, (our lives), in the ditch and just walk away out into the wilderness. We get lost and never find that road again.

I will be honest with you. I had this call to go deeper and to write about this wonderful experience 40 years ago. OH yes! I am slow to learn. But I would call MY GOD and he would pull my vehicle, (my life), back on the spiritual road time and time again. If my life was a car, and you followed me down my spiritual road, you would see a lot of car parts in the ditch. YEP! You would see an engine, a transmission, flat tires, bumper and a busted headlight. However, you will not see as many car parts at the end of my road as you saw at the beginning.

You have to understand, salvation is not legislated by the o<u>ne thing you do,</u> or by the <u>one thing you understand about GOD.</u> Salvation is the process of growth. This is why Paul started **ROMANS 8:39** with, *I AM PERSUADED,* and why he went on to say -- *nobody, and no situation, present or future can separate him from GOD.* Persuaded means to <u>cause one to Believe</u>. This Faith can only happen by continually filling your heart, your bag, with penny's worth of understanding. It is a daily relationship with GOD through his Word.

Marriage is a good example of the difference between a legislated relationship, and a relationship based on one's actions. A BIG wedding ring on a bride's finger does not guarantee your relationship will last. A lasting relationship is the process of continually, on a daily basis, doing the many little things <u>you know</u> pleases your partner. Process means, a series of actions directed toward a specific aim. Do not misunderstand our conversation in reference to actions. No one act, or multitude of acts on our part can make us righteous, because our nature itself is evil. Only Faith in GOD'S ability to change that nature is what brings new thoughts and actions into our lives. [14]*For when the Gentiles, which have not the law, do by <u>nature</u> the things contained in the law, these, having not the law, are a law unto themselves:* Rom. 2:14. By faith, you are allowing

GOD to give you HIS nature. This is why Zacchaeus immediately changed AFT<u>ER</u> **HE PERSONALLY SAW** Jesus enter his home, his heart.

Now to explain what we mean in reference to your actions building a relationship. It is through your actions of study and fellowshipping with GOD through prayer and meditation. This is how you learn about GOD'S likes and dislikes. Your aim, through this process of fellowship, is to allow GOD the opportunity to change you. To fully match HIS, ·as you learn what HIS nature looks like.

The Last point we want to discuss is an answer to a question many new Christians ask, "WHEN AM I SAVED?" The answer is—SALVATION <u>starts</u> the minute You **Truly** Believe. GOD uses the actions of the high priest to teach us how **<u>true</u>** faith is established.

Faith <u>that produces</u> **ACTION** opens the door to GOD. This act of faith puts you into fellowship with GOD. Look! When we say it opens the door to GOD, we mean—these steps are helping you to SEE, or to ACCEPT the FACT that GOD <u>IS</u> now a part of your life. You must fully accept this fact before you will be able to truly trust in GOD'S abilities. It is a simple process, but very difficult for US to allow, because we are complicated creations. We are eternal beings wrapped in a temporary house of FLESH that desires to satisfy those natural cravings.

Remember, symbolically, there is now only one room in The Holy Tent. The heavy curtain that divided the Tent was removed when Jesus Christ was crucified. The Holy Place is where the "lifeless" body of Christ, the Word of GOD was represented. Why did we say the <u>lifeless</u> body? Answer—The Word "alone" has not got the power to change our nature. The Word by itself, brought spiritual death and separation from GOD. We need the *active* <u>spirit</u> of GOD in us to bring the Word to life. The Most Holy Place was where GOD spoke and was actively involved in fellowship with the Priest. When the sins of mankind was paid for through the sacrifice of Christ. GOD symbolically stepped through his door and filled the entire tent with HIS active presence, thus making salvation a basic two-step process. First you hear the Word. And Secondly, you <u>SOLIDIFY</u> that newly found faith in your heart by doing what the Word said.

Do you remember the two doors we talked about? We symbolically come through the door at one end to meet GOD, who has already come through his door at the other end of the tent. We meet at the body of Christ, this being the Word of GOD. It is the joining of our hands through the Word. It is us grasping hold of GOD'S effort.

The moment you truly believe, puts you inside the Holy Tent grasping the body of Jesus. The moment the curtain dividing the tent was removed, allowed GOD to grasp again the DEAD body of Christ. This touch again brought life into the body of Christ. The Word is now ALIVE due to the active presence of GOD. That life became GOD'S permanent hand. When ***we grasp*** hold of GOD'S hand with our hand of faith, we become one. We have entered the Holy Tent and grasped the **<u>resurrected</u>** body of Christ, through the acceptance of the Word, which in turn resurrects us to a new life brought about by the active presence of GOD fulfilling that Word. This simply means—The <u>Word is no longer dead to us,</u> but is now <u>brought to life in us by the active presence of GOD</u>. This union will immediately produce some instinctive desires and actions in our hearts. Such as, a strong desire to actively fulfill the Word as it is exposed to us. *[13] For it is God which worketh in you both to will and to do of his good pleasure.* Phil. 2:13. Immediately after GOD and I embraced hands, I just could not stop praising HIM. The very next morning, I was compelled to walk three miles just to apologize to someone I had wronged. This was the result of that new GODLY nature which had just become a part of me. Remember, Zacchaeus showed no signs of a changed heart after the first contact with Jesus.

However, he did not give up until he made the second touch. True <u>faith</u> showed its face when Jesus got into his house, his heart. The <u>spontaneous</u> action was a change for the better in how he dealt with people.

GOD represented part of the cross outside the Holy Tent to show us there was more to **<u>establishing</u>** faith than just saying I believe. When you *fully* believe, is when you and GOD will embrace one another. It is essential for us to "understand" <u>why</u> GOD divided the holy tent into two rooms. Why the **WEST** end represented HIS actual spiritual presence, and Why the EAST end, (The Holy Place), represented the "<u>dead body</u>" of Christ on the cross, which in turn represented the Word WITHOUT the active presence of GOD.

ANSWER—The Tabernacle gives us a visual <u>picture</u> of the **spiritual mechanics** involved in the salvation process of uniting us with Him. This is why HE put the Word, which reveals his nature, between us. Not only in the Tabernacle, but on the cross as well. In the Tabernacle, <u>The Holy Place</u> was "between" the outer courtyard and <u>The Most Holy Place.</u> On the cross, Christ was suspended "between" <u>earth</u> below and <u>heaven</u> above. Remember that old saying—SEEING is BELIEVING. It is hard for mankind to grasp **JOHN 1:1** -- *In the beginning was the Word, and the Word was with God, and the <u>Word was GOD</u>.* The Lord, in the Old Tabernacle, drew a line of separation between HIS Word—and HIS spirit by using the curtain that divided the two rooms. Disobedience to the Word is what separated mankind from GOD. *²⁴ So he drove out the <u>man</u>; and he placed at the east of the garden of Eden Cherubims, and a flaming <u>sword</u> which <u>turned every way</u>, to keep the way of the tree of life.* Gen. 3:24.

Notice, it said the **<u>sword</u>** was placed **East** of the Garden. Eden represented GOD'S presence. HE talked directly to Adam in Eden, and talked directly to the high priest in The Most Holy Place. Both, <u>The Most Holy Place</u> and <u>Eden</u> represented a place GOD choose to speak directly to mankind. The flaming sword, GOD'S Word, separated man from Eden. The Holy Place at the East end of the tent stood between The Most Holy Place and mankind, all of whom is represented in the outer-courtyard.

GENESIS 3:24, in GOD'S mind, was partly responsible for inspiring the design of the Tabernacle itself. Notice again, the Sword (the WORD), was placed in between Eden and Man. If you want to understand something, backtrack to where it began, and then follow it forward to where it stops. WE, mankind, separated ourselves from GOD by introducing condemnation into our lives through disobedience. HE has developed a plan to remove it and to renew our relationship.

WINDOWS serve two basic purposes, they let LIGHT in, and allow us to SEE beyond the wall of the room we are in. Light ILLUMINATES, allowing us to SEE all the cobwebs, dirt, and little bugs hiding within. This is what the two testaments do in our lives.

These two Spiritual WINDOWS also allows us to SEE into the Soul of GOD. Have you ever hear this old saying—the EYES are the WINDOWS to the Soul? The Old and New Testaments ARE the EYES of GOD. As WE **look** into them, they reveal to us how GOD sees and reacts to all things.

Do you want to be seen and acknowledged by GOD? Then YOU haft to step into HIS WINDOW of VISION to be seen and acknowledged by HIM. To do this, YOU have to follow the high priest into the Tabernacle—through the Altar of Sacrifice—the washing at the Brazen Laver—and finally, into The Holy Tent of Meeting. This being the place representing the Spiritual bonding between mankind and GOD. This is how you will avoid hearing GOD SAY, *[21] Not every one that saith unto me, Lord, Lord, shall enter into the kingdom of heaven; but he that doeth the will of my Father which is in heaven. [23] And then will I profess unto them, I never knew you: depart from me, ye that work iniquity.* Matt. 7:21, 23.

How to Catch and Hold the Truth

One day when watching college football, and after a controversial call by the referee stopped the game, GOD spoke to me. HE said, "Pay close attention as to how the referees arrive at the right call. The running back fumbled the ball at the one yard line and the other team recovered the ball, or at least that was the ruling made by the referees. However, the team who fumbled the ball challenged the ruling on the field. They said it should not be called a fumble because the ball carrier's knee touched the ground before he lost the ball.

We will explain for you that do not understand this rule. A play is officially over when any part of the body, except for the ball carrier's hands, touches the ground. The problem here, was the fact that nobody got a good look at that play in regard to the timing of the fumble and whether the ball came free before or after the runner's knee touched the ground. The referee's view, <u>at ground level,</u> was somewhat blocked because the play happened so fast and the bodies on both teams were <u>piled</u> on top of the ball carrier. The <u>referees only saw</u> the ball rolling around and the other team recovering it.

They, like all of us, made their initial call from what the **natural eye** captured. The referees realized they needed a DEEPER look. So they ask for a <u>view through the eye in the sky.</u> They knew their opinion might be wrong concerning this play, so they stopped the game and called for instant replay. This was developed to assist the referees in rightly judging any controversial play. It stops it, and allows the referee more time to view that particular play from at least three different **locations.** The referees ruling on the field was eventually changed. The team who fumbled the ball was given the ball back. The play was ruled officially over before the running back lost the ball, because it came free after his knee touched the ground. In the end, the right call was made because of the extra time given to the referee who sat high up in the review box. HE viewed the play through **THREE camera locations.** This referee used these **THREE** angles of view to reveal the truth. This was to eliminate all confusion as to allow the game to continue. OH—I almost forgot to remind everybody about one important fact concerning instant replay. There was only *"ONE"* referee stationed high above the playing field. HE used **THREE** camera locations to "reveal" and "confirm" the truth to all that was affected by that play.

Instant replay was what GOD drew my attention too. HE said, "There is a parallel between instant replay and rightly judging all life's situations and understanding all truth." The parallel is, Location-Location-Location. The referees eventually got the call right because of the three views they had been given. GOD reminded me that HE had established three WINDOWS providing three angles of view to help in our understanding of all things.

Again, these are the two Testaments and GOD'S Spirit, (Father-Son-Holy Ghost) represented on the six shafts of the Candlestick.

The referees caught the truth—it could not escape. They were able to slow the play down to a snail's pace and look from three locations. Three WINDOWS of OPPORTUNITY providing three angles of VIEW concerning ONE game changing situation. Spiritual Truth is revealed in the same manner. Our three WINDOWS is information collected while LOOKING through the Old and New Testaments, and from GOD'S personal assessment of that information.

GOD'S children have to learn how to build a spiritual trap in order to capture and hold the truth. For example, take a hundred straight ten foot sections of fence. Out of that hundred, how many sections would it take to build the simplest pen in which a person could completely surround and hold one little critter? Let us ask you in another way? If you had to use the least amount of "straight" lines, what would be the most efficient and simplest geometric shape to completely surround a single object? It would have to be a Triangle. Remember, GOD deals in straight lines. *¹⁴Because strait is the gate, and narrow is the way, which leadeth unto life, and few there be that find it.* Matt. 7:14. The three sides forming this spiritual shaped pen is found in **1st JOHN 5:8,** *there are three that bear witness in earth, the Spirit, and the water, and the blood: and these three agree in one.* The Spirit is GOD, and the water is the Word of GOD, and the blood is GOD confirming his Word through the **life** of Jesus Christ. The last part of **LEVITICUS 17:14** says, *for the life of all flesh is the blood.* All things are revealed, (by GOD), as **We LOOK** through the Old and New Testaments.

We want you to consider the word ***truth*** as representing a beautiful furry little critter, a creature that you would like the time to get to know. But this critter is in the habit of moving around, and naturally, he wants to get away. So GOD gave us three equally long sections of spiritual fence from which to build a pen. We then attach the three spiritual sections of fence together to form a three sided triangular pen. This gives us three windows of opportunity *"through"* which to view and study a single truth. This three-sided pen is how we will solve all difficult situations that forces their way into our lives. We can "view" that little critter from three angles, seeing every inch of that creature and learn about its nature—safely. I guess I forgot to tell you that this little critter called truth has sharp teeth, and sometimes will give you a painful bite if it does not agree with the way you handle it. In other words, the truth can hurt, especially if it is contrary to what you have believed in all your life.

I had an experience with a wild baby raccoon several years ago. The noise of my dog barking feverishly at my back door caused me to step outside to *see* what the commotion was all about. When I stepped out, a little ball of fur caught my attention. It was wedged in between the house and the air conditioner. I slowly reached down and picked it up by the back of its neck. I expected the raccoon to put up a fight the very minute I touched it, however, it did not. Spiritually, some truth does not put up a fight when we first touch it. Nor does it gain our attention when we first start our walk with GOD, because we simply do not have enough knowledge. This little critter, which was about three months old, was frozen with fear. So I put it into a pen I used to keep rabbits in. Latter, I notice it was moving around, like it was looking for something. I thought, "Maybe it is hungry, I will give it something to eat." So I went out to feed it. As I opened the door to the pen it rushed forward, catching me off guard and bit me in the hand. I knew raccoons are prone to carry rabies. I also knew rabies shots were very painful. To avoid taking the shots, I would have to keep the raccoon under close observation for at least thirty to sixty days. If the raccoon showed no sign of rabies after that time, I would probably be okay. However, in my haste to get to the house to clean and bandage my wound, I had forgotten to properly lock the cage door. The next day, when I went to feed the raccoon, it was gone. I now had to **suffer** through the "pain" of those terrible rabies shots, because I let the little furry critter escape before I got a good long look at it. I lost the chance to learn the truth concerning my situation because I was in a hurry and neglected to properly surround the truth, to entrap it so it could not get away. You that do not have an abundant knowledge of the Old and the New Testament, is similar to me leaving the gate open. I lost the raccoon and the chance to avoid the pain of those shots. You on the other hand, will suffer pain because you lost the chance to observe the truth, the answer to a problem. You lost the little critter because you had no way to block his escape due to your neglect of study and meditating. *[6] My people are destroyed for lack of knowledge:* Hosea 4:6a. I suffered physically, but you who have little or no knowledge of the Word will absolutely suffer spiritual pain, because you have no way to catch and hold the SOLUTION to your problem. The only way GOD can answer your questions and change your life is through HIS Word.

GOD first developed the Old and the New Testaments so we would have two more WINDOWS of OPPORTUNITY, two more angles of view from which to judge all things. The Old and New Testaments are the first two sides of the spiritual pen. The third is GOD'S active influence in our lives, not only in our actions but also in our minds.

⁴ And when he putteth forth his own sheep, he goeth before them, and the sheep follow him: for they know his voice. John 10:4. The words he goeth before them simply means, GOD first developed the Old and the New Testaments before we received HIS spirit, and these three will always agree. Spiritual critters, are the "understanding" of all things "buried" in the scriptures. **Understanding** the structure and the mechanics of this spiritual triangle is why GOD gave us the story of Gideon, who divided his men into three groups and surrounded the enemy, which was the problem that confronted them in the valley below. The people viewed and attacked their problem from THREE LOCATIONS which provided THREE angles of VIEW, and because of this, gained the victory. *¹¹ Thy word have **I** hid in mine heart, that I might not sin against thee.* Psalm 119:11. *¹³ Howbeit when he, the Spirit of truth, is come, he will guide you into all truth:* John 16:13a. GOD is the only one that reveals the absolute truth. Notice, the scripture said—*I have hidden the Word in my heart.* You have to study the Bible. You need the two sides of the spiritual pen. You then need to stop the play, the activity in your life, for a moment through meditation. This allows the third side of the pen to be put into place, which is GOD'S input, (HIS voice).

I know we have been somewhat redundant concerning these three bowls with knops and flowers represented on the Golden Candlestick. However, there is a good reason for this—redundancy. We have just entered into a spiritual cave that has just enough natural light, (man's opinion), to cause most of the church world to misread the images painted on the cave's wall by GOD'S Word. It is not a misread that will keep you from having a relationship with HIM, nor is it one that will keep you out of Heaven. It is however, another pennies worth of understanding to put into your bag which will bring you closer to GOD. When you understand one thought, that in turn opens up other truths hidden in the Bible. A close relationship with the Lord comes from accumulating understanding of those individual thoughts. More pennies in the bag the closer to GOD you will be.

Would you like to have a close relationship like John the apostle had? He knew Judas would betray Christ before any of the other apostles. GOD told John "through" Christ at the last supper, *²¹ When Jesus had thus said, he was troubled in spirit, and testified, and said, Verily, verily, I say unto you, that one of you shall betray me. ²² Then the disciples looked one on another, doubting of whom he spake. ²³ Now there was leaning on Jesus' bosom one of his disciples, whom Jesus loved. ²⁴ Simon Peter therefore beckoned to him, that he should ask who it should be of whom he spake. ²⁵ He then lying on Jesus' breast saith unto him, Lord, <u>who is it?</u> ²⁶ <u>Jesus answered</u>, He it is, to whom I shall give a sop, when I have dipped it. And when he had dipped the sop, he gave it to Judas Iscariot, the son of Simon.* John 13:21-26. At that particular moment, twelve men at that last super had a relationship with GOD through Christ. Judas had a *cold* one, ten others had a good one, and John had a great one with the Lord. If you study about John, you will see the other apostles were somewhat jealous of John's relationship with Jesus. John's head upon the breast of Jesus, and the Lord revealing to John the identity of the one who would betray HIM, symbolized a great fellowship with GOD. This comes only through the Word and the Spirit. *¹In the beginning was the Word, and the Word was with God, and the Word was God.* John 1:1. *¹⁴ And the Word was made flesh, and dwelt among us.* John 1:14a. John's head against the <u>flesh</u> of Jesus symbolized what lies between, separating man from GOD. HE gave us the written Word and then brought it to life in Christ. Mankind must first believe and <u>embrace</u> this Word, this Christ. Which life is the confirmation of the character and promises of GOD.

This is confirmed in the Old Testament Tabernacle. The priest entered The Holy Place from the East end and GOD entered The Holy Place from the West end, out of the area called The Most Holy Place. Symbolically, what **lay** between, and separated GOD and mankind in The Holy Place? It was mankind's inability to fulfill HIS Word, because our natures are not a like. So GOD—stitched—into his eternal makeup the experiences of the flesh, what mankind has to deal with on a daily basis. GOD adorned that flesh from within and without with all righteous thoughts and actions, fulfilling every law HE spoke into existence. Jesus Christ, whose name means GOD with MAN, or GOD in union with the flesh, was tempted in all things, and yet, he did not sin. Jesus Christ was GOD exposing himself to all the muddy waters we have to walk through. The sinless life of Christ confirmed GOD'S righteous nature. This is why GOD called this life of Christ, HIS right arm. This experience has now become a permanent part of GOD. Henceforth, Christ will always be the visual expression of GOD. Remember, GOD is the INVISIBLE Spirit who inhabits all eternity and all space as HE so chooses. Jesus Christ is the VISIBLE expression of GOD. Since GOD proved, by example, to be absolutely one hundred percent trust worthy. We, with all confidence, can grasp the promises confirmed by the Word.

Through FAITH, we can grasp this promise of having HIS nature at work in our lives. Confidence allowed the priest to enter The Holy Place to grasp the promise of GOD'S personal involvement to come, represented within The Most Holy Place.

Some men misinterpreted the picture painted on the spiritual cave's wall by GOD'S Word and passed it on to the church. There are not THREE separate and **distinct individuals,** such as a Father, a Son, and a Holy Ghost teaching us what we have inherited. There are however, *THREE LOCATIONS,* **THREE WINDOWS** established throughout time, which GOD uses to teach through.

God began to establish these THREE locations as far back as the exodus of Israel out of Egypt. During their exodus, GOD had the people of Israel turn around and head back toward their enemy. They faced that enemy at a spot **surrounded** by **(3)** cities, Pihahiroth, Migdol, and Baalzephon. The 14th chapter of Exodus tells us, this was done to draw out King Pharaoh and the Egyptians so GOD could remove this problem out their lives forever. Like Job, the Israelites still carried the FEAR of Egypt in their hearts even though GOD was with them. **EXODUS 14:10-12** said the Israelites wanted to return to be slaves back in Egypt at the first sign of trouble. The fear of this sinful problem overtaking and controlling them had to be overcome before they could move on in their relationship. This was done from within the boundaries of **three** cities, Pihahiroth, Migdol, and Baalzephon. Three angles of view for the purpose of "capturing" all truth and defeating all enemies. **Pihahiroth** means temple or house, which spiritually is the body of Christ. This is the New Testament WINDOW, the perspective angle of view WE see through the *Son.* **Migdol** is watchtower, this spiritually represented the Word of the Father, our GOD.

A tower is a high place from which to speak to a large group, preparing the people to receive deliverance and victory. This is the perspective view WE **see** through the WINDOW of the *Father*—the Old Testament where GOD prepared mankind to receive Jesus Christ. **Baalzephon,** is Lord of the North, the active Spirit of GOD. This city represented the perspective angle of view WE **see** through the WINDOW of the *Spirit,* (the Holy Ghost). This is GOD *explaining* what we **SEE** while looking THROUGH the Old and the New Testaments. GOD built the trap amidst **three** locations from which the Israelites will witness the victory over evil, represented by Pharaoh. GOD will bring victory to all that believe through the view we get through the three ***WINDOWS***, *Father—Son—Holy Ghost.* These HE established at **three** locations in time. The Old Testament, the New Testament, and when HE poured out HIS Spirit to all believers on the day of Pentecost.

GOD confirmed this judging of sin through three WINDOWS of authority in the life of Samuel. He represented GOD in the days of the first Kings of Israel. Samuel served Israel, not only as a **prophet,** but as a circuit-walking **judge** <u>settling disputes</u>. His circuit formed a triangle of **three** cities in central Israel—*Mizpah, Bethel,* and *Gilgal.* **Mizpah** in Hebrew is watchtower. **Bethel** in Hebrew is house of GOD. **Gilgal** means circle, which points to actions inspired by the Spirit. Gilgal is where the Israelites, under the "direction" of GOD'S Spirit, were told to take twelve stones out of the Jordan River and piled them in a circle. That command at Gilgal represented GOD using the stones of information out of the two Testaments. Mizpah the watchtower, the Word—is the WINDOW called the *Father* preparing us to receive the Victory. Bethel—the house is Christ, the WINDOW called the *Son* through which we see the victory. Gilgal, is the WINDOW called the *Holy Ghost.* GOD'S voice confirming the Word in the mind of the believer. As <u>one person,</u> **one spirit,** Samuel judged Israel from three LOCATIONS.

The book of Job is a good example of this triangular approach to teaching. Job is broken down into three segments, all of which represented the three WINDOWS of opportunity. The <u>Spirit's WINDOW</u>, is when GOD literally spoke into the mind of Job explaining the words that he heard from the first two witnesses. The first witness was the group of three friends, and Elihu was the second witness. We see these THREE WINDOWS being used in the life of Job, after the muddy waters rolled over his head and the arrows of life penetrated his soul.

Job's three friends, Eliphaz, Bildad, and Zophar represented the <u>office of the Father,</u> the Old Testament through which GOD first introduced his law to mankind. They declared GOD'S sovereignty, exposed wickedness, reproved sin, and showed the blessings of repentance. In addition, the Old Testament by itself was <u>unable</u> to <u>solve</u> mankind's problem. Elihu, the second witness, confirmed in **JOB 32:5** this lack of power to help in regards to the three friends. Elihu represented the perspective view we get when LOOKING through the Son's WINDOW, the New

Testament. Who, as it said in **JOB 32:6,** was young and did not begin to speak until after the three friends were silent. This silence represented the four hundred years before the birth of Jesus Christ. This was the span of time that GOD stopped speaking through the prophets to Israel. Elihu translated means, this truly is GOD, and, this truly is an expression of GOD. **HEBREWS 1:2-6** said Jesus was the express image of GOD. Expression is the conveying of thoughts or feelings through a work of art. This work of art—**is Christ.** Elihu, according to **JOB 32:5,** came because the three friends had "no answer" to his problem. Job claimed he was righteous because of his good deeds, and that GOD was being unjust. In the mind of Job, this trouble was GOD'S fault, does that sound familiar? JOB **33:1-6** will confirm Elihu as representing Jesus Christ and the New Testament. *¹, Wherefore, Job I pray thee, hear my speeches, and hearken to all my words. ², behold, now I have opened my mouth, my tongue hath spoken in my mouth. ³, my words shall be the uprightness of my heart, and my lips shall utter knowledge clearly. ⁴, the spirit of GOD hath made me, and the breath of the almighty hath given me life. ⁵, if thou canst answer me, set thy words in order before me, stand up. ⁶, behold, I am according to thy wish in GOD'S stead; I also am formed out of clay.*

Job's three friends represented the Old and Elihu the New. The Old Testament, like the three friends, established the sovereignty of GOD as being the Father, who alone has the right to judge us all. However, obeying the laws of GOD could not change the nature of man. Like Job, hearing GOD'S Word by itself cannot solve mankind's problem. But the information given by the three friends prepared Job for the next witness. Both Elihu and Christ tried to explain the Word more clearly. Through the Son, GOD furthered the knowledge and understanding of scripture. "Preparing" the people to receive the Spirit, the actual voice and strength of GOD operating in their lives.

Job still did not understand, even though he had received information from two sources. In our case, the Old and the New Testaments. The first two sections of the spiritual pen was in place. Job only needed that <u>third</u> section to complete the pen. That came in the **thirty-eighth** chapter where GOD began to explain, **<u>personally,</u>** the words Job <u>heard</u>. *¹Moreover the* L<small>ORD</small> *answered Job, and said, ² Shall he that contendeth with the Almighty instruct him? he that <u>reproveth</u> God, let him answer it.* Job 40:1-2. *Then Job answered the Lord, and said. Behold, <u>I am vile</u>, what shall I answer thee? I will lay mine hand upon my mouth. Once have I spoken; but I will not answer: yea,* **<u>twice:</u>** *but will proceed no further.* Job 40:3-5. Job finally got smart, he learned to shut-up and listen.

Job found peace and gained the victory after GOD got through "tying" all those words of wisdom together. *⁵ I have heard of thee by the hearing of the ear: but now mine eye seeth thee.* Job 42:5. Remember that old saying, Seeing is Believing. Meditation is that period when we allow GOD time to put the last section of our spiritual fence in place. It is about using our spiritual cameras, (our imaginations), to hold in our minds the Word of GOD so as to allow HIM the time to explain.

Let us go back to the Old Tabernacle for a moment. Because there is something that you may not know about the area called The Most Holy Place? It is where the Ark of the Covenant was placed. It was a gold-covered box, two and half cubits long by one and a half cubits wide with two golden cherubs on top. Each cherubim was beaten into shape out of a **<u>single</u>** piece of gold. Each had two wings stretched outward. These cherubs were attached to the ends of the golden lid that covered the box, with both facing each other and the cover itself. The wings pointed toward each other and formed a covering over the mercy seat where the high priest sprinkled the blood of the sacrifice. This mercy seat is where GOD talked to the high priest.

Here is something you may not know. The cherubim's body to the left, or **south,** represented the Old Testament. This cherubim's two wings, extending from that body, represented Moses and the Prophets. The cherubim's body to the right, or **north,** represented the New Testament. This cherubim's two wings, extending from that body, represented Jesus and the Apostles.

GOD said in **EXODUS 25:22,** *and there I will meet with thee, and I will commune with thee from ⁻above the mercy seat, from* **between** *the two cherubims which are upon the ark of the testimony, of* all things *which* I will give thee in commandment *unto the children of Israel.* Here again, we find GOD in fellowship with his people from within the boundaries of the Old and New Testament. The SPIRITUAL **three** sided triangular trap.

There is an example in the New Testament where GOD specks to the church from "between" the two cherubs. **MATHEW** 17: 1-7 said, Jesus took Peter James and John up into a high mountain. Jesus was then transfigured before them. HIS face shined like the sun, and his clothes was white as the light. Then Moses, who represented GOD in the Old Testament, and Elias who represented the prophets, appeared and talked with Jesus. Moses and Elias represented the two wings of one cherub, which in turn represented the Old Testament. Jesus and the apostles represented the two wings on the other cherub, which in turn represented the New Testament. Then the bible said in **MATHEW 17:5,** *while he yet spake, behold, a bright cloud overshadowed them: and behold* **a voice** out of the cloud, *which said, this is my beloved son, in whom I am well pleased; hear ye him.*

GOD'S purpose was to get the Israelites to put their trust in Jesus. To bring that trust up to the same high level and hopefully beyond as they had in Moses, who was given a god like status in the Old Testament. **EXODUS 7:1,** *and the Lord said unto* Moses, *See, I have made thee a* **god** *to Pharaoh: and* Aaron *thy brother* shall be thy prophet. Do you know what Peter James and John was doing when GOD spoke out of that cloud of glory? Nothing! They were watching and listening to the third section of the spiritual fence. Their <u>eyes</u> received the first two sections and the voice o<u>f GOD interpreted</u> what their eyes had just seen. They received understanding out of the Old and New Testaments through the <u>*voice*</u> of GOD. These are the three WINDOWS of opportunity that forms the spiritual triangle, "through" which comes all knowledge and understanding.

New Christians get the idea that fellowship with GOD is furthered by doing things in the church. Such as, parking attendant, singing in the choir, asking people to come to church, and visiting the sick. However, that is not the case. A relationship with GOD is established and maintained through the understanding of the Word, brought about by the spirit of GOD. I have heard many young and old Christians say, "<u>I do not "know" much of anything about the</u> Bible, <u>I just like to keep busy and do things for GOD</u>." Doing things to further the Kingdom of GOD is the SECOND calling all Christians <u>should</u> fulfill. However, the **FIRST** and most important calling is that daily commitment of time spent in the **WORD** with just you and GOD. Remember when Jesus was in the house of the two sisters. Martha was **<u>busy</u>** waiting on all the people who came to see and hear Jesus. However, Martha became <u>bitter</u> and started <u>complaining</u>. Mary on the other hand sat at the feet of Jesus and listened. Look again at what Jesus said to Martha when she complained about Mary not helping. **LUKE 10:42,** *but <u>one thing</u> is <u>needful</u>, and Mary hath chosen that <u>good</u> part, which shall not be taken away from her.* We will be far less likely to develop a complaining attitude if we start the day in fellowship with GOD through the Word. All the things you do to further the Kingdom of GOD, after that personal time with the Lord, will be done with much greater zeal. One Mary, who sat at the feet of Jesus bathing those feet with her tears—<u>Ran</u>—to testify to others of the Lord's resurrection. The Bible said in **MATHEW 22:37-39,** that the first commandment is to *love the Lord,* and the second commandment is to *love your neighbor.* Doing things to help the church to grow, no matter how insignificant it may seem, is very-very-important and very-very necessary. But do not forget that personal time with GOD from whence comes the inspiration to do those other things.

Father-Son-Holy Ghost, representing three WINDOWS providing THREE ANGLES through which to EVALUATE all questions and situations, will be seen in operation in chapter Eight. You will "SEE" Elisha, who represented GOD, opening up a WINDOW in order to ANSWER a problem presented by Jehoash the King of Israel. That WINDOW being the ANGLE of View provided by the Old Testament.

You will "SEE" two stories involving Elisha, recorded one right after the other, used to explain a spiritual truth. Both stories took place at different LOCATIONS in Time. Yet both revolve around the same subject. This being the purpose and manner in which to apply the Water Baptism experience. One story runs immediately into the second story. This parallels the Old Testament story running into the New Testament story. These TWO STORIES are the TWO WINDOWS of OPPROTUNITY placed by GOD in the "church," which HE uses to expose all things. The first story shows the King shooting an arrow through an OPEN WINDOW, this being the view we get as we look through the Old Testament.

The second story has us looking into the OPEN grave of Elisha and SEEING a man brought back to life, this being the view we get as we LOOK through the New Testament WINDOW.

Elisha **VERBALLY** exposing the Kings misunderstanding is the third WINOW of OPPROTUNITY labeled the Holy Ghost. It is GOD personally explaining scripture in the mind of the believer.

My Two Birds

Before I introduce you to my birds, you need to know that GOD gave them to me for my own personal growth. This was GOD'S response to my request for more understanding. I am giving you my two little imaginary friends, my two personal tools which has helped me tremendously, in hope that they will help you.

After I "seriously" asked him, GOD begin to establish two <u>things</u> I would need in order for him to take me deeper into his mind. First, I would need one hundred percent trust. Yes! I do mean, 100% trust in HIS ability to reveal all things. Second, I will need two little <u>imaginary birds</u> which HE will affix to each one of my shoulders.

The first of these two things will be the acceptance and application of two scriptures. One of these scriptures has a powerful promise within its wording which has been somewhat overlooked: But when combined with another scripture, will give you spiritually speaking, the power equal to a nuclear bomb. They together have power to destroy or blow away anything other than the absolute truth. This includes the answer to any situation or question that might arise. The first scripture, often quoted throughout the church world is **MATTHEW 7:7**, *Ask, and it shall be given you; seek, and ye shall find; knock, and it shall be opened unto you.* The second scripture, which contains the nucleus of the atom to the spiritual bomb of revelation, is **PHILIPPIANS 3:15,** *let us therefore, as many as be perfect, be thus minded: and <u>if in anything ye be</u> **"otherwise minded"**, <u>**GOD "shall" reveal** even this unto you</u>.* Stop and think about the last half of this scripture for a minute—GOD is promising to NEVER STOP TRYING to bring to your attention, any changes you need to make in your actions or thinking regarding your beliefs. The problem is, many churches and individuals unknowingly reject each attempt GOD makes to change our way of thinking, due to our adherence to traditions and prior teaching. Often we reject information out of the Bible because it came to us from a person not famous, or who is not a high ranking official in the church. I once tried talking to a preacher about a new twist on an old belief he and his church had embraced forever. Before we could get STARTED into the subject, he cut me off. He said, "I have held this belief in this particular fashion all my life, and <u>I will not</u> change my view on this subject now <u>or ever</u>." The preacher then said, "Besides, who are you to think you can add anything new to a subject that has been taught by the "<u>great</u> men" of our church organization?" There is that fence again, blocking the advancement of fellowship with GOD. A fellowship furthered by the <u>flow</u> of information that could lead to "greater" understanding. The Bible says, *⁴ Ye are the light of the world. A **<u>city</u>** that is set on an hill cannot be hid.* Matt. 5:14. GOD, through Christ, compared us to a city. A city grows from a <u>constant flow</u> of people moving in. A city's growth depends on the many roads leading into it. The city has wide expressways with several lanes, plus it has four lane roads, two lane roads, and alley ways. All of these help the city to grow and be productive. If any of the main roads are shut down, they will use a secondary road to keep the flow of people coming into the city. We, as spiritual cities, operate in like manner. Sometimes our spiritual super highway, our understanding and acceptance of scripture, is blocked or broken down. If GOD cannot **flow** new and vital information to us through normal spiritual channels, such as reading HIS Word or through the ministry of preaching, then he will use secondary avenues into our lives. The Fifth chapter of 2nd KINGS tells us how a <u>little servant girl</u> brought to the great and powerful General Naaman of Syria, the information that eventually lead to the healing of his leprosy. The Bible says, *² Be not forgetful to entertain strangers: for thereby some have entertained <u>angels</u> unawares.* Heb. 13:2. The translation of angels is <u>messengers</u>. This means somebody carrying a message or somebody running an errand for somebody else, and also, a paid courier. Yes, this includes preachers.

Any child of GOD that wants to grow should never say, "Who are you to be giving advice in regard to GOD'S Word?" We should always ask ourselves, "What did GOD say, and why did he say it?" We who love the Lord always have to take into consideration **ROMANS 8:28,** *we know that **ALL** things work together for good to them that love GOD.* Take note again of what **PHILIPPIANS 3:15** said. The church world (GOD'S children), if they are to be perfect, collectively, should be *thus minded.* Have you ever asked yourself why there are so many different-minded churches? We've got Baptist, Methodist, Catholic, Lutherans, Assembly of God, Pentecostals, Jehovah Witness, and so on. Each of these church groups has built their own fences around themselves. This makes it difficult, if not impossible for them to receive anything other than what their group believes.

We, GOD'S children, even have two basic ideas that we have to deal with at work in the church community, pertaining to the identity of GOD. One of these basic beliefs is held by most of the church world. That is—GOD is represented by a Father, a Son, and a Holy Ghost, these being three **separate** and **distinct** individuals called the holy trinity. The definition of trinity means, three separate and **distinct** things. The other basic belief is held by a large number of believers calling themselves the Oneness people. They believe the Father-Son-Holy Ghost to be three **offices** of authority that manifest the one and only GOD. These two beliefs have separated GOD'S children far too long. The sad truth is, 99.9999% of the people in either group cannot properly explain what they believe in regard to the subject of GOD'S identity, because they themselves do not understand.

Remember this -- your salvation is not determined by whether you believe in GOD'S identity as Trinity or Oneness. Salvation is determined by your acceptance of the life and sacrifice of Jesus Christ as being GOD'S only plan to reunite us to HIM. However, the understanding of GOD'S identity; meaning, GOD'S relationship to the life or the body of Christ will strengthen this relationship. Here, we will make a bold guarantee. You will understand better than ever after you read the Chapter, "**GOD Is.**" It will put another penny in your relationship bag. Again, more pennies of understanding in your bag migrates to a closer relationship with GOD.

Some say, "It is not meant for man to understand GOD." To them I say, "That is not true. GOD gave us the Bible so <u>**all**</u> things could be revealed, even his identity." It is our "GOD given right" as HIS children to know and to understand all things, except for the exact moment Jesus again appears on earth. All we need, are the tools and the know-how in which to use these tools. This book is all about exposing <u>some</u> of those spiritual tools, and showing how to use them to bring unity of thought throughout the church world.

My two little "imaginary" birds, which GOD created for me, will help you in your quest to go deeper into HIS mind. Both birds are now permanently perched on each of my shoulders. Both are about six inches tall and have the appearance of two little Owls. Their height includes four inch bodies and two inch legs. Each has only one eye of a different color. They have a little beak just below the eye, one leg, and one foot that looks like a man's hand. We started to build these two imaginary birds just after I had read the story of Adam and Eve for the hundredth time, or so it seemed.

Yes, I said WE! Meaning, GOD allowed me to give my input concerning their creation. Granted, GOD only allowed me to pick the color of their eyes as long as they were both different colors. GOD explained the difference. He said, "These two birds represent two words, and these words will always bring into view all things in just a little different manner. Once you have these two words firmly attached in your life, I will use them to reveal all things in the Bible whenever you—<u>**openly**</u>—ask, <u>seek</u>, and <u>knock</u>." GOD also revealed why he choose a man's hand to be their feet, instead of the "natural" choice that I wanted—a bird's foot. I understood that the foot of each bird represented the supernatural hand of GOD, (Jesus Christ), which life keeps us bound together with HIM. The overall six inch height of the birds reminds me of the Bible. Their two inch legs represent the New Testament, which covered approximately two thousand years of man's existence. The four inch body represent the Old Testament, which covered approximately four thousand years of mankind's history. The fact that they looked like one legged little owls always reminds me of the word WHO, because that is the sound the WISE owl makes when HE speaks. So when I am confronted by a question, information, or a situation, I know the only WHO to ask—GOD—through reading the Bible, prayer, and meditation. I do this before I come to a conclusion regardless of how long it takes. This is why their little beaks, just below their eyes, are always poked inside my ears chirping away, reminding me to check it out with GOD.

Can you fill in the blanks? The name of the first bird is _____, and the name of the second bird is _____. Can you tell me the reason GOD considers these two words spiritual power tools? We will give you a hint. The story of Adam and Eve revealed the devil knew the power of these two words, if applied properly. He knew they could change a person's mind and the path an individual would take in life. Have you guessed the names of the two birds yet? Remember, the devil said to Eve -- *hath GOD said ye shall not eat of every tree in the garden?* Remember Eve's words in response to that question in GENESIS 3:3, *Ye shall not eat it, neither shall ye touch it, lest ye die.* Eve left out one important word used by GOD, *you will—*<u>SURELY</u>*—die.* The devil was checking Eve to see if she knew what GOD said. The devil knew Eve was weak in the knowledge and understanding of GOD'S Word when she could not repeat it correctly. The devil then gave Eve his version of what GOD said. "*You will—*NOT*—surely die.*" Then after the devil changed the what, he went after the why. He said, [5] *For God doth know that in the day ye eat thereof, then* *your eyes shall be opened, and ye shall be as gods, knowing good and evil.* Gen. 3:5. The devil used the power of what and why to change the path that all mankind would take.

Say hello to my two little birds, **What** and **Why.** They are constantly chirping into my ears, "What did GOD say—Why did HE say it?" In my youth, a teacher once said to our class, "Pay attention to the 5-W's (Who-What-Why-Where-When), because they are tools that will bring you knowledge understanding and power." We will focus only on What and Why, since when and where is self-explanatory, and the Bible has already exposed the only *Who* that matters.

These two powerful scriptures, MATHEW 7:7 and PHILIPPIANS 3:15, contain a promise from GOD to **answer** all questions and to **eliminate** all confusion in your life. To receive the promises these two scriptures expose. One must first ask GOD, then *completely* believe HE will deliver. One must live with great expectation and patience for the answer to come even while you're going about your everyday life. Some answers will come immediately, and others may take years, due to our thick heads and neglect of study.

Much of GOD'S mind was exposed as I researched those four rivers. I first had to ask GOD **What** HE had to say about them, and **Why** did HE include them in the Bible. What and Why are the shovels of spiritual discovery. They will inspire you to DIG Deep into the mind of GOD. Great treasure will "only" be found by digging or searching for it. You may discover a small piece of the treasure by chance or opportunity? But you will never discover the mother lode without great effort.

The Atocha and Margarita were Spanish treasure ships filled with gold, silver, and jewels from the New World. In September of 1622, they sank in a hurricane. Naturally ha-ha, as many would testify to, the "Margarita" was found and her treasure was recovered. The Atocha however, landed on a reef in 55 feet of water.

Before they could figure out how to retrieve its treasure, another hurricane swept the Atocha off to a new location.

Mel Fisher is a treasure hunter. In 1969 he decided to see **What** information he could find concerning the Atocha. He started his search in the area that the maritime logs recorded the ship's last known position. After finding nothing, Mel brought together specialists in ancient maps, oceanography, and weather. The specialists came up with a reason why he should look in this new area. Mel listened, and in 1985 Kane Fisher (Mel's son) who captained the salvage ship Dauntless, sent this jubilant message, "Put away the charts, we found the main pile." You see, in 1973 they found three silver bars which could be confirmed as belonging to the Atocha. They stumbled onto a piece of the treasure. However, it took them 12 more years to find the mother lode. Its current value is near one billion dollars.

[44] Again, the kingdom of heaven is like unto treasure hid in a field; the which when a man hath found, he hideth, and for joy thereof goeth and selleth all that he hath, and buyeth that field. Matt. 13:44. You cannot find great treasure without digging and searching for it. This treasure the man discovered in the field was not yet his. He had to own the land where the treasure lay, and so, he had to first buy it. To buy the land means, one must spend his hard earned currency. Spiritual money is, **TIME SPENT.** In this story, the *treasure* in the field is spiritual understanding. The *field* is information that hides and surrounds this treasure.

Information comes to us by ways of reading the Bible, preachers, teachers, the media, and angels unaware, who are seemingly unimportant individuals. It is our responsibility to take **What** and **Why,** the two spiritual shovels, and put them to work by digging through the field of information. That is where you will find the treasure, the mother lode, the "understanding" of scripture. Now, I do not discredit any information received just because of the status of the individual who brought it to me. On the contrary, I look forward to questions and information coming my way regardless of who brings it. I now ask GOD, "**What** did you say and **Why** did you say it?" That is why my relationship with GOD is not dependent on the success or failure of any church organization, preacher, or individual that is connected to the church. Later in the book, we will use my two birds to dig below the surface of some well documented subjects. Before we go on, I would like to give you this joke about something below the surface.

This married man allowed his wife's domineering mother to move in with them. The mother-in-law constantly talked about going to Israel. She even stated that she would love to be buried there. After many years, the husband gave in and took his wife and his mother-in-law to Israel. While there, the mother-in-law died. His wife said, "Let's bury mom here in Israel." The husband replied, "No, let's take her back home to the good old U.S.A." The wife asked, "Why, it would be much cheaper, and besides, she wanted to be buried here in Israel?" Then the husband got all teary-eyed: With great emotion and a quivering voice he answered, "You and I loved her greatly; and we'll miss her; and if she stayed in Israel, we would not be able to visit her grave." Well, upon hearing this compassionate grief filled response from her husband, the wife said, "You are the most loving and considerate man I have ever known." It cost him a lot, but he took his mother-in-law back and buried her in the good old U.S.A. Sometime later, a close friend asked him **What** it cost, and **Why** did he ship his mother-in-law back to the U.S.? The husband replied, "It cost a lot; however, the why is, a little over 2000 years ago; rumor has it; a man called Jesus rose from the dead in that land of Israel. I could not afford to take the chance that it might happen again."

What and Why are the tools used in digging up the truth. [7] *Ask, and it **shall** be given you; seek, and ye **shall** find; knock, and it **shall** be opened unto you:* Matt. 7:7. [15] *Let us* *therefore, as many as be perfect, be thus minded: and if in <u>any thing ye be otherwise minded</u>, God shall <u>reveal even this unto you</u>.* Phil. 3:15. Look at three of the definitions that describes the word **SHALL**. 1st, something in the future <u>will</u> happen. 2nd, used especially in formal speech and writing to indicate determination on the part of the speaker, that something <u>will</u> happen, or somebody <u>will</u> do something. 3rd, indicating that something <u>must</u> happen, or somebody is <u>OBLIGED</u> to do something because of a **rule** or **law.** We want to give you a couple of examples of how the promise of GOD, within these two scriptures, helped me.

I got the overwhelming urge to write this book approximately two years before I started. At that time, my wife and I had loved each other and been best friends for over (38) years. However, even that great union could not stop the spontaneous outburst of laughter, and these words bursting forth from her mouth, "YOU,—ARE YOU KIDDING ME?" Here is the sad part, I laughed just as hard as she did. I even said, "GOD boo-booed this time. Man did he ever lay an egg." We <u>both</u> felt <u>completely justified</u> with how we responded, due to our prior knowledge in regard to any skill that I might have in the field of writing. I (kan nott) spell, and I barely passed English with a D-, only because my high-school teacher did not want the school system to suffer one more year of my presence. Two fingers do the typing while the other eight sit back and enjoy the ride. In addition, any word containing more than (3) letters has a 50% chance of being tracked down in the dictionary. There was at that time one very important qualification that I did possess, which my wife and I agreed upon. That was, time spent in the presence of GOD. For eight years prior to this book I was spending two hours a day in fellowship with GOD through prayer and meditation, "listening" to GOD. On a few occasions, up to four hours. After which, I could not even speak because of the overwhelming glory of GOD. During these prayer-filled sessions. I would cry due to the burdens GOD carried, Laugh because of HIS joyful presence and see many wonderful things which could not be explained to others in just a few words.

Here is how GOD changed my mind from—I am not called—to—I am called to write this book. *15 and if in <u>any thing ye be otherwise minded</u>, God **shall** reveal even <u>this unto you</u>.* Phil. 3:15b. Again, this scripture means, GOD will never stop trying. HE will use all avenues to realign your thinking and actions with HIS. The change of mind was a slow one to two year process, due to doubt. This was the result of me looking at my abilities and not GOD'S. It started with my wife saying to me, "If GOD has called you to write a book, then HE will confirm that call in many ways until all doubt is gone.

To save time, I will group a lot of these inspirations together under the category of media. It seemed like every program I watched from then on, including the Discovery and History channels, told how writers changed the world. One program that "leap out" and <u>took me in its grasp,</u> was a conspiracy mystery. The lead character said to another man, "Just write what I have shown you, and I will take care of the rest."

Then one night <u>I had a dream</u>. It was a dream out of the ordinary. I hardly ever dream, and when I do, I can hardly recall anything about the dream. But this one was different. To this day I remember every little detail. I was sitting on the couch all alone, twiddling with my pencil, pondering over my inability to write. All of sudden, I found myself at a podium accepting an award for selling **25 million** copies that changed countless lives. Later in the day, I was watching an old rerun of Tool Time starring Tim Allen. Tim was <u>paid in advance</u> to write his first book. He agreed to turn in a couple of chapters by a certain date. Tim kept making excuses why he could not start the book, until finally, the weekend before the due date had arrived. Tim told his wife on Saturday morning, "Take the kids and go to your mom's house and stay the weekend, because I need solitude." After they left, Tim sat twiddling with his pencil for hours. Unable to get started, he finally fell off to sleep. Tim, <u>in a dream,</u> found himself standing at a podium accepting an award for selling millions of copies that changed countless lives. You see, I had told my wife about my <u>dream</u> that morning, a few hours before the program aired. So I immediately started to walk nonchalantly upstairs to tell the wife, thinking all the while, "What a coincidence." All of a sudden, I stop dead in my tracks. I suddenly realized there was another little fact about Tim's dream I almost overlooked. Both Tim and I sold 25 **million** copies. I flew up the last half of those stairs hollering to my wife, "WHOA BABY WHOA BABY WHOA." Some will call that another coincidence, but I knew better. I know I will not sell 25 million copies. But without a doubt, I know at the very least, GOD will use one copy to change somebody's life.

The final situation set up by GOD came the day I went to the Tag Agency to renew my car's license plate. I ran into a man I had not seen in five years. He invited me to a revival being held by two brothers, missionaries from South America. This was at little church out in the boondocks I never heard of before. There was about 60 people at church, none of whom I knew. Even the man that invited me was not there. Twenty minutes into the service, and just before the one brother delivered the sermon. The other brother, who takes care of the music, rushed to the podium and asked for the microphone. He said, "I hardly ever do this, but I feel overwhelmed to say—if GOD told you to write a book, you had better write the book." I could not wait to get home to tell my wife. And yes, once through the door, you guessed it—WHOA BABY WHOA BABY WHOA. You see, I was not spiritual enough to get it on the first <u>ten</u> tries. GOD, to redirect my life, used secondary avenues such as the media and angels unaware—meaning, ordinary people. Even great men, at one time or the other, had to have their minds changed by GOD through secondary avenues.

Elijah, as recorded in 2nd **KINGS 2:11,** never saw death and was taken up into heaven on a chariot of fire. Yet, 1st **KINGS 18:22** tells us of a problem that Elijah held in his heart. The problem was, Elijah thought he was the last prophet and the only one left in Israel that loved and served GOD. Elijah did not, but the Lord knew that eventually this attitude would lead Elijah into a place of discouragement and depression. This eventually came to pass in **1ˢᵗ KINGS 19:4-5.** There, we find Elijah in the desert under a bush telling GOD, *It is enough; now, O LORD, take away my life; for I am not better than my fathers.* Think about this—here is arguably one of the greatest prophets of all time setting under a desert bush telling GOD, "I've had enough, just kill me now."

This belief Elijah held in his heart, about him being the only one who loved and served GOD, was not true. GOD attempted, through secondary avenues, to enlighten Elijah to this fact. We will look at these avenues used to change Elijah's thinking. Remember, this story took place before Elijah was taken up into heaven. This is an example, at the top of the spiritual hierarchy, of how blind we are to our own weaknesses. This story also confirmed the promise in **PHILIPPIANS 3:15,** that GOD will never give up trying to realign your thinking with HIS.

It all started with GOD sending Elijah to tell Ahab, the King of Israel, that HE will send rain and end the drought. At that same time, Ahab sent a servant named Obadiah to search for Elijah. GOD had two objectives in mind at that time. First, HE wanted to turn the hearts of **all** Israel back to HIM. Secondly, HE wanted to remove that self-important attitude Elijah held in his heart. When they met, Elijah told Obadiah in **1ˢᵗ KINGS 18:8,** *go tell thy lord that I am here.* Obadiah, in the next few verses, basically said, "Do you hate me so much to deliver *'thy servant'* into the hand of Ahab. I know at any time the spirit of the Lord might carry you off where I cannot find you. And Ahab will kill me if I return without you."

Obadiah tried to convince Elijah that he was not Ahab's servant, but his servant, and a faithful servant of GOD. Take note of what Obadiah said in the last part of verse **12**—*but I **thy servant** fear the Lord from my youth.* Then he said in verse **13**—*was it not told my lord what I did when Jezebel slew the prophets of the Lord, how I hid a hundred of the Lord's prophets by fifty in a cave, and fed them with bread and water.* King Ahab and his wife Jezebel were evil representatives of the devil. But Obadiah, at great risk to his own life, remained a faithful servant to GOD through those perilous times. However, look at the "opinion" Elijah held in regard to Obadiah. In **Verse 8** Elijah said—*go tell **thy lord.*** Deep down in his heart. Elijah saw himself at the top of the spiritual hierarchy chart, and unable to see low enough to find Obadiah on the same chart. And so, considered Obadiah a servant of the devil. Otherwise, if Elijah had considered Obadiah a fellow servant of GOD. He would have said, "Go tell the King," and not, "Go tell thy lord." Plus, Elijah would not have said he was the only one left who served GOD. Remember, Ahab who was evil represented the devil. It hurt Obadiah, and was a personal hit below the belt to have someone say to him, "Ahab is *thy lord,*" which is the same as someone saying, you are the servant of evil.

Because of his high opinion of himself, Elijah **rejected** Obadiah and the message from GOD he carried, which was, you're not the only one. The failure of GOD'S first attempt to change Elijah's thinking is an example of the warning HE gave us in **HEBREWS 13:1,** *be not forgetful to entertain strangers: for thereby some have entertained angel unawares.* The word *entertain* means to receive. And *angels unawares* means, someone on an errand for someone else, or someone with a message to deliver.

Next, we find Elijah in 1st **KINGS 18:19.** Calling all Israel to come and see an old fashion duel between him and 450 false prophets of Baal. It was like a high noon spiritual gunfight at the O. K. Corral. Again, Elijah said to all the people, *²² Then said*

Elijah unto the people, I, even I only, remain a prophet of the LORD; but Baal's prophets are four hundred and fifty men. 1 Kings 18:22. Elijah still carried that "high minded opinion" of himself. So the spiritual duel went like this. Elijah told the 450 prophets to sacrifice a bull. And put it on an altar on top of some wood, but put no fire under it and he will do the same. Then Elijah said, "The god that consumes the sacrifice with fire, will from that time on be the GOD of choice in Israel." So the 450 prophets put their sacrifice on the altar and begin to call on their god. From morning until noon they cried out to Baal. They even leaped on the alter cutting themselves while asking Baal to take their sacrifice by fire. Elijah began to mock them. *²⁷ Cry aloud: for he is a god; either he is talking, or he is pursuing, or he is in a journey, or peradventure he sleepeth, and must be awaked.* 1 Kings 18:27b. As you can see, he still displayed that cockiness which is a by-product of the attitude, "I AM the only one." Finally, after no answer came, the 450 prophets gave up.

Elijah not only put his bull on the altar over some wood, but poured water over the sacrifice until it filled the trench around the altar. Then, Elijah said, *³⁶ LORD God of Abraham, Isaac, and of Israel, let it be known this day that thou art God in Israel, and that I am thy servant, and that I have done all these things at thy word.* 1 Kings 18:36. In **Verse 38,** *GOD* answered by consuming the wood, the stones of the altar itself, even the dust, and **_licked_** up the **water** as well. Afterwards, the people worshipped the Lord saying—he is GOD. **"Elijah** then said" to the people, "You take all those 450 prophets of Baal and destroy them." To us, these prophets represent anything we put above GOD in our lives.

After this great display of power on GOD'S part, we find Elijah fleeing for his life because of a threat made by Queen Jezebel to avenge her slain prophets. Next, in 1st **KINGS 19:4,** we find him in the desert under a bush telling GOD -- *it is enough; now, O Lord, take away my life.* Then Elijah **went to _sleep,_** only to be awakened by an angel who said arise and eat. Like Elijah, we all unknowingly fall off to sleep spiritually and need "angels unawares" to kick us in the seat of our pants to wake us up. *⁶ And he looked, and, behold, there was a cake baken on the coals, and a <u>cruse of water</u> at <u>his head</u>. And he did eat and drink, and laid him down again. ⁷ And the angel of the* L<small>ORD</small> *came again the second time, and touched him, and said, Arise and eat; because the journey is too great for thee. ⁸ And he arose, and did eat and drink, and went in the strength of that meat forty days and forty nights unto Horeb the mount of God.* 1 Kings 19:6-8. The cake baking on coals is telling Elijah and us—GOD has a work in progress within the situation at hand.

The cruse placed by Elijah's head was a jug that held water. Spiritually, this water is all of those individual events that has led Elijah into a nasty situation. The jug is the culmination of all those events, it is the situation. Another example in the Bible is <u>Jonah</u> in the belly of the whale. The <u>whale</u> was the **jug,** the situation Jonah was in. The water in the jug was the individual events that led Jonah to be toss overboard into the sea. The whale was the culmination of all those events.

WHY do Christians lose FAITH in GOD during a crisis? Answer—they forget that part of the water in Elijah's **jug,** was spiritual water. Along with the Natural occurrences, there was Spiritual events orchestrated by GOD mixed in as well. In Jonah's case, the Whale was an added event produced by the Spiritual River. *¹⁷ Now the* **L<small>ORD</small>** *had* **prepared** *a great fish to swallow up Jonah. And Jonah was in the belly of the fish three days and three nights.* Jonah 1:17. At first glance, that fish seemed to be part of the problem, and not the solution to Jonah's situation. However, that fish kept him from drowning. And in the end, it delivered Jonah on dry ground headed in the right direction.

Some say—<u>Blind Faith</u> is all you need. Beware! This is a trap you do not want to fall into. Definitions of Blind—1st unable to see—2nd unquestioning—3rd <u>unable</u>

to recognize or unwilling or unable to understand something. Abraham is known as the father of the FAITHFUL due to his relationship with GOD. He was 1st—able to see the present and future. He saw the angel who told him Sarah was going to have a son named Isaac. 2nd—He questioned GOD concerning the destruction of Sodom and Gomorrah. 3rd—He recognized GOD'S involvement due to the Lord's explanation. He understood the situation concerning the life of Lot, a family member who lived in Sodom. *15 The simple believeth every word: but the prudent man looketh well (gives thought) to his going.* Prov. 14:15. **2ND CORINTHIANS,** we **LOOK** not at *the things which are seen, but AT things which are unseen.* These unseen things we have to see is found in the Word. **ROMANS 14:1-23** arrives at this conclusion—each one should be fully convinced in his own mind. *Now faith is the substance (assurance) of things hoped for, the evidence (conviction) of things not seen.* Heb. 11:1. Elisha saw the chariot of fire, and he picked up the mantel of Elijah. Together, these gave him the understanding and the full assurance that GOD was involved in his life. Blind faith costs very little. You do not have to invest much of your time to purchase it. However, when life smacks you around, it will not last, it will not go the distance. Faith founded on understanding, brought about through study and meditation while in GOD'S presence, will last, it will go the distance.

CONFIDENCE and ASSURANCE produces the strong Faith. These two are treasures from the word and presence of GOD. Job at the end said, "Before, I just heard about GOD'S greatness, but now I SEE his greatness." Faith is the product of prior contact between you and GOD through HIS Word and listening to HIS voice. Blind is a word used "many times" by the devil to lull you to sleep. It gives you an "excuse to stand on limited effort" in regard to your relationship to GOD concerning these bad situations.

The positioning of the jug of water by Elijah's head, and him going back to sleep. Was symbolic of the fact that Elijah, at that time, still did not get GOD'S message;

nor did he fully understand why or how he got into his present situation. In other words, the answer lay just beyond his grasp. This is why the angel came back the second time and fed, watered, and sent Elijah on a 40 day journey across the desert to mount HOREB, the "mountain" of GOD. Eating the cake and drinking the water for the second time, is a symbolic statement by GOD to all. This being—you will eventually understand and overcome as long as you <u>continue</u> to eat and drink from the Word and the presence of GOD.

Elijah fell prey to the same failure we all experience when standing on top of the mountain. We can see everything around us, but we cannot see the pebble that we are standing on, because it is hidden under our own feet. When you climb up a mountain from the valley below, you are more likely to see the pebble before it becomes hidden under your feet. Spiritually, you're more likely to see your faults on the way up the mountain. The **angle of view** as you climb gives your eyes a better chance to see every pebble in your path, <u>as you climb over them</u> on your way up the mountain.

GOD allowed Elijah to be pushed off the top of the mountain, so he could see the pebble that was hidden under his own feet by having him climb back up the "mountain" again. Next, we find Elijah again climbing the "mountain" of GOD and hiding in a **cave.** I put cave in bold letters, because it finally drew my attention to something hidden deep within this story that I had missed. I could not figure out why the Lord kept urging me to read it over and over until I saw the answer during meditation. We have labeled it, The Threads of Similarities and committed the next chapter to this subject. But for now, back to Elijah in the cave.

*[11] And he said, Go forth, and stand upon the mount before the LORD. And, behold, the LORD **passed by**, and a great and strong wind rent the mountains, and brake in pieces the rocks before the LORD; but the LORD was not in the wind: and after the wind an earthquake; but the LORD was not in the earthquake: [12] And after the earthquake a fire;*

but the LORD *was not in the fire: and after the fire a still small voice.* ¹³ *And it was so, when Elijah heard it, that <u>he wrapped his face in his mantle</u>, and went out, and stood in the entering in of the cave. And, behold, <u>there came a **voice** unto him</u>, and said, What doest thou here, Elijah?* 1 Kings 19:11-13. Where the scripture said—behold, the Lord passed by—tells us the answer Elijah sought could not be found by him in anyone of the individual manifestations GOD sent his way. Notice it said, Elijah wrapped his face in his mantle, and <u>afterwards</u> came a voice to him. The mantle is the Word, and the voice heard by him was GOD'S. Elijah's problem was solved only after he encountered all three manifestations of GOD. The wind, earthquake, and fire represented the three angels GOD sent to Elijah. Obadiah, was the angel unaware, along with the two other angels in the story. The other two angels represented the two Testaments. And Obadiah, represented the voice of the Lord that Elijah ignored when they made their initial contact with one another.

In the cave, GOD used the three sided spiritual TRAP to catch and hold the little fury critter called truth, long enough as to allow Elijah to get a good look at it. This Truth, was his self-important attitude. We recognize this three sided trap as being the two Testaments, and GOD'S voice, HIS active involvement. We are no better than Elijah. We too need all three sides of the trap in order to reveal and to solve all our problems.

In addition, this story of Elijah defeating the 450 prophets on the mountain suggests that we cannot see the little pebbles: The weaknesses in our lives because they are <u>covered</u> over by the invincible feeling we sometimes get from being on that mountain, seeing GOD in action. It is the feeling we get when GOD allows us to participate in a situation that displayed HIS power in the lives of others. Paul said ⁷ *And lest I should be exalted above measure through the abundance of the revelations, there was given to me a thorn in the flesh, the messenger of Satan to buffet me, lest I should be exalted above measure.* 2 Cor. 12:7. This thorn, was the attack by false teachers on Paul's character and authority in regard to his apostleship. In the following verses, GOD said to Paul—do not worry about it, my strength is made perfect in your weakness. Notice! Paul <u>did not</u> rely on <u>Blind</u> faith in regard to his perplexing problem. Paul went to GOD for the answer. Changes <u>in our lives</u> comes from climbing the mountain ourselves and not from seeing the great power of GOD displayed in the lives of others. Elijah's mountain top was the defeat of 450 false prophets. We get pumped up when we are participants in the display of the spectacular power of GOD. However, that mountain top experience does not always reveal what lies beneath, within our own hearts.

The still small voice Elijah heard, is GOD reintroducing into our minds all his attempts to reveal and eliminate problems hidden within our lives. This is generally done during the time of quiet meditation. It is when you give GOD the chance to parade through your mind, all the words and experiences that was connected to the situation that had engulfed your life. For example, Elijah had an encounter with three different angels before he ended up a changed man. Obadiah, an angel unaware was one of the three. GOD having Elijah stand at the entrance of the cave, after the wind earthquake and fire passed by, represented the time given to meditation. It is when Elijah and GOD together, revisited all events encountered during that dark period of his life. This is way the answer finally penetrated into the mind and life of Elijah.

I was an unfortunate witness to the destruction of a good preacher's ministry, due to the same high minded attitude that Elijah temporarily had. In the year 2000, this preacher and his church underwent a change of views and ideas. This caused a separation between them and the church organization they were affiliated with. During that time, some people left. My wife and I started going to this preacher's church just shortly after the departure of those. The very week we started, the preacher asked for volunteers to come and spend two hours in prayer every morning. The purpose was to ask GOD to bring stability and direction to him, his staff, and all the believers in the church. This preacher loved GOD and was very humble and approachable to all at that time. However, that begin to change after stability settled in, and the church began to grow due to many answered prayers and miracles. There was excitement in the air with love and boundless joy among the people. Then the young ministers, teachers, and board members, those close to this preacher began to notice a change in his attitude. This change coincided with the return of his **self-confidence,** which later <u>migrated</u> into **self-importance.** At first it was his little comments that begin to reveal this growing self-important attitude. Here are a few of those comments—I deserve to have a big church. I am the only one in my church capable of teaching the Word of GOD properly. There was one story he told from the pulpit during the Sunday sermon that startled many. He talked about this one woman who fought against his ministry a few years back, and how he had asked GOD in prayer, to save her or **kill** her. He then told the congregation the woman died with cancer within two years—so do not fight against **my** ministry, because I am GOD'S representative.

This part of the preacher's story may seem similar to the killing of the 450 false prophets. So we want to remind you of something. GOD did not kill those prophets, nor did HE give Elijah the order to kill them. GOD wanted to *turn the hearts of <u>**all**</u> Israel back to HIM.* Elijah ordered the death of those 450 prophets. They too should have been given the chance to change. This command from Elijah, to kill, came while under the influence of that **Self-Important Attitude.** This is why Elijah's ministry went <u>immediately</u> downhill and landed in the valley of despair. The cancer that took the lady, most likely was the product of that natural River of Life. However, it did not stop Elijah, or this preacher from converting that mountain experience into energy to feed that ever growing attitude—I am the MAN.

One sermon was on loyalty to him. He stated, and I quote, "If you do not line up to what I preach in this church, you will find yourself prayed right out the door." This message he would later confirm by throwing out several, (angels unawares), who questioned his motives. He demanded his subordinates to sign letters of **absolute** loyalty to him. He told everyone not to talk to anyone who left **his** church because that would be disloyal to him. More than one assistant, and several people in the church tried to inform him of the reason for the departure of many. However, they too were asked to leave his church. One was thrown out of church in the middle of worship service just so he could display his power and authority. He had the few subordinates that were left, wash his feet in a special service to see who was still loyal and submissive. "HIS" church went from 300 people down to a few within two years. During this time, he managed to replace all the original board members of the church with family and business associates.

These new board members did not attend his church. Some even lived outside the state hundreds of miles away. In the end, he made a secret deal to give this debt free church, worth over 2 million dollars, to another church who wanted to expand. After months of secret negotiations, he made the announcement to the rest of the church several days "after" the deal was already completed. The new church would pay off his home and give him a big severance pay. In addition, he and his wife would receive a large salary for years to come as board members, even though they moved far off in another state. There was one more contributing factor in the downward spiral of this preacher. It was the hiring of a man who promised he could quadruple the growth of the church. GOD, on many occasions and through many **avenues,** tried to reveal to the preacher that this man was not sent by HIM. This guy was a servant of the devil, disguised as an angel, only interested in financial gain.

Remember we said the devil is very observant. Well, he was instrumental in bringing these two men together. The devil was able to deduce, there is a good chance these two will join hands and walk the same path together. The devil saw that the preacher wanted power fame and fortune. This man, as was discovered later, had duped other preachers with the same promise. I remember one trick this man used to gain the confidence of our preacher. He had an unknown woman come and tell our preacher that she had a vision as she drove by his church. In this vision, she saw the church growing due to the union of the preacher and this man he hired. Our preacher was so smitten with pride, that he asked the woman to repeat this vision to the church during Sunday morning's service. Also, "by chance," there was a man with her who confirmed that "all" her visions come to past. Ha-Ha—right, if you can believe that one.

Concerning visions and dreams—YES, GOD does use them as avenues into our lives. However, they will always run parallel with the Word of GOD. If they do not, ignore them. GOD is not about inspiring us with power fame and fortune in this world.

So remember, do not immediately reject, especially from your wife, the information they present. But go to GOD, and yes, you are more than welcome to use my two little birds. Remember again, it might be an angel unaware, a secondary avenue used to change your life. Do not get offended when a specific belief of yours is continually challenged. Because it just might be GOD trying to change your mind and the direction you take in life.

The Threads of Similarities

We have discussed secondary avenues used to change our lives. Briefly, we want to expose an example of GOD'S brilliant use of the main SPIRITUAL expressway, the Bible. This example lies beneath the surface in the story of Elijah and Obadiah. This example shows us the importance of knowing **What** words are in the Bible, and Why <u>every</u> Word becomes important when placed in the hands of GOD. Placed in HIS hands means, trusting in HIS ability to use every Word and situation to lead us into understanding, revelation, and victory.

Have you ever experienced a memory that happened years earlier in your life, which was initiated by a word or a similar experience? They may have only one little point in common.

However, that little similarity <u>pulled</u> your mind over and made a connection with a prior experience. For example, one day my wife and I saw a door that the top or the bottom could be opened separately. This door pulled our minds over and made a connection with a memory in our past history we had forgotten. An embarrassing moment we experienced together. Around 1974, we were newlyweds at a special gathering of several churches being held at a building in our small town. Our church was responsible for providing food and drink. At the end of the function, we immediately put all the folding chairs in the storage room behind a door that the top or bottom could be opened separately. My wife and I started to take the leftovers out to the car. Most of the people, including the district leaders, stood around that storage room talking. A friend spoke to me as I was walking past the storage room, so I stopped and leaned against that door while I talked with him. The bottom part was closed and the top part was open, exposing all those metal chairs leaning against one another at a slight angle. The row of folding chairs extended almost to the door itself. There I was, waiting for my wife, leaning against that door as I talked to some people and holding a covered glass container of leftovers in each hand. Just as my young beautiful wife begin to pass by me, the door I thought was secured, flew open. As I fell backwards, my wife came rushing toward me in an attempt to help, only to trip over my size fourteen feet. My back, once in contact with those chairs, caused them to slide underneath me. When my fall was completed. I was on my back on top of those chairs with both legs sticking straight up in the air, while still holding those two containers of leftovers. My wife's fall was completed shortly thereafter, with her body on top of me between my sky-ward out stretched legs. The noise of us falling on top of those chairs attracted all to come see what happened. What they saw was—a young newlywed couple bouncing up and down. What they heard was—an intense groaning noise, and—OH-MY-OH-MY-OH-MY coming from the little wife. The up and down motion was me using my 6'4" body to help my wife get to her feet. The groaning was caused from the pain of those chairs under my back, and the weight of my 4' 11"wife pushing down on my chest in an attempt to get to her feet. The—OH-MY-OH-MY-OH-MY was my wife's response, due to her attempt to free her entangled feet from those chairs as she squirmed back and forth on top of my body. YES! It looked like you think it looked. But I will tell you this—I never dropped one green bean or one kernel of corn.

One day, and at the ripe old age of sixteen, long before I met my wife. I had an encounter with a girl, a bottle, and a surgeon. The gorgeous sixteen year old blond was running with the football. She was trying to score a touch-down. I, being on the opposing team, was in hot pursuit with every intention of tackling her before she scored. This I accomplished in the knee-high grass in our make-shift football field. Afterward, I stood up feeling extremely sorry to end that ten second blissful experience of embracing such a beautiful woman. As I walked away with my <u>head</u>

<u>in the clouds</u>, ready to resume play, someone said, "Hey man, you're bleeding."

Sure enough, there was blood running down the side of my right leg. The broken coke bottle hidden under the tall grass was so sharp, that I did not notice the wound, even after walking several feet. It took the intervention on the part of a friend to bring me off that blissful mountain top experience long enough to focus my attention on my wound. Funny thing, how we humans react when we realize we have been wounded. We just fall over and give up. Oh yeah, as soon as I saw that wound, I couldn't take another step. I had to be carried to the car, even though I had just walked fifty feet. Afterward at the hospital, the surgeon told my dad. "Your son is going to need **two** sets of stitches **sewed** into that wound, one set inside, and one set outside. The wound is to the bone, and the wound will have to be pulled together in <u>***stages,***</u> from the inside out, otherwise it will not heal."

Spiritual wounds cut to the bone as well, and require more than one row of stitches to be sewed in, starting deep within and working their way to the surface. A tear in the flesh needs strong threads sowed into the wound in order to pull that separation together, as to allow the wound to heal. We need the threads of input from GOD'S Word to close our spiritual wounds. Some of these wounds can be, fear, depression, hate, lack of direction in one's life, lack of peace, lack of joy, partial understanding of certain truths, and a wrong attitude such as Elijah had.

Spiritual threads are the similar characteristics between one or more words of a story in relationship to another story in the Bible. GOD will take as little as one word in a story, and use it to pull your mind over to make a connection with another story in order to bring change and healing into our lives. My wife and I did not remember that embarrassing moment until we saw one object that had a connection to the original story, which was the similarity between the doors. GOD starts the healing process by using **similar** words from one Bible story and ties them to another Bible story, and then HE pulls the stories together. This in turn leads to understanding, from which comes freedom and victory. *³² And ye shall <u>know</u> the truth, and the truth shall make you free.* John 8:32. GOD always closes spiritual wounds from the inside out. The last stitch to be inserted into the wound and pulled together is at the surface. The spiritual surface is the point in which all the people around us will see the change in our lives. The wound is closed up, peace has returned, and joy will be witnessed by all.

Water Baptism is an outward sign of a stitch being sewed into the spiritual wound of a new Christian. The wound is—the I am all alone feeling due to the RIVER of Life firing its arrows of woe into our lives. Water Baptism is <u>one more</u> STEP in ESTABLISHING **<u>faith</u>** in GOD'S ability. It is this statement of faith in GOD that we make to **ourselves**—(that without a doubt, I <u>know I am no longer alone</u>). Every Word and story in the Bible is used by GOD to bring healing and victory into our lives. It is up to us to provide GOD with the threads, so he can tie them together in order to pull those wounds shut and complete the healing process. If our knowledge of the Bible is limited, GOD'S sources are likewise limited in regard to the threads of similarities HE can use to close wounds?

I would not walk from the moment I realized my leg wound until the surgeon sewed it up. It was not because I could not walk. I simply did not want to walk. I was in pain and I wanted sympathy. I had just gone from the mountain-top experience of tackling the blond beauty to a wounded man filled with pain and depression.

Elijah was like the rest of us wounded soles. He wanted to sit under an old desert brush, wallow in self-pity, and die. It took GOD using **threads of similarities,** between his situation and the story that Obadiah told him, to help heal and change Elijah. Obadiah hid 100 prophets in two caves in groups of 50, and gave them food and water because Jezebel was out to kill them. GOD sent two angels with food and water to Elijah while he was on the run from Jezebel, who was also out to kill him. Both Elijah and the 100 prophets were HIDDEN IN A CAVE, fed, and watered by someone else.

The final thread that GOD sowed into the wound in Elijah's life, came at the "opening" of the cave. Elijah went and stood in the cave's entrance, *¹³And, behold, there came a voice unto him, and said, What doest thou here, Elijah?* 1 Kings 19:13b. According to **verse 12,** a small voice, like a whisper said—*what are you doing here, Elijah?* Later in **verse 18,** the voice said—*yet, I have seven thousand in Israel, all of the knees which have not bowed unto Baal, and every mouth which have not kissed him.*

Again! Elijah returning from the interior part of the cave to its entrance represented the TIME spent revisiting, in our minds, those things we encountered during the dark situation that had swallowed us up. GOD used those similarities to draw a complete picture in the mind of Elijah. GOD uses similarities within our everyday lives, and ties them to similarities within a Bible story. This reveals to us that we are not alone and we are not the only one to suffer such a specific trial or tribulation. This was exactly Elijah's problem, who thought he was alone and that he was the only one. GOD brought together two stories that had similarities he could use in changing Elijah's mind set and attitude. Once GOD had those similarities walking around in Elijah's mind, HE SPOKE and brought clarity, understanding, peace, strength, and victory back into Elijah's life. The last thread sowed into the wound in Elijah's life was the voice of GOD explaining all things.

The last thread to be sown into any DEEP wound is at the surface, whether or not it is a natural or a spiritual wound. It is the point in which the closing and the healing of the wound can be witnessed by all through the natural eye. Such was the case with Elijah. We all witnessed the positive change in Elijah's attitude after GOD'S voice sowed that last thread into the wound.

Don't let mankind's interpretation of "humility" cause you to reject **spiritual threads** connecting you to great men recorded in the Bible. For example—God may connect, through similar situations that have been experienced by both you and men such as Abraham, Moses, Elijah, Elisha, Paul, and Peter. Mankind-inspired humility will respond with, "You're no Moses or Paul," but spiritual humility responds with, "At this very moment, yes I am."

All scripture *is given by inspiration of God, and is **profitable** for doctrine, for reproof, for correction, for instruction in righteousness.* 2 Tim. 3:16.

If you reject that THREAD, you actually will be rejecting GOD'S help. So don't listen to someone's negative response of, "You're no Paul."

Water Baptism

It is just a cheap bath. Baptism is about making a statement to the world that you have accepted Christ into your life. Our church says, in the name of the Father-Son-Holy Ghost while applying water baptism to a new Christian, because that is how Jesus said to do it. Some will say in protest, "Well, our church says in the name of Jesus as we apply it, otherwise the baptism experience does you no good, because the power lies in the using of the name." Others say, "You do not need to be baptized in water at all. You only have to believe." Some say, "You have to be totally immersed in water." Finally, others say, "Our church only sprinkles a little water on you during baptism."

There is a lot of confusion wrapped around this subject of Water Baptism, in regards to the why and manner in which to apply it. Confusion concerning spiritual subjects is the same as having a deep-to-the bone wound. It needs to be sewed shut. This wound of confusion has been allowed to fester far too long.

Understanding is the only treasured remedy that will close it. In order to find this treasure, we will have to use our <u>currency of time</u> to <u>buy the field</u> that <u>holds the treasure</u>. We will have to take our two spiritual shovels out and start digging. Who-Who -Who-Who goes my two little birds. Man, they are anxious to start the dig.

What did GOD say in regard to the proper way to apply this Water Baptism experience? *[18] And Jesus came and spake unto them, saying, All power is given unto me in heaven and in earth. [19] Go ye therefore, and teach all nations, baptizing them in the name of the Father, and of the Son, and of the Holy Ghost:* Matt. 28:18-19. *[38] Then Peter said unto them, Repent, and be baptized every one of you in the name of Jesus Christ for the remission of sins, and <u>ye **shall** receive</u> the gift of the Holy Ghost.* Acts 2:38.

Who-Who goes **Why,** digging for the reason GOD put in the Bible two ways in which to verbally apply the Water Baptism experience. You have to ask yourself, "Why did GOD open the door to controversy?" The ones who baptize in Jesus name will say, "Peter understood and properly translated the command Jesus gave in MATTHEW 28:19, to baptize all in the <u>name</u> of the Father—Son—Holy Ghost." Again they say, "Jesus said, baptizing all in the <u>name,</u> which is singular and not plural." They say, "The Father's name is Jesus because he said—I come in my Father's name, and we all know that the Son's name is Jesus, and the Holy Spirit was the spirit of Jesus that ascended up into heaven." Those that say, "Peter in ACTS 2:38 translated MATTHEW 28:19 properly," still have to answer this question. Why did <u>GOD</u> open the door to controversy where a translation was necessary in the first place? If GOD would have had Jesus say in **MATTHEW 28:19,** go ye therefore, and teach all nations, baptizing them in the name of <u>Jesus Christ,</u> there would not have been the door of controversy to go through to begin with. There would have been no argument possible. No two doors to go through. No two paths to travel—end of story. However, GOD did, and so we have to ask ourselves—WHY?

Generating the need to revisit Water Baptism through deep study is the purpose GOD had intended all along. HE does not do or say anything without a reason regardless of how trivial it seems. There is something HE treasures dearly hidden deep within this Water Baptism experience HE wants us to **see,** especially new believers. GOD knew the best way to provoke a study would be through controversy. Man has that competitive nature, and has the need to be the one who is right. So let us take our two little shovels, What and Why, and stick them into this field of information and flip some spiritual dirt.

First, we can conclude that GOD wants total immersion in water, because it points to total commitment, vs. the sprinkling of water, which points to partial commitment. Baptism itself means to **<u>totally immerse</u>** in a liquid. We also have the suggestive nature of many scriptures which points to total immersion in water verses the sprinkling of water. *¹⁶ And Jesus, when he was baptized, went up <u>straightway out of the water</u>: and, lo, the heavens were opened unto him, and <u>he saw</u> the Spirit of God descending like a dove, and lighting upon him:* Matt. 3:16. Also, a strong <u>suggestive</u> influence comes from nature itself. Earth is totally surrounded by a watery atmosphere, which **allows** the rays of the Sun to be productive instead of destructive. Water Baptism allows the Word of GOD to be productive in our lives instead of destructive. This watery experience **helps** to align or lives with HIS Word through the elimination of condemnation. This natural comparison is brought to our attention in the Book of Romans. *²⁰ For the <u>invisible things</u> of him from the creation of the world are clearly seen, being <u>understood</u> by the <u>things that are made</u>, even his eternal power and Godhead; so that they are without excuse:* Rom. 1:20. Even the construction of the Old Testament Tabernacle suggested total immersion in water. Remember, the outer walls and the area within the compound represented the waters of life. And those waters totally surrounded and touched the Holy Tent, where mankind met with GOD.

Since we're again in the Old Tabernacle, we want to show you how and why GOD has sewn, or **stitched** together, the use of natural water with a spiritual purpose. The priest washing and then entering the Holy Tent to fellowship GOD, represented how a new Christian should start this relationship. GOD has **tied** the natural act of washing with water to his Word under one act of obedience. We have to ask ourselves, why is understanding this act of obedience so important? Look again at the passage in Matthew. *¹⁶ And Jesus, when he was baptized, went up <u>straightway out of the water</u>: and, lo, **the heavens were <u>opened</u>** unto him, and **<u>he saw</u>** the Spirit of God descending like a dove, and lighting upon him:* Matt. 3:16. Notice it said<u>, the heavens were opened unto him</u>. This is telling those individuals who have come through this watery experience, they now have the **access** and the **right** to **know** and **understand** all things. However, there is still yet a condition one must satisfy before that flow of knowledge and understanding of spiritual things can begin. That condition is exposed in this scripture as well; *and **he saw** the spirit of GOD descending like a dove, and <u>lighting upon him.</u>* HE SAW the Spirit of GOD simply means, by the time we come out of the water; we need to <u>**know**</u> and believe <u>without a doubt;</u> GOD is a part of our lives from then on; influencing our thoughts and actions. Bottom line—we have to <u>SEE</u> GOD as being a part of our lives. Faith should be the inspiration behind your act of obedience. Faith in what seemingly looks to be, <u>on the surface,</u> a foolish ritual, will only come through understanding. We all need to know the What and the Why we are doing this, preferably before, or immediately after you go through this spiritual washing. Because it is the same short walk of faith the priest made in the Old Tabernacle, from the Alter of repentance on through the "washing process" at the Brazen Laver and on into The Holy Tent.

Many make contact with the cross and even make it through Water Baptism. However, they still fail to make that inner connection with GOD. They fail to make it through the curtain door of the Holy Tent. They do not SEE themselves actually possessing the power of GOD. They did not "spiritually" touch the body or the life of Jesus. They did not grasp or take hold of the PROMISE of GOD. To grasp, or to take hold of the Word means—one must know and understand GOD'S Word concerning the purpose of Water Baptism. Those that do not understand, are the ones that cannot quite make the "spiritual" connection. They cannot possess any of the promises of deliverance when the <u>pressure</u> is put on them by the River of Life. They failed to climb that short distance on the cross between the ground and the body of Jesus, whose body is the Word of GOD. That distance can only be crossed by faith. <u>Understanding</u> the natural washing process **helps** greatly in the **acceptance** of the spiritual washing **process.**

Memorize this statement; FAITH IS NOT EASY TO COME BY, nor CAN IT BE HELD ONTO WITHOUT THE <u>**ASSISTANCE**</u> OF KNOWLEDGE AND UNDERSTANDING. If you think life changing Faith is easy to come by, then you need to read the Bible again. Only Noah, in his generation, had Faith in GOD'S Word; whose faith was confirmed by his act of building the Ark. The Ark, which eventually saved Noah, was built on a daily basis. Noah had to understand what materials were to be used, and what size should the boat be. This came through constant study, meditation, and fellowship with GOD. Also, ask the crowd that did not receive anything from Jesus. You know, the group thronging and grabbing Jesus. The ones the lady with the rare blood disease had to push her way through before she got healed. Yes, that lady, the only one out of that crowd with the Faith to GRASP the promise of deliverance. Remember the passage in Matthew, *²¹ For <u>she said</u> **<u>within</u> <u>herself,</u>** If I may but touch his garment, I shall be whole.* Matt. 9:21. The great faith possessed by Noah and the Lady, which is necessary in regard to salvation, is easy to recognize due to their great effort. Remember this in regard to your personal walk with GOD. **Action does not create Faith. Faith creates Action.**

I know some will say—those touching Jesus, that the little lady had to push her way through, also had faith. Our answer to that is, yes they did. However, their faith was in their actions. This is the same as doing what someone tells you to do, or doing it because you saw someone else do it, without you ever understanding the **What** or **Why.** Their faith was in the physical outward touch. They thought, "If we do what we see others do, we will be healed." Where the scripture says—<u>*she said* **within** *herself*</u>—*if I may but touch his garment*—tells us the lady put in some extra time and thought as she made her attempt to touch the Lord. The spiritual definition of *Garment* is righteousness, this being GOD'S Word. "*She said within herself,*" represented the extra time of meditation and study that we all need to put in. *"If I may but touch his garment,"* represented what that extra time should be spent on, and that is the meditation and study of GOD'S Word. <u>Understanding</u> produced her faith, and that faith created her actions which led to her healing. The other people's actions were inspired by hearing and not understanding. Those souls went away empty handed, they never got healed. *⁷ Ever learning, and <u>never able</u> to come to the knowledge of the truth."* 2 Tim. 3:7. Now do not get all shook up or discouraged, and say to yourself, "I've got zero chance of having this kind of Faith," because, you will have this kind of faith after you "understand" the purpose of Water Baptism.

WHO SNOOZE—WHO SNOOZE—WHO SNOOZE—WHO SNOOZE—WHO SNOOZE. Excuse me! But as you can see, What and Why feel off to sleep and were snoring away: Can you believe that? Excuse me again! I just got informed it was me who was snoring away, because What and Why never sleep. Hey, certainly you all understand. I mean, who likes to admit being the one snoring anyway. Especially when you did not catch yourself snoring in the first place. Hey! It is hard to take someone else's word in regard to one point in your life, when you think it would have been impossible to get something so obvious by you. Well, I am awake now. So take us the rest of the way, What and Why.

We now know the purpose of the wording in MATTHEW and ACTS concerning the way in which to apply the Water Baptism experience. It was GOD using controversy to force mankind into an in-depth study of this subject in order to give us the "necessary" understanding. Here are the answers we gathered. One all Bible scholars will agree upon, is revealed through the understanding of Watchtowers, which is the safety found under the **<u>umbrella</u>** of GOD'S Word. A Watchtower, in ancient times, was a secured tall building from which to "view" your enemy. It was a fortress that provided weapons, and a safe place in which to **plan** your enemy's demise. HIS Word is our

Watchtower. Let us say, you accidentally smash your thumb with a hammer and cuss, or you knowingly disobey GOD. Your enemy, Condemnation, will try its best to keep you from renewing your relationship with GOD. So you run into the Watchtower of GOD'S Word and ask—**What** did HE say that covers my present situation? Under the protective cover means, you first must **know** and **understand** and **believe.** For instance, just before you get to church you lose your temper and cussed: Now what do you do? You try to raise your hands to worship during song service, but you cannot. Condemnation is telling you, "Man, you are one sinful dude and unworthy to praise GOD because he is perfect and righteous." So what do you do? Well, you pull out **ACTS 2:38,** the spiritual agreement you signed through faith which you confirmed through your act of obedience. It is the scripture that came just after the people asked Peter—**What** must we do to be saved? You see, **condemnation** had gripped the hearts of all the people when they heard Peter explain, how <u>all</u> of us because of our sins was responsible for putting Jesus Christ on the cross.

Many will ask, why use **ACTS 2:38** and not MATTHEW 28:19? The reason is, <u>*simplicity,*</u> because it is the only scripture that contains all three steps necessary in establishing salvation. All three steps are confirmed by the priest in the Old Testament Tabernacle. **First**—the DEATH—Peter said repent. This experience of dying to self-paralleled the death the priest experienced at the Altar of Burnt Offering. **Second**—the BURIAL—Peter said to be baptized for the remission of sins. This means the forgiveness of sins. This paralleled the priest washing at the Brazen Laver. Faith in the Word produced the priest act of obedience. The priest entering The Holy Place symbolized the grasping hold of the Word. Standing "inside" the tent symbolized an <u>acceptance</u> of the forgiveness and the **guaranteed** fellowship of GOD <u>**to come**</u>**.** If a new Christian does not fully believe in these promises, his relationship with GOD will begin to erode and eventually die. Again we ask this question, does action create faith or does faith create action? The priest, entering the Holy Tent, is a great example of Faith creating action. He had to know within himself he had been forgiven before he entered that Tent. Such confidence could have only come through the "understanding" of GOD'S directions.

There is something critically important we need to know in regard to this second step. That is, in order for anyone to receive forgiveness, we must "first" forgive others. Question—WHO is the very first person we have to forgive? Answer—<u>ourselves,</u> which at times is not easy. Our mistakes are boulders that lay between us and GOD. They are too heavy for us to move on our own. We need a spiritual tractor (GOD'S word), and a spiritual Rope (our faith). We wrap our rope of faith around the boulder of mistake and attach the other end to HIS Word. We then let the power of the Word pull the boulder out of the way. This is why GOD wants all new believers to establish and understand these steps taken by the priest. They "solidify" the strong foundation on which our relationship and growth with GOD will be built upon. They teach us how to let the Word and the power of GOD remove the boulders out of our lives.

The **Third** step is the RESURRECTION. Peter said—*and you* <u>**shall**</u> *receive the gift of the Holy Ghost.* This is when you fully, and I mean 100% accept the fact that GOD IS an **ACTIVE** participant in your thoughts and actions. Understanding and obeying the first two steps helps <u>greatly</u> in clearing the boulders of doubt and condemnation out of the way. This active spiritual relationship with GOD is paralleled by the priest entering into the second room called The Most Holy Place. It is where the priest and GOD actually talked to one another.

Again my little bird asks, what do you do when condemnation will not allow you to forgive yourself, or to continue your fellowship with GOD? Answer—You pull out, in your mind, that agreement GOD signed with the blood of Christ, and you signed with your faith. Yes, that one giving you <u>the right to fellowship HIM at any time,</u> even if you made a mistake just one minute earlier. Yea, you pull out that Sword of GOD. And if that condemning enemy does not run away immediately like a Bat out of—Hell. Which is exactly what condemnation is, a Bat trying to suck GOD out of your life. You grip the <u>handle</u> of faith. You swing the <u>blade</u> of GOD'S Word. And you <u>hack the head of condemnation</u> off with the <u>sharp cutting edge</u> of Understanding.

Here is another quick example of the power you give the Word of GOD through your faith. Consider how, and why the dead was removed off the wooden ships in the earlier centuries. The why is—that dead body, if left on board the ship would bring disease and death to the crew as it decayed. The how is—they would tie the dead to some heavy weight and throw the body over the side into the sea. The purpose of the weights was to <u>sink</u> the dead out of sight as soon as possible. Otherwise, the body might continue to float alongside the "slow moving ship" and **<u>spook</u>** the men, driving them <u>insane</u> with <u>FEAR</u>. This very thing happened when the British finally caught and defeated Black Beard the pirate. The British cut the pirate's head off and tossed his body into the sea. The pirate's body floated around the ship several times, spooking the sailors so bad they could never get that picture out of their minds. Have you ever heard of that old saying, Out Of Sight and Out Of Mind? And so it is with our lives, our vessels. We immediately toss our mistakes over the side into the sea. However, in order to get them to sink out of sight and out of mind—**below the water**—we will have to get some rope and tie weights to them. The weights are the promises of GOD exposed by HIS Word.

Mistakes are like dead bodies. They will bring the disease of condemnation if allowed to linger IN the ship, which in turn breeds doubt. Paul said, *[13] Brethren, I count not myself to have apprehended: but this one thing I do, <u>forgetting</u> those things which are <u>behind</u>, and <u>reaching forth</u> unto those things which are before,* Phil. 3:13. We attach our rope of faith to HIS promises and the other end to our mistakes. Then we toss them over the side while waving our hands skyward in praise as the Word pulls them **beneath** the water, out of sight and out of mind.

"What," asked my little bird, "is hidden beneath the surface of this Water Baptism experience?" Most Bible scholars would say faith, and they are correct. However, the hidden and easily overlooked element of spiritual faith is, there are two kinds called Mustard-Seed-Faith and Growing-Faith. The problem in viewing them as separate individuals, is they are so closely related. Both are sired from GOD'S Word. Both have the same last name. However, the resemblance ends with the name. Mustard-Seed-Faith revolves around the hearing of GOD'S Word. Growing-Faith revolves around the Understanding of GOD'S Word. [17] *So then faith cometh by hearing, and hearing by the word of God.* Rom. 10:17. Mustard-Seed-Faith is not easy to identify because it hides under the surface. It is immature and never grows up and has very little knowledge of the Word. Mustard-Seed-Faith is an Emotional mess. We constantly find it **"begging"** over and over for forgiveness. It is like, Mustard-Seed-Faith does not understand what GOD has given him? This confusion constantly causes him to ask, "AM I SAVED?"

Growing-Faith on the other hand is easy to identify. It is Emotionally Sound, full of knowledge and understanding purchased through Time Spent in study, prayer, and actual fellowship with GOD.

[24] *But let him that glorieth glory in this, that he understandeth and knoweth me,* Jer. 9:24a. [6] *For the* LORD *giveth wisdom: out of his mouth cometh knowledge and understanding.* Prov. 2:6. [32] *And ye shall **know** the truth, and the truth shall make you free.* John 8:32. [15] *Study to shew thyself approved unto God, a workman that needeth not to be ashamed, rightly dividing the word of truth.* 2 Tim. 2:15.

Growing-Faith is easy to spot, because it is seen above the surface. [31] *It is like a grain* *of mustard seed, which, when it is sown in the earth, is less than all the seeds that <u>be in the earth</u>: ³² But when it is sown,* **it groweth** *up, and becometh greater than all herbs, and <u>shooteth out great branches</u>; so that the fowls of the air may lodge under the shadow of it.* Mark 4:31-32. Yes! We know, that the <u>fowls</u> of the air may lodge under the shadow of it means—despicable characters will hide within the borders of the ever growing church. However, this scripture also runs parallel to how faith should not remain a seed underground, but should be seen <u>growing</u> into a mighty tree. Growing-Faith is always full of praise and thankfulness. He never has to **beg** for forgiveness because he "knows" and "understands" what GOD has given him. Mustard-Seed-Faith quits when he witnesses the failures of those in the church, but Growing-Faith continues on his journey with GOD.

One of the secrets hidden deep within the purpose of Water Baptism, is the ability, and I repeat, the **ability** to **identify** and **separate** the two Faith brothers; also, why you want to avoid embracing one, and why you should seek to <u>embrace</u> the other. Do you think it wise to take a closer look at these two brothers?

MATTHEW 25:1-12, *Then shall the kingdom of heaven be likened unto ten virgins, which took their lamps, and went forth to meet the bridegroom. And five of them were wise and five were foolish. They that were foolish took their lamps, and took* **no oil** *with them. But the wise took oil in their vessels with their lamps. While the bridegroom tarried, they all slumbered and slept. And at midnight there was a cry made, Behold, the bridegroom cometh; go ye out to meet him. Then all the virgins arose, and trimmed their lamps. And the foolish said to the wise, give us of your oil; for our lamps are gone out. But the wise answered, saying; Not so; lest there be* **not enough** *for us and you: but* **go ye** *rather to them that sell, and <u>BUY</u> for yourselves. And while they went to buy, the bridegroom came; and they that were ready went in with him to the marriage: and the door was shut. Afterward came also the other virgins; saying, Lord, Lord, open unto us.*

But he answered and said, Verily I say unto you, I knew you not. **MATTHEW 25:14, for** *the kingdom of heaven is as a man traveling into afar country; who called his* **own** *servants, and delivered unto them* **his goods.** **MATTHEW 25:25-28,** *And I was afraid, and went and <u>hid thy talent in the earth</u>:lo, there thou hast that is thine. His Lord answered and said, thou wicked and slothful servant, thou know<u>est</u> that I reap where I sowed not, and gathered where I have not strawed. Thou oughtest therefore to have put my money to the exchangers, and then at my coming I should have received mine own with usury. Take therefore the talent from him, and give it unto to him which hath ten talents.* Oh by the way, where it said, hid thy **talent in the earth** means—"<u>burying</u>" oneself in the things and cares of this life. There is common ground between these two stories of the <u>ten virgins</u> and the <u>servants</u> with the talents. Together they had an invisible line that separated two areas, and each area had **two** groups residing within. One side of the line is the area we call the DANGER-ZONE, and the other side of the line we call the SAFE-ZONE. The two groups in the SAFE-ZONE were saved because they put "enough" to "more than enough" effort into their relationship with GOD. The two groups in the DANGER-ZONE were lost because they put **<u>little</u>** to **no** effort into their relationship with GOD. "What-What-What-What," stuttered my excited little bird? Asking, "What is this line, spiritually speaking, between <u>nothing at all</u> to <u>not quite enough</u>—vs.—<u>enough</u> to <u>more</u> than <u>enough</u>?" Well as the ten virgins found out, it was oil or no oil. And as the servant with one talent found out, it was more than the little that he had.

Here is where a lot of us misinterpret the problem exposed in these two stories. The real problem many who call themselves believers want to ignore is, they may be on the wrong side of the line along with the nonbelievers. Some argue that the five foolish virgins represented people who never believed, because the scripture said that group had no oil at all. And we agree, the line between the two groups is easily seen and understood.

Oil—No Oil, You Know GOD—You Do not Know GOD. However, the story of the lazy servant clearly puts this person in the group called believers. MATTHEW 25:14 clearly stated, the master gave **HIS talent** to **HIS servants.** Plus, GOD said to the lazy servant—***thou knowest*** what I require. GOD clearly put the lazy servant in the same group with the five foolish virgins. This being the same group called the have nots. Again, the problems that needs to be answered is, where is the line that separates the DANGER-ZONE and the SAFE-ZONE? And how can we stay on the side of the five wise virgins?

The natural line that separates Mustard-Seed from the great plant that it grows into is easy to see. It is the surface of the earth. The SPIRITUAL dividing line between Mustard-Seed-Faith (the danger-zone) and Growing-Faith (the safe-zone), is much more difficult to find. So we will again travel back to the Old Testament Tabernacle in order to answer this question.

GOD gave examples of two types of fire that was used in the Old Tabernacle. The Altar fire "outside" The Holy Tent in the open courtyard represented a consuming fire that brought death. The fire burning on the candlestick "inside" the Tent represented the fire of salvation that brought life. This light inside represented healing, enlightenment, and strength. We have a destructive fire that can be seen at work in the outer courtyard. And there is the healing fire of salvation at work inside The Holy Tent. The people outside The Holy Tent in the courtyard, are subject to the rays of light given off by the destructive fire of death. The people inside The Holy Tent, are subject to the rays of light given off by the salvation fire of life. Here is the Questions to be answered. Can you draw a line at the exact point between the two "spiritual" fires, where the destructive fire becomes a healing fire? Also, can you draw a line at the exact point in our atmosphere, where the Sun's rays stops being destructive and starts being productive? The difficulty in finding this dividing line in our atmosphere, parallels the difficulty in finding the spiritual line of salvation. This invisible line is also represented somewhere within the stories of the ten virgins and the lazy servant.

Here is another way to look at setting a line between too distances. You are standing somewhere on a football field in between the two gold posts. And the field has no markings on it whatsoever. Now walk up and draw a line at the **exact** half-way point between the two gold posts. It is impossible to do without some measuring device. A spiritual line is impossible to find without the aid of a spiritual measuring device.

Answer this—what is the power of the old fashion twelve inch **wooden ruler?** Most would say it is a measuring device, and we agree. Question—what gives this ruler the power to be a measuring device? Answer -- it is the individual lines of measurement on the twelve-inch piece of wood. Without those lines of measurement, it is just an ordinary piece of wood. The Cross is the spiritual wooden ruler. The measuring lines marked down on the cross is the life of Jesus Christ. That life being the written Word of GOD. The Word is the measuring lines on the spiritual ruler. However, simply holding a ruler in hand does not give us the power to find the center line if we do not know how to use it? We have to understand the measurements of "Space" in **Between those** lines on the wood ruler, such as -1/4-1/2-3/4.

The Cross becomes powerful if we understand those **spiritual lines and how to apply them.** Those being the life of Christ, the Word. Here is GOD talking to us all.

ISAIAH 28:9-13, *Whom shall he teach knowledge? And whom shall "he make" to understand doctrine? Them that are **weaned from milk** and drawn from the beasts. **10**, for precept upon precept, precept upon precept; line upon line, line upon line; here a little and there a little. **11**, for with stammering lips and another tongue will he speak to this people. **12,** to whom he said, this is the rest wherewith ye may cause the weary to rest; and this is the refreshing: yet they would not. **13,** but the word of the Lord was unto them precept upon precept, precept upon precept; line upon line, line upon line; here a little, and there little; that they might go, and fall backward, and broken, and snared,* *and taken.* Precept means directions and Line means the Word, from which, comes the "understanding" of those directions. The repeating of precept upon precept, precept upon precept, and line upon line, and line upon line means—you get your understanding from the study of the Old and New Testaments. Where it said, here a little and there a little means—with GOD'S assistance, we will get little threads of information, (threads of similarities) from both the Old and New Testaments.

Excuse me, I had to take a time out because the brilliance of GOD has caught me off guard as I wrote down those last five scriptures. HE has a way of putting so much into so few words. ISAIAH 28: 9-13 captures the entire purpose, or the essence of this book. This being—the **understanding** of scripture will bring "rest" and "refreshing" to one's spirit. And <u>refusing</u> to search for those precepts through the lines of scriptures will lead to separation and destruction.

Remember we told you earlier, a preacher said, "Most only want a basic salvation." Remember the definition of **basic**—the bare essential; the starting point; the minimum; <u>without or before</u> <u>the **addition** of anything extra</u>. Does not this sound like a description of the lazy servant, who showed "no" increase. GOD said, whom shall he teach knowledge, and whom shall he <u>make</u> to **understand** doctrine; them that are <u>weaned from milk</u> and that are drawn from the beast. People who **have not** been **weaned** from spiritual milk—The BASICS—are the ones who still embrace Mustard-Seed-Faith. They have "little" to "no" understanding of scriptures, nor do they desire such. They are the ones living in the DANGER-ZONE. Who, when the pressures of life are applied, will be drawn to the beast. This being the cares or things of this life.

We need to clarify what we mean in regard to separating and drawing a line between Mustard-Seed-Faith and Growing-Faith. Both make up the ONE group called believers. However, we at any time can sever our relationship with GOD. Notice! I said we—*[14] But every man is tempted, when <u>he</u> is <u>drawn away of his own lust,</u>*

and enticed. James 1:14. GOD provoked the study of Water Baptism in order to pull us back to the Tabernacle, so he could draw in our minds a more complete picture of the **woes of being a new believer.** HE wanted HIS new born children to learn **early on,** how to spiritually walk and in what direction. HE wanted to help us babes in Christ to see and cross as soon as possible that line of—I am "more" interested in GOD than the things of the world. HE wants us to come to grip with this fact—we can still be lost. Paul, arguably one the greatest apostles of all time said, *²⁷ But I keep under my body, and bring it into subjection: lest that by any means, when* **I have preached** *to others,* **I myself** *should be a* **castaway***.* 1 Cor. 9:27. Where Paul said, *I keep under my body* meant, through faith in the power of GOD was his body made to "submit" and "conform" to the Word. Maybe you think you have a closer relationship with GOD than Paul. GOD used the Tabernacle to show us exactly where HE has drawn this spiritual line separating those in the SAFE-ZONE that will be saved, and those in the DANGER ZONE that have a real good chance of being lost. This spiritual line is visible in the Old Tabernacle. It is just past Water Baptism which the priest experienced at the Brazen Laver. Yes! We said—**PAST**—or slightly beyond. The priest still had to "PUSH" the curtain door open and enter the Tent. Inside was where he received GOD. This entry curtain represented that spiritual LINE we all have to cross before, during, or after experiencing Water Baptism. One side of this invisible line is inhabited by SOME DOUBT, and on the other, TOTAL BELIEF GOD is now active within ones heart and mind. Repentance and Water Baptism are simple SPIRITUAL TOOLS to help us push doubt behind and enter the TENT of Fellowship. The Tabernacle gives a VISUAL of the SPIRITUAL MECHANICS involved.

The separating LINE is the Holy Tent wall. The priest had to PUSH open the heavy curtain door to enter the area called the Holy Place, the Tent of Meeting. This area represented fellowship with GOD through **understanding.** This being the "product" of the **active** presence of GOD in ONE'S MIND and HEART. Outside the Holy Tent represented the area of little to no understanding.

In the outer courtyard there is a key to help us to see where, and to understand Why GOD put this spiritual line just past two of the three steps to salvation. That key is the "distance" between the Altar of Burnt Offering and the Holy Tent. Your SALVATION, your relationship with GOD, starts as soon as you believe and ask GOD to forgive your sins. This is Mustard-Seed-Faith in action, because "you were **told** to do it" in order to connect with HIM. In the Old Tabernacle, the starting point of SALVATION is repentance. This being represented at the Alter of Burnt Offering. However, Growing-Faith is a *budding* relationship with GOD founded on the "understanding" of HIS Word, due to the active presence of GOD in **your** mind and heart. YES! It is GOD influencing your thoughts and your actions. This is why a minister might say—GOD SAID TO ME. This kind of faith, or relationship, is represented INSIDE the Holy Tent. It takes practice in learning to recognize the voice of GOD. One must Read, Pray, and Listen through quiet meditation.

Mustard-Seed-Faith, founded on **little** to **no** understanding, is represented OUTSIDE in the open area around the Holy Tent. This includes the distance from the Altar of Burnt Offering to the Holy Tent door just past the Brazen Laver. Growing-Faith is the understanding of GOD'S Word which comes through effort of study, meditation, and prayer. These point in the "direction of travel" GOD is trying to get all newborns to walk early on in their relationship with HIM. Mustard-Seed-Faith comes from, and revolves around Hearing only.

I saw a scientific experiment on the Discovery channel explaining the nature of water. It showed the flow of water was made up of individual droplets with a Space in Between. The naked eye could not see this separation. It took special cameras to slow the flow of water down to a crawl in order to see the space between the droplets. And so it is with the separation between Mustard-Seed-Faith (the danger-zone), and Growing-Faith (the safe-zone). We need GOD'S special equipment, HIS Word in order to SEE this separation between the two.

Remember! The area of the cross, from the feet to the top of Christ's head, represented the area inside the Tent <u>between</u> the <u>entry curtain</u> to the <u>dividing curtain</u> which separated the Holy Place from the Most Holy Place. The head of Christ being represented by the Alter of Incense against the dividing curtain. The barren part between HIS feet to the earth is represented outside the Tent, an area were the lost and those struggling to connect "spiritually" with GOD are represented.

The entire cross Christ was crucified on is represented in the Old Tabernacle. The imaginary main beam starts at the Altar of Burnt Offering—it runs through the Brazen Laver—on into The Holy Place—On through the Alter of Incense—up through the heavy curtain wall of The Most Holy Place and stops at the Ark of the covenant. The imaginary cross beam that held the hands of Jesus in place, ran between and through the Candlestick and the table of Show Bread. You would have the outline of a cross if you drew a line and connected ALL those items.

Here are questions asked by my little bird. Why did GOD represent part of the Salvation process in the DANGER ZONE? Why did GOD give us a visual picture, placing New Christians in the same DANGER ZONE with the nonbelievers, those who reject GOD'S offer? **Answer**—GOD wanted us to see early on, the right spiritual direction to walk, and to understand the importance of getting on that path as soon as possible.

Our spiritual walk starts from the area called Mustard-Seed- Faith, which **revolves** around **hearing** the Word preached. But it <u>should "cross the line" into the area of Growing-Faith,</u> which is understanding given you by GOD'S active <u>presence</u> in your mind and heart. All new believers, and some of us old believers need prodding to get us going in the right direction. GOD used controversy to pull us back to the Old Tabernacle in order to give us a visible picture of the **spiritually insecure** position of a new believer. In order to connect, GOD showed what spiritual building blocks are required and the equipment necessary to put those in place. HE has drawn us a _picture_ showing how to procure it and what salvation looks like. And we can give you a 100% guarantee that it is not—BASIC salvation. It on the other hand, is most definitely the gathering of UNDERSTANDING from **Between** the **Lines** with GOD'S _PERSONAL_ assistance.

The area of the cross -- above the head of Jesus—represented the room called The Most Holy Place. GOD choose to enter The Holy Place from that room through the curtain of flesh. By raising Christ from the dead, HE painted another picture showing us that HE will bring the Word to life in every individual who reaches higher and grasps the Word. The heavy curtain that divided the tent into two compartments, represented the sins of the flesh separating us from GOD. The death of Christ is a statement to us that HE has torn that curtain open and crossed the line. HE **"pushed"** open the door of HIS heart by putting great effort into establishing this fellowship **"through"** HIS Word. We have to **push** through the curtain door and come in at the other end. We have to cross the line. We have to keep open the door of or heart through constant effort. And where, through our effort do we meet with GOD? It is in the Word lying ON the CROSS _between_ us formed from earth and GOD from above.

To reveal HIS mind, GOD uses every part of the cross. Both the part covered by the body of Christ, and the uncovered part. There is two reasons why GOD chose the Cross to put the body of Jesus on. First reason, as we have just discovered, was a **visual** example of the Word positioned between GOD above and mankind below. This is confirmed in the design of the Old Tabernacle. You have the outer courtyard where all of mankind is represented. You have The Most Holy Place where GOD'S presence _alone_ is represented. In between the two—you have the room called The

Holy Place. This room is the Word, which is where the life and body of Christ is represented. GOD drew us a picture, with HIM coming through one door and mankind coming through the other, and we all meet at the Word. HE wants us to consider the Holy Place the dining room table, and the food to be consumed, is his Word. *²⁰ Behold, I stand at the door, and knock: if any man hear my voice, and **open** the door, I will come in to him, and will **sup** with him, and he with me. Rev. 3:20.*

The Second reason GOD choose the Cross was to provide a space to visually expose that LINE between the five foolish—and five wise virgins. This space, is the uncovered distance from where the cross entered the ground to where the body of Jesus began. The ground represented all mankind. The uncovered distance on the cross, between the ground and the feet of Jesus, is the individual who climbs above the mass of humanity to lay hold of the promise. Lazarus climbing the tree above the mass of people was a good example.

The story of Lot and his wife in the **nineteenth chapter** of GENESIS gives us a good view of this dividing line in an action sequence. It clearly shows "two groups" living **foolishly** in the DANGER ZONE, and "two groups" living **wisely** in the SAFE ZONE. The story begins with three angels stopping off at Abraham's place, who happened to be Lot's uncle. The angels told Abraham that GOD was going to destroy Sodom, where Lot lived, and the town of Gomorrah because of their sins. Abraham pleaded to save the righteous, so God sent two angels into the wicked city of Sodom to warn Lot. He tried to warn the others, but none would listen. Lot, his wife, and two daughters made it out with the **help** of those angels. Once out of the city, *they* told the family not to look back, however, Lot's wife did. *²⁶ But his wife looked back from **behind him**, and she became a pillar of salt.* Gen. 19:26. Her heart still had too many attachments back in that wicked city. Like the *lazy servant,* she had *hidden her talent in the earth*. She had a relationship with GOD which was represented by her leaving town with the angels. However, her actions revealed her heart was across that line with the five foolish virgins. Still struggling with her desires and the love for the things in the city.

Here is what we want you to see. Those in the wicked cities represented the five foolish virgins, the people who had **no oil,** no relationship with GOD at all. Lot's wife represented the lazy servant, "believers" who have not enough of a relationship to keep from turning around. Lot represented those that have enough, and Abraham those who have more than enough because of his great distance away from those wicked cities. That invisible line of **understanding,** which separates the DANGER ZONE and the SAFE ZONE, was located somewhere in *between* Lot and his Wife. Lot understood the situation, this produced faith which allowed the obedience to GOD'S Word into his life. This being, do not look back. Lot understood that if he looked back, he would experience the same fate as those in the cities. Lot's wife "did not understand" their situation. This confusion produced doubt and opened the door to her heart in which disobedience stepped in, as it did in the lives of Adam and Eve. Abraham, (who had more than enough) and Lot (who had just enough), were the two groups in the SAFE ZONE who were saved. The people in the cities (who had nothing at all) and Lot's wife (who had a little but not enough), are the two groups in the DANGER ZONE who were lost. Be **honest** with yourself. Which group are you in?

Answer this, how far is far and how close is close and where is the dividing line between the two? When flying from Thailand to Guam in 1971 on a military plane, our number 3 engine caught fire. The pilot was able to extinguish the fire. However, because of the damage to the plane, he had to make a decision on whether to continue on to Guam or to return to Thailand. The determining factor came down to this—which destination was closer? Are you closer to GOD than the things of this world?

Every stressful situation has a line called the DECIDING LINE. One side of the line goes away from GOD, and the other goes toward GOD. This line is as thin as the blade of a knife, which makes it impossible to stand on. You will fall on one side or the other. Either you will fall toward GOD or away from GOD.

Have you seen the movie Top Gun? It was about a modern Aircraft Carrier whose planes fought in one air to air combat mission. One of the theme songs in the movie was, We Fly Through the Danger-Zone. Christians should sing this song every morning as soon as we wake up. Then we might be more compelled to start the day by taking our spiritual currency—time—and spend it **buying** GOD'S strength and inspiration.

In air to air dog-fights, both combatant's planes try to destroy and bring each other crashing to the ground. The arrows fired by life's everyday situations and the unseen spiritual forces are attempting to destroy us. The "crash" and "burn" of a life can only happen if separated from GOD. There is two basic ways to bring down a jet fighter. One, is to <u>shoot it down</u> and the other, the jet <u>runs out of fuel</u>, a situation most of us have experienced that leaves one feeling awfully stupid. Now be honest and admit, the only way to run out is through neglect. *³How shall we **escape**, if we **neglect** so **great** salvation;* Heb. 2:3a. How will you escape those difficult situations life tries to engulf you in? I constantly got on to my wife and daughters when they drove the car on fumes, and just because they did not like to spend their "TIME" at the gas station. Now the other way to knock a jet out of the sky is to shoot it down. There are two basic things a pilot needs to shoot his opponent's jet down. One, a better jet or secondly, better skills. Spiritually speaking, we are sitting in the cockpit and have our hands on the control stick of the greatest fighter of all time—GOD'S Word. So if we get shot down, it will not be due to an inferior weapon, it will be due to our **inferior skill** in regard to the handling of this weapon.

Now to approach another type of line that lies between and divides GOD'S church. Those that apply Water Baptism in the name of the Father-Son-Holy Ghost as stated in MATTHEW 28:19—vs. those that apply Water Baptism in the name of Jesus Christ in obedience to ACTS 2:38. Before we go any farther, we want those that have been baptized in the titles of Father-Son-Holy Ghost to know—You **DO NOT** have to be re-baptized. However, one exception to this rule is those who have been **sprinkled** only, and not been totally immersed in water. To be "sprinkled," does not establish the commitment in your heart necessary in connecting spiritually with GOD, because it is founded on <u>**total**</u> misunderstanding.

According to the bible, GOD'S preferred way to verbally apply Water Baptism is in the name of Jesus Christ. However, the verbal application <u>**is not,**</u> and <u>we repeat, **not**</u> the power of this experience. We say this in regard to the Oneness belief which says—your Water Baptism is null and void if it was not applied while saying in the name of Jesus Christ.

The verbal application applies to the outside, but the "power" of Water Baptism lies on the inside. This power is produced by understanding the spiritual mechanics involved.

My birds asked these questions. What is more important, to do something you are told to do, or to do it because deep within you <u>understand</u> that it is the right thing to do? Let us see what Paul has to say. *⁶Who also hath made us able ministers of the new testament; not of the letter, but of the spirit: for the letter killeth, but the spirit giveth life.* 2 Cor. 3:6. Remember, the spirit leads and guides and <u>explains</u> the letter of the law. Paul is saying—GOD gives us the understanding which produces the faith that will allow HIM to implement the Word in our lives. Our power is that FAITH in HIM which "only" comes from understanding HIS Word. This again is confirmed in the Book of John. *³²And ye shall **know** the truth, and the truth shall <u>make you free</u>.*

John 8:32. GOD, through the <u>understanding</u> of scripture, will eventually lead you to freedom in every situation. You cannot please GOD by simply doing what someone else told you was the right thing to do. GOD is pleased if you have allowed HIM to give you, from within, the understanding and the INSPIRATION. GOD will use those roads into your life, such as preachers, teachers, nature itself, and angels unaware to help you gain this understanding. True fellowship with GOD is, *[30] He must increase, but I must decrease.* John 3:30.

Again, the necessity of understanding is why GOD provoked this controversy within MATTHEW 28:19 and ACTS 2:38. Through this study, we would gain a spiritual map pointing us in the direction one must go in order to establish this unbreakable relationship with GOD.

GOD painted this story in my mind while meditating on the importance of understanding how to use spiritual weapons. Two dudes in the Old West were <u>pinned down</u> **behind** some ***rocks***—(the Word), hiding from wave after wave of arrows. Suddenly a man appeared from out of nowhere. He handed each man a brand new 1860 Henry Rifle. One old timer said, "Hey, I know the <u>three separate</u> characteristics that gives this gun its power." So that old timer stood up with his gun and *He waved it <u>above</u> his head while <u>shouting</u> at the enemy,* "This is a **_13 shot-repeating-rifle._**" However, the arrows kept on coming. Frustrated, the old man jumped back in behind the rocks and said to his partner, "Man, this here thing did not scare the enemy at all." The other man said, "The power lies in using the <u>creator's name</u>." So he stood up and <u>shouted</u> loudly at the enemy while *waving the gun <u>above</u> his head,* "This is a **HENRY** rifle, so you all better run." However, the enemy just stayed put and kept on firing those arrows. He too, jumped back into his hiding spot and looked over to his partner saying, "You're right, this here thing did not scare our enemy one bit." Then as the two frustrated old men begun to lose all hope of being saved, the stranger appeared again. He said to the men,

"The power of the thing in your hands is inside the weapon, and it is called the bullet." Then the men said to the stranger, "You cannot call these things you gave us, weapons, because they do not work. This here bullet did not scare the enemy one bit." Then the stranger said to the men, "You have to "understand" the **mechanics** involved. You have to know how the components that make up this weapon are used to send the bullet." After the stranger "explained" how to load, cock, aim, and pull the trigger of the gun, the two men stood up and started firing. After a few volleys, the men turned to the stranger and said, "WOW, what a weapon, look at our enemies run.

Some hold the belief that speaking the name of Jesus <u>over the head,</u> as they submerse the new believer in water, is the power of Water Baptism. They believe, you have to verbally apply the name of Jesus in order for you to be saved. In other words, you had to pronounce the name of Jesus Christ (over the head) as you put the person under the water for the experience to work. To confirm this belief, they would use as example our present day check cashing system. They say—the power that controls the direction the money travels in the checking system, is the name on the check. Before a check can be cashed, the owner of the account has to apply his signature in order to okay the transaction. However, and quite by accident, or so I thought, I found out differently. While studying Water Baptism, this example of the name being the power of the checking system came up again in my mind. So I said to GOD—this example made sense. Then, due to the urging of my little bird. I asked GOD—What do you Lord have to say in regard to this example?

Here again, is the brilliant use GOD makes of those secondary avenues into our lives. I had just been approved for a large amount of life insurance. <u>So I ran down</u>—hey, <u>we live on a high hill</u>—to my agent and pulled out my check book and paid 550 dollars to put that policy into effect. One week later my daughter came and asked, "Dad, did you cash a 550 dollar check on my account?" Well, I immediately said no.

However, she showed me a copy of the check which had my signature Okaying the transaction.

Here is the problem in believing the application of the name on the check is the power that controls the direction the money flows. My daughter, who is married, no longer has my last name. The bank cashed that check, even though my daughter and her husband's name was at the top, and my unauthorized name, or signature was at the bottom. Here is what happened just a couple days before I paid for my policy. My daughter borrowed my car and accidentally left her check book in my glove compartment. When I got into my car, I put my check book in the glove box. I grabbed her check book by mistake and paid for my policy.

Here is why I think GOD was a little more involved in this situation than I originally thought. While getting into my car, I bumped my head and knocked my ten dollar pair of glasses off. They broke as soon as they hit the concrete. This is why I did not see I had the wrong check book. In addition, I am in my sixties and have only experience this particular situation once ever in my life. And it happened just after I asked for GOD'S help in regard to the power of the check cashing system.

OH, EXCUSE ME! We almost forgot to expose the real power of this system. Paul Harvey, through his radio broadcast, told the true story of a man who committed one of the first big high tech bank robberies. This man used his knowledge of computers and the banking system. He somehow took blank deposit slips and put his own "routing number" at the bottom. Then he placed them back on the table in the bank. When people came to make a deposit, they would unknowingly use the deposit slips that already had his "routing number" on them. That **routing number** tells the computer where the money should go, and not the <u>name</u> on the <u>surface</u> of the deposit slips and checks. The bank only remembered a man withdrawing a few hundred thousand dollars just a couple of days after the account was open. They never caught the thief. This guy, early on in the computer age, **understood** the **internal workings** of the banking system and walked away rich. So the power is not what is applied at the surface. It is on the other hand, the understanding of the internal mechanics of the system.

Some believers at this point, with bugged out eyes and hands over their mouths, are mumbling—did this guy deny the power that is in the name of Jesus Christ? NO—I know all power lies—IN—the name. And we repeat—**IN**—the name. You have to understand, the power does not lie in the verbal using of the name. It does lie in "YOUR" connection with that name. This connection with the life of Jesus comes only through the bonding of your spirit with GOD'S. Jesus Christ is the life that fulfills the Word of GOD. This bonding of our spirits, which begins to fulfill the Word of GOD in our lives, can only happen through faith. This kind of FAITH can only be generated through understanding.

Water Baptism was not set up to break down the wall in GOD'S heart, separating him from us. It is to break down the wall of doubt and ignorance in our hearts, separating us from him.

Through controversy, GOD pulled us back to the Old Tabernacle so HE could clearly *show us the line* that separates a good and bad relationship. That "line" is the **understanding** of scriptures. This understanding of scripture can only come through your active connection with the Spirit of GOD.

If you think the power lies in using the name, just asked the seven sons of one Jew named Sceva. *[13] Then certain of the vagabond Jews, exorcists, took upon them to **call over them** which had evil spirits the **name** of the L<small>ORD</small> Jesus, saying, We adjure you by Jesus whom Paul preacheth. Acts 19:13. [15] And the evil spirit answered and said, Jesus I know, and Paul I know; but who are ye? Acts 19:15. [16] And the man in whom the evil spirit was leaped on them, and overcame them, and **prevailed** against them, so that they fled out of that house **naked** and **wounded**. Acts 19:16.*

Here again in the Old Testament, GOD brings together two separate stories. Painting us a picture, confirming that the power of Water Baptism lies in the **understanding** of the internal workings of this experience. The Syrians were marching against Israel. King Joash, (Jehoash), came to Elisha, who was sick and **dying,** asking for help. **Second KINGS 13: 15-21,** *and Elisha said unto him, take bow and arrows. and he took unto him bow and <u>arrows</u>.* **16,** *And he said to the King of Israel, put thine hand upon the bow. And he put his hand upon it: and Elisha put his hands upon the King's hands.* **17,** *And he said, open the window* **Eastward.** *And he opened it. Then Elisha said, shoot, and he shot. And he said, the* **arrow** *of the Lord's deliverance, and the* **arrow** *of deliverance from Syria: for thou shalt smite the Syrians in Aphek, till thou have consumed them.* **18,** *And he said, take the arrows. And he took them. And he said unto the King of Israel, smite upon the ground. And he smote thrice, and stayed.* **19,** *And the man of GOD was wroth with him, and said, thou shouldest have smitten five or six times; then hadst thou smitten Syria till thou hadst consumed it: whereas now thou shalt smite Syria but thrice.* <u>Here is the second story</u>. **Verse 20,** *And Elisha died, and they buried him. And the band of Moabites invaded the land at the coming in of the year.* 21, *And it came to pass, as they were burying a man, that, behold, they spied a band of men; and they cast the man into the sepulchre of Elisha: and when the man was let down, and touch the bones of Elisha, he revived, and stood up on his feet.*

GOD brilliantly painted a picture of the internal spiritual mechanics of Water Baptism in these two stories. Have you ever seen in a store on display, a mechanical device cut in-half, revealing all the internal parts and how they work? Well, that is exactly what GOD has done with Water Baptism. He has cut this experience in half by removing the water so we can see the parts inside and how they work. We know these two stories together represent Water Baptism, because they have death, burial, and resurrection in them.

You will see the **"room"** where Jehoash met with Elisha, and that Elisha eventually died in, represented the room called The Holy Place. The Tabernacle room where the body of Jesus, (GOD'S Word), is also represented. Elisha represented Jesus, and Jehoash represented the priest in the Old Tabernacle who fellowshipped GOD by faith through the Word. The Words directing Jehoash actions came to him in that room through the lips of Elisha. It is also the room where the body of Elisha was to be found later on. This room paralleled The Holy Place, where the body of Jesus, (the Word of GOD) was represented. In addition, that room where they met had only one recorded, and I repeat, <u>recorded</u> opening. It was the "WINDOW" to the East. This paralleled the entrance to The Holy Tent, which also was positioned at the East end of the Tent. GOD is using those threads of similarities. He ties The Holy Tent together with the room where Elisha and the King met to show us something. This is why it is so important to fully understand the Old Testament Tabernacle, because it confirms and opens doors to so many things.

The "WINDOW" the King <u>had to push open</u> represented the entry curtain into The Holy Tent. Opening that window, represented the effort we put forth in opening up our hearts in order to fellowship with GOD through the Word.

Question—Why did Elisha have the King open the East window? Remember, salvation started at the East end of the Tabernacle. Water Baptism was represented at the Brazen Laver at the East end just outside The Holy Tent. Elisha and Jehoash looking through the East WINDOW, spiritually speaking, are in fellowship in The Holy Tent. Together, they are **"looking back"** through the entry curtain toward the Brazen Laver. GOD is telling the church to step back into the Water for the second time, through **Study.** HE is saying—look again deeply into Water Baptism, even if you have already gone through this experience. It is absolutely necessary that we understand what parts are involved and how they work. This is the reason GOD provoked the controversy between MATTHEW 28:19 and ACT 2:38. The parts are, determination to seek out and follow the Word through understanding, because this is how faith is produced. Elisha was mad because the <u>King did not fulfill</u> the ***SPIRIT of the word,*** which was—shoot **one** arrow.

Remember, only **one** arrow was sanctioned in defeating the enemy by Elisha through the laying on of hands. Only one arrow sanctified by GOD whom Elisha represented. The THREE arrows the King <u>applied</u> to the "ground" revealed his lack of *perfect* understanding—it was mankind's interpretation. Remember when the two of them shot the one arrow through the window. Jehoash, at that time, had many more arrows in his quiver. However, only one was ordained by Elisha. When the King used more than one arrow. Elisha said in anger, "You should have shot them all." This was said to show Jehoash's lack of determination in following directions laid out in the Word. There was only **one** arrow ordained by GOD. This number being confirmed by the arrow they shot together while both had their hands on the bow. Jehoash's lackadaisical attitude caused him to overlook that little detail.

When we were children, we would play a game called Simon Says. One kid on one side of the room was in control of the game, and he would be Simon. All the other kids would stand against the wall on the other side of the room and follow the commands only of, Simon Says. Then the **<u>one in control</u>** would say, "<u>Simon says</u> take one step forward." Anybody who did not follow his command would be out of the game. Then the kid in control might say, "Take three steps forward." Those that took the three steps would also be out of the game, because the "kid in control "did not say, "<u>Simon says</u> take three steps forward." You had to pay attention to detail or you would be out of the game. Now do not be fearful and stop studying. Because no one in this life will ever gain all the knowledge that the Bible holds. This is just more of those little seemingly insignificant little details. This story shows how GOD TESTS and REVEALS our understanding or lack thereof.

Jehoash should have asked for Elisha's help before he shot those three arrows if he did not understand the purpose behind the command. However, he did not ask one question before or after the shooting of those arrows. No questions directed to GOD was the same mistake Adam and Eve made. The last half of 1st **CORINTHIANS 10:5** says, *bringing into captivity **every thought** to the obedience of Christ.* "Of Christ" means, in line with the Word of GOD, regardless of ours or anyone's opinion. There are so many little pieces of information we discard for one reason or another—especially because of pride.

GOD provoked his children to look again into Water Baptism for a reason. HE placed deep within this burial chamber an example. And look who it is, Elisha. He, in these two stories, also represented the life of Christ. GOD wants us to look at his life because he also went through the Water experience. However, what most Bible scholars have overlooked is, Elisha went through Water Baptism—**twice.** The first time was when he followed Elijah through the water of the River Jordan. This represented the experience of physically being put under the water in compliance to the Word. The second time, is when we find Elisha in the waters of the Jordan River alone with the mantel of Elijah. This represented the reentry into Water Baptism through the **STUDY** of GOD'S Word.

In 2nd **KINGS 2:1-6,** it tells us that many sons of the prophets knew Elijah, Elisha's master, would be taken up into heaven by GOD. Many times he was told by others to stay behind and leave Elijah's side. Even Elijah himself told Elisha to stay behind. In **Verse 6,** *Elijah said unto him, Tarry; I pray thee, here; for the Lord has sent me to Jordan. And he said, as the Lord liveth, and as my soul liveth, I will not leave thee. And the two went on.* Notice the determination to keep his eye on the

Master. This is the same as keeping one's eye on the Word. Keeping one's eye on the Word means—seek the understanding, or the *SPIRIT* of the Word.

In **verses 7-11** we see Elisha experiencing Water Baptism for the first time with 50 witnesses in attendance. 2nd KINGS 2:7-11, *and fifty men of the sons of the prophets went, and <u>stood to view afar off;</u> and they two stood by Jordan.* So we have 50 believers ready to watch Elijah and Elisha enter the water. **Verse 8,** *and Elijah took his <u>mantle</u>, and wrapped it together, and smote the waters, and they were divided hither and thither, so that they <u>two</u> went over on dry ground.* Elijah represented GOD, and the mantle represented the Word. *Wrapped it together* meant, he was completely absorbed in the word. This is why we know GOD can never fail in fulfilling his Word, because HE is his Word.

Verse 9, *and it came to pass, when they were gone over, that Elijah said unto to Elisha: <u>**Ask**</u> what I shall do for thee, before I be taken away from thee. And Elisha said, I **pray** thee, let a double portion of <u>**thy spirit**</u> be upon me.* Notice, and after he first followed His Master through the water, <u>Elisha still sought to possess the same powerful spirit</u> Elijah had working in his life. Elisha following his master through the water parallels us being Baptism in compliance with the Word, but without having the full understanding we need in order to connect spiritually, **Verse 10,** *and he said, <u>Thou hast asked a **hard thing;**</u> nevertheless, <u>if you SEE me</u> when I am taken from thee, it shall be so unto thee; <u>but if not, it shall not be so</u>.* Remember **JOB 42:5,** *I have heard of thee by the hearing of the ear: but now mine eye **seeth** thee.* Great faith is generated through understanding. **Verse 11,** *and it came to pass, as they still went on, and <u>talked</u>, that, behold, there appeared a chariot of fire, and horses of fire, and parted them both asunder, and Elijah went up by a <u>**whirlwind**</u> into heaven.* <u>Elisha still sought the power</u> after he **first** followed Elijah, (his Lord), through the Water Baptism experience. However, Elisha did not receive that power until he <u>re-entered</u>

the Water with the Mantle, (GOD'S Word) in his GRASP.

2nd KINGS 2:14, *And he took the mantle of Elijah that fell from him, and smote the waters, and said, Where is the Lord God of Elijah? And when he had smitten the waters, they parted hither and thither; and Elisha went over.* The first Water Baptism represented obedience to the Word, but without the necessary understanding. The second Water Baptism represented understanding brought about through the study of the Word.

Elisha's story is telling all of us, and especially the new believers. If you do not fully understand what you have been given, keep on asking and searching because you will in the end. Elisha, after that **whirlwind experience,** was finally able to **SEE.** And from that time forward, **he knew** that the power of GOD was in his life. In order to have FAITH in the belief that YOU have the POWER of GOD. You first must SEE yourself as having it. In order to **SEE** yourself as having that power, you must first understand the purpose and the spiritual mechanics involved in Water Baptism. Know the parts and how they work and you will be able to harness the power of this spiritual weapon.

[12] And Elisha saw it, and he cried, My father, my father, the chariot of Israel, and the horsemen thereof. And he saw him no more: and he took hold of his own clothes, and rent them in two pieces. 2 Kings 2:12. Elisha's clothes represented his righteousness. The tearing of his clothes confirmed mankind's thoughts or actions was not acceptable to GOD. The two separate pieces his clothes were torn into, represented the Old and the New Testaments. It is GOD reaffirming to all, that these two testaments will have to be gone through in order to receive the full power of the mantle, GOD'S righteousness and power. *[13] He took up also the mantle of Elijah that fell from him, and went back, and stood by the bank of Jordan; 2 Kings 2:13.* In verse 13, Elijah's mantle represented the Word fulfilled by the power of GOD. And where

it said, *the mantle Fell **from Him,*** represented the spirit of GOD being passed on to Elisha through the understanding and obedience to GOD'S Word. In short, WE have to tear through, *(study through),* the Old and New Testaments with GOD from whom comes the understanding of all things. Hey, there is that three sided triangular pen that catches and holds all those little critters of truth.

We all need to tread through Water Baptism the second time through study. This is confirmed through the lives of the Israelites. They also went through Water Baptism—Twice. The first time was through the Red Sea, and the second time was through the Jordan River. The Red Sea represented the physical experience of being put under the water. The Jordan River represented the reentry into Water Baptism **through study** in order to understand how to utilize its power. The Israelites still lived in a state of doubt and confusion after the Red Sea Baptism. This is why they could not enter the promise land for forty more years. They did not understand what they had been given. God, through forty years of teaching opened their eyes to this overcoming power. During the second Water Baptism in the Jordan River, the Israelites carried out 12 stones. This meant, they now fully understood the power they had received from GOD. My two birds want you, with all sincerity, to answer this question. Do you see yourself as having that power?

GOD gave us an action sequence inside Elisha's grave that shows us how one gains this overcoming power. That man coming back to life, after touching the bones of Elisha, is a VISUAL guarantee from GOD. That all who follow Elisha into the water the second time, through intensive study, will gain the control over the waters of life. Elisha knew Who held the answers. He had the determination to seek out the What and Why. He fully believed he would receive the answer and the promise of GOD.

In addition, GOD having us go through the Water twice, is trying to establish within us a new habit. That is, to revisit the Word more than once, of all things that you have heard preached or taught.

Now to talk about that **single** arrow Elisha and the King shot through the window. But before we enter this cave of controversy, we want to discuss determination. GOD'S determination is to bring <u>all</u> his children's thoughts, views, and actions in line with his. GOD'S goal is to eradicate church denominations. HE wants his children to be in alignment on **all points** no matter how small or insignificant they seem to us. GOD wants his church to be like the restaurant chain called The Cracker Barrel. This restaurant group is consistently reliable. I know the "special dish" being served on Thursday is Turkey and Dressing regardless of the State or town I am in. GOD wants all churches to serve up the same special dish of understanding, regardless of the location or (mental **state**) one finds himself in.

This <u>single</u> arrow, which means one, represented Jesus Christ. *² And he hath made my mouth like a <u>sharp sword</u>; in the <u>shadow of his hand hath he hid me,</u> and made me a <u>polished shaft</u>; in his <u>quiver</u> hath he hid me;* Isa. 49:2. Polished shaft means, branch, rod; a reed, stalk; by extension: a <u>measure</u> of length. Jesus Christ is that <u>branch</u> by which all things are <u>measured</u>. *¹⁴ And the LORD shall be seen over them, and his arrow shall go forth as the lightning* Zech. 9:14a. Jesus Christ is <u>the arrow</u> Elisha and King Jehoash applied together through the <u>open</u> (Old Testament) *WINDOW* called the Father. *¹In the beginning was the Word, and the Word was with God, and the Word was God.* John 1:1. The (New Testament) WINDOW labeled the *Son,* is the view we get as we look down through the open grave of Elisha, where we SEE the resurrection of the life that touched HIS BODY. The third spiritual WINDOW of OPPORTUNITY labeled the Holy Ghost, is the ***WORDS*** of DIRECTION and promise of VICTORY to come given through Elisha. Three ANGLES of VIEW through *three* spiritual WINDOWS called the *Father-Son-Holy Ghost* in order to answer all questions and solve all mysteries.

The name of Jesus Christ should be applied when a new Christian is Baptized. That is if you are determined to follow the Word more perfectly. When you pronounce that name over the individual being Baptized, you are applying the one arrow—the Word. Elisha using the East window, is GOD redirecting our attention back to the Brazen Laver, which symbolically represented Water Baptism. GOD wanted us to see this one arrow as representing the exact way in which to apply it to a life. Saying, in the name of the Father-Son-Holy Ghost over the individual being Baptized, is equal to the three arrows shot into the ground by the King. The three <u>arrows</u> Jehoash <u>applied</u> **into** the <u>ground</u> also represented Water Baptism, because it is a process of being buried.

The <u>three arrows</u> represented <u>misunderstanding</u> of GOD'S command. Like in the kids game Simon Says, Elisha did not say, "Shoot three arrows."[19] *Go ye therefore, and teach all nations, baptizing them in the **name** of the Father, and of the Son, and of the Holy Ghost:* Matt. 28:19. Notice, it did say in the name, which is singular. Jesus said, *I come in my <u>father's</u> name,* and the <u>Son</u>'s name as we all know, is Jesus, and the <u>Holy Spirit</u> was the spirit of Jesus. The **name** representing the Father is Jesus, the **name** representing the Son is Jesus, and the **name** representing the Holy Ghost is Jesus. Peter did understand what GOD said through Christ in MATTHEW 28:19. That is way he told the people the second chapter of Acts, *[38] Repent, and be baptized every one of you in the **name** of Jesus Christ for the remission of sins, and ye shall receive the gift of the Holy Ghost.* Acts 2:38b. In this scripture, there are two things taking place in the one event of Water Baptism. They are, the remission of your sins, and you receiving the Holy Ghost. Where it said, you **<u>shall</u>** receive the Holy Ghost, is a statement giving you the <u>absolute</u> GUARANTEE that GOD will be an active part of your life from then on, <u>if we allow</u>. You receive both promises through **one** act of obedience sanctified through **one** name, Jesus Christ. We repeat: <u>you do not have to be baptized again</u> if you have already been PUT UNDER WATER in the titles of Father-Son-Holy Ghost. As we have already stated, the power lies in understanding the "purpose" and the "spiritual mechanics" involved. However, using three arrows was not exactly in compliance with GOD'S command. That is why, even though he was upset with the King, Elisha basically said, "You will defeat your enemy, but you should have been determined to follow the Word more closely."

Jehoash won his battle, but he passed on to his descendants his lack of determination to fully understand GOD'S Word. This resulted in his descendants being defeated by that very same enemy later on. GOD, in these last days, is attempting to bring his people together on **all points.** That means—we Baptists, we Pentecostals, we Methodists, we Assemblies of GOD, and so on, should seek to be like minded in **all points** of the Word. This promotes more confidence in those who are not Christians. This in turn will lead to more growth in **GOD'S** church. Good habits are hard to start and bad habits are even harder to stop. The danger in refusing to change due to pride, feeds that self-important, I AM THE ONLY ONE attitude displayed by Elijah. We want to stay In Between the Lines of GOD'S thoughts and actions verses outside the lines, where man's thoughts and actions dominate.

There is another thread of similarity we want to show you. And it lies in the number, "**Two.**" GOD, in the New Testament, gave **Two** commands to apply Water Baptism. One being MATTHEW 28:19 and the other ACTS 2:38. GOD, by way of the mouth of Elisha, gave Jehoash **Two** commands to shoot the arrow. Spiritually speaking, **Two** commands to apply Water Baptism. We have also shown Elisha himself going through Water Baptism Two times. In addition, the Old Testament tells us the Nation of Israel went through the experience of Water Baptism **Two** times. One through the Red Sea, and after, through the Jordan River. Israel found themselves in the Wilderness of confusion and doubt after the Red Sea Baptism.

After the Jordan Baptism, they found themselves in the Promised Land of confidence and overcoming power. The "Wilderness" represented little to no faith due to the lack of knowledge and understanding. The "Promised Land" represented overcoming faith produced through knowledge and understanding. This came through 40 years of *study* spent with GOD in the wilderness.

The Bible will always flow in a positive progression, from some to more, from clear to clearer, and from darkness to light. In the Old Tabernacle, the priest traveled in one direction in his relationship with GOD, from the East to the West. He followed the path of the Sun. To us, this symbolized following GOD through the light of HIS Word. The direction GOD'S Word travels is always a positive progression. From a view through a clouded haze to a clear and unclouded view, and from in general to precise, just like in **EXODUS 14:20,** where GOD placed a cloud between the Egyptians and the fleeing Israelites. Darkness covered the Egyptian camp and light covered the Israelites camp, but in between the darkness and the light—was a cloud. GOD, through his Word, will always takes us from the darkness of no understanding—through the cloud of partial understanding—to the light of perfect understanding. For one reason or another, we on many excursions through the Word stop in the first two areas.

In the New Testament, MATTHEW 28:19 was the first command given in regard to applying Water Baptism, and ACTS 2:38 was the second. MATTHEW 28:19 was a command under a clouded haze—it was not clear. It gave us a decision to make. Should we baptize in the titles Father-Son-Holy Ghost, or should we baptize in the **one name** that represented each? ACTS 2:38 was the progressive second command. It removed the clouded haze on how to apply Water Baptism. It made clear that the one name of Jesus Christ represented the Father-Son-Holy Ghost. It followed the progressive direction of the Word of GOD.

Remember this, <u>neither the Israelites nor Elisha "carried anything out" of their first entry into the Water Baptism experience. However, both carried something out of the Water Baptism experience on their second attempt</u>. The Israelites carried out 12 stones in their hands. And Elisha carried in his hand, the Mantle of Elijah. Both objects represented the Power of GOD. This Power can only be received through the reentry into Water Baptism the second time, by way of **study.**

The first command to be Baptized in MATTHEW 28:19 was given to the apostles "before" they received the Spirit of Truth. The second command to be Baptized in ACTS 2:38 was given "after" they had received the Spirit of Truth. This follows the positive progression the Word of GOD always flows in, from in general, to precise and, from cloudy to clear.

GENESIS 28:10-12, *and Jacob went out from Beersheba, and went toward Haran. 11, and he lighted upon a certain place, and tarried there all night, because the sun was set; and he took the stones of that place, and put them for his pillow, and lay down in that place to sleep. 12, and he <u>**dreamed**</u>. and behold a <u>ladder</u> set up on the earth, and at the top of it reached to heaven: and behold the angels of GOD ascending and descending on it.* There is one last thing we want you to remember. Water Baptism is all about "you" making a statement of commitment to **"yourself."** This ladder Jacob saw had three basic components. Most ladders have two basic parts that make up its framework, two long parallel members and the steps affixed to them for <u>climbing.</u> However, Jacob's had a third part. There were angels ascending and descending, which is why we know this is a spiritual ladder.

The two long parallel members of a spiritual ladder represent the Old and the New Testaments. Each step connecting those spiritual beams is the understanding received from between the lines of scriptures. The "angels ascending" represent our request for that understanding. The "ones descending" represent the answers to those requests.

Notice in Verse twelve—the angels of GOD ascending came first before the descending angels. This is GOD'S way of confirming what HE said in **MATTHEW** 7:7, you have to <u>**first,**</u> *ASK, SEEK,* and *KNOCK*

The definition of understanding is, the ability to **grasp**, meaning, it is the ability to <u>perceive</u> and <u>explain</u> the <u>nature</u> of somebody or something. Spiritually speaking—we call understanding the Word, the grasping of the SPIRIT OF THE WORD. My little bird asked—what is the part of the ladder we **"grasp"** to pull ourselves up? It is those two long parallel members—it is the two Testaments. My little bird again asked—what supports our weight as we, with GOD'S help, pull ourselves up this spiritual latter? It is the connecting steps coming out those two long parallel members. These steps being the understanding that comes from out of the two Testaments. In short, with GOD'S assistance, we gain understanding from "between the lines" of scripture, and this help comes through preachers, teachers, evangelists, books, life situations, and angels unaware.

Water Baptism is about promoting, at the outset in your walk with GOD, the right mind set and attitude. It is about you establishing your own spiritual ladder early into in your relationship with GOD. Jacob cheated his brother Esau out of his inheritance and was fleeing for his life. Oh by the way, Esau was a great hunter and deadly with the Bow. He reflects the deadly skill of the devil when it comes to shooting arrows. Read the rest of Jacob's story in **GENESIS 28:13-22.** You will see him making a commitment to follow the Word just after his first encounter with GOD. This commitment came immediately <u>after</u> Jacob <u>understood,</u> that GOD was the author of his dream. That is when he realized those promises of protection and blessing was his for the taking. This dream of Jacob happened "after" he <u>laid his head</u>—on the ***rock.*** That stone represented GOD'S Word. Jacob's head on that rock reminds us that we need to fill our minds with the Word.

Many put the **emphasis** on Water Baptism as you making a statement to the world you are a believer, a Christian. However, that statement comes later and more gradual through the change in your attitude, speech, and actions. *²⁰ Wherefore <u>by their fruits</u> ye shall know them*. Matt. 7:20. And how will these changes come about to begin with? Well, <u>it will be due to the determined commitment you made to yourself, through the understanding of Why you were Baptized to begin with</u>. Remember, the Bible said 50 priests witnessed Elisha going through the water with Elijah, a <u>Far off</u>. This meant, Elisha alone had to make the commitment in his heart to follow GOD in order <u>to receive the promise of power.</u> He did this by pursuing his Master, even after his FIRST trip through the water. The Bible said nothing about anyone watching him go through the Water the second time. It is our individual determination to follow the Word through the <u>door of understanding by way of study</u>. This is what GOD wants to establish in our hearts early as possible. This is why Jesus said to Peter in **JOHN** 21:21-22, <u>follow *me*</u> and do not worry about what the other apostles are going to do.

As the Bible flows in a progressive, positive direction, so should our lives flow, because this is salvation at work. And how are GOD'S new born children pointed in the right direction to start with? Well, it is through the "understanding" of why you complied with GOD'S command to be baptized in Water.

Jacob's Ladder affirms this absolute necessity of seeing yourself as having the power of GOD. Jacob's spiritual relationship with the Lord did not began until he SAW the ladder and the messengers of GOD flowing into his life. Water Baptism was designed by GOD to totally convince the convert that "you" have received GOD'S forgiveness and HIS abiding presence. This my brothers and sisters gives us the right to have—all questions answered—receive all knowledge—to understand all things. GOD has never failed to give the treasure of understanding to any question I have asked him, due to my digging in the field of information with What and Why, my two spiritual shovels. It has not always been what I expected or wanted.

Remember—the proper way to climb a ladder is to first **grasp hold** of those two long beams. This allows you to pull yourself upward. Those little steps that comes out of the two main support beams is the reason you can climb higher. They allow you to **"rest" your weight on them**. So it is with the two Testaments. The understanding that comes out of them supports our weight, our faith. This faith allows us to climb higher above the ground, leaving Mustard-Seed-Faith behind. Jacob's Ladder is all about reminding us, that understanding the Word of GOD is the KEY ingredient necessary in climbing closer to GOD.

God Is Chapter 9

Chapter 9 is one <u>law</u> in the United States that helps municipalities, such as a city, in eliminating its huge debt. We are the bankrupt cities that have no ability to pay our enormous spiritual dept. GOD alone is that <u>one law</u> who **"single" handedly** removed our dept.

Some of you probably think I am affiliated with a particular denomination—well you're wrong. I am unaffiliated, and I believe some Baptists, Assemblies of God, Pentecostals, and so on, are GOD'S children and will be found in Heaven. My only goal is to close that distance <u>we all have</u> in-regard to our relationship with GOD, through the <u>understanding</u> of scriptures. In **JOHN 21:15-17,** Jesus said to *Peter, feed my sheep.* Jesus never said, clip, groom, or beat my sheep. I feel it is not my responsibility to point my finger at any individual and say—you are saved, or you are not saved. I do not know your level of fellowship with GOD. I can make a good guess with the help of the Word. However, my opinion will make no difference in you being saved or lost. I on the other hand can help point out the right direction one needs to walk to establish and maintain a relationship with GOD.

We have shown that "understanding" the Word is the **<u>dividing line</u>** between the Danger-Zone and the Safe-Zone. This is why I do not tell people they are saved or not when asked. I simply asked them to tell me why they doubt they are saved? I then explain to them, they might be too close or even across that line in the Danger-Zone where the <u>confused</u> and <u>lost</u> are found, which is basically what Paul did.

ACTS 19:1-7, *and it came to pass, that while Apollos was at Corinth, Paul having passed through the upper coasts came to Ephesus: and finding certain <u>disciples</u>.* **2,** *he said unto them, have ye received the Holy Ghost <u>since ye believed</u>? And they said unto* *him, <u>We have not so much as **heard**</u> whether there be any Holy Ghost. **3,** and he said unto them, unto what then were ye baptized? And they said, unto John's baptism. **4,** Then said Paul, John verily baptized with the baptism of repentance, saying unto the people, that they should believe on him which should come after him, that is, on Christ Jesus. **5,** <u>when they **heard** this</u>. they were baptized in the name of the Lord Jesus. **6,** and when Paul had **laid his <u>hands</u>** upon them, the Holy Ghost came on them; and they spake with tongues and prophesied. 7, and all the men were about tw<u>el</u>ve.*

Notice in verse six it said <u>Paul laid his hands on them,</u> and afterwards, the Holy Ghost came on them. This meant—through Paul's influence and tutelage, they **understood** how to better receive the promises of GOD. Paul simply pointed them in the right direction.

I had a similar hands on experience that changed my direction in life. One morning I was sitting at my desk in fifth grade. All of a sudden, two familiar **hands** grabbed my shoulders from behind. Had I at that young age known about the rapture, I would have concluded—GOD, at that moment, was taking me up to heaven. My body suddenly left my desk, shooting straight upward. Yep—as my "bottom" left the chair, followed quickly by my feet, I knew I had been engulfed in a new spiritual experience. While at home, hours after the burning sensation left my bottom, it dawned on me. My father's **two hands,** which suddenly took <u>hold of my life</u> at school, was trying to teach me something. You see, my fifth grade teacher snuck my parents into the coatroom which happened to be just behind my desk at the back of the classroom. I do not know whose brainstorm it was to put an eight-inch window in that coatroom door. Personally, I think it was a bad idea. My teacher told my parents to watch how I disrupt class, shooting spit wads, rubber bands, and eating noisy potato chips. Hey! History books taught us, that in the beginning, mankind was comprised of hunters and gathers. Well in my mind, every student's hand being raised to gain the attention of the teacher, looked like a bird of prey leaving the ground. It was up to a great hunter such as myself, who was well armed and well fed, to bring that bird of prey down before it hurt the reputation of me and my fellow students. That bird of prey, that "hand waving" in the air to get the teacher's attention, represented knowledge me and the others did not have. I and my fellow students would have looked stupid had the student, with the hand in the air, been allowed to answer the question presented by our teacher. I was simply trying to use the skills and the equipment in my possession to help others. Later that night at home it became apparent to me, I needed **hands-on help** from someone else in order to <u>**learn** a better way</u> in which to help my fellow students.

People should not have to be told they are saved. If so, something is wrong? I knew my natural father because we spent time together. I know my spiritual father because we spend time talking to one another. I do not know if you have noticed that throughout this book you will read, We this or We that. GOD'S immeasurable mind, together with my two fingers punching the keys to my computer have brought you this book. I am less than ordinary. Yet, I know my GOD'S voice, his likes and dislikes, and His identity.

Who is GOD, and what is the relationship between HIM and Jesus Christ. Here is another confusing and controversial subject, which <u>has no bearing on whither you are saved or lost</u>. It is a subject, once understood, that will quicken and close that distance between you and GOD.

There are two men in identical homes sited in identical chairs with identical weapons behind closet doors. Each weapon was exactly the same distance from the two men. However, one man had two additional doors to open before he could get to the closet door that separated him from his weapon. Suddenly, two burglars burst through both men's doors at the exact same time. Both men have, in their closet, the power to stop the burglar. Question: Though both men are **equal** in <u>ability</u> and <u>speed,</u> who will retrieve their weapon first? It will be the man who has only one door to go through. So it is with the difference between those who embrace the three spiritual doors of the trinity, verses those that embrace the one door, a singular version of GOD. **Both** groups have a good solid relationship with their weapon of choice—GOD. However, in this story, we see one man ***SIMPLIFYING*** the connecting to his weapon by the removing of two doors. The same principal applies spiritually if you hold "deep within your heart" the trinity belief. Mathematics can be used to solve a spiritual as will a natural equation. This subject may seem too small and insignificant to you, but let us remind you—salvation is the ongoing process of gathering little things.

Here is an example of three doors slowing down a child of GOD getting to his spiritual weapon. In church, I overheard the prayers of an individual. He first delivered his request to the Father. Then he repeated the same exact request to the Son. And again, repeated the same exact request to the Holy Spirit. I realized he believed in giving all three **equal time** and **respect.** This subject of the singularity of GOD and Christ is a relationship issue, and not a salvation issue. However, this subject once understood, will open areas in the Bible you have been unable to go into.

Moses is one of the greatest friends of GOD recorded in the Bible. Yet, he never set foot in the Promised Land where other Israelites walked. He rejected a truth due to a lack of understanding. This lack, in turn, led to disbelief and rejection of that particular truth. EXODUS chapter seventeen and NUMBERS chapter twenty tells how GOD, through Moses, brought fourth water from a rock to satisfy the thirst of the Israelites. In EXODUS, GOD told Moses to stand upon and smite this rock in Mt. Horeb, and water would come forth. Later in NUMBERS, GOD told Moses to simply **Speak** to the rock, and water would come forth. However, Moses again smote the rock. GOD did not hide from our eyes HIS best friend's failure to follow that "positive progression" HE wanted his Word to flow in. Instead, GOD used it as a tool to teach us a truth. This rejection kept Moses from entering the Promised Land with the rest of the Israelites. The point is—if you reject truth from one scripture, you will be unable to receive truth from another related scripture. GOD'S Word is the Promised Land. You may not be able to go into a scripture and get what someone else has gotten out that same verse, simply because you did not understand another related scripture.

For example, GOD uses the similarities between two stories in regards to the **only two** kings anointed by Samuel to lead Israel. GOD exposes many truths through these two stories, but we will only expose one.

First SAMUEL 31 1-4, *now the Philistines fought against Israel: and the men of Israel fled from before the Philistines, and fell down slain in mount Gilboa.* **2,** *and the Philistines followed hard upon Saul and upon his sons; and the Philistines slew Jonathon, and Abinadab, and Melchishua, Saul's sons.* **3,** *and the battle went sore against Saul, and the archers hit him; and he was sore wounded of the archers.* **4,** *then said Saul unto his armor bearer, Draw thy sword, and thrust me through therewith; lest these uncircumcised come and thrust me through, and abuse me. But his armor bearer would not; for he was sore afraid. Therefore Saul took a sword, and fell upon it.* The other story is a little lengthy. So we will give you the general idea of what the story is about. In 2nd **SAMUEL** chapters **eleven** and **twelve,** King David sleeps with Bathsheba, who happened to be the wife of Uriah. Later, David is told by Bathsheba that she is with child. He then set her husband Uriah up to be killed. Just after the baby was born, it fell sick. Seven days straight King David would not eat. During which time he sought GOD in behalf of the child, but the child died. During that time, the King was so <u>distressed</u> that his servants feared for his life.

Out of both stories comes one point we want to bring to your attention. Both King Saul and King David suffered pain due to the **<u>death</u>** of their "<u>first</u> born child." However, there was a difference in the pain suffered by both. David suffered **emotional** pain and Saul suffered both, **emotional** and **physical** pain. David <u>watched</u> his first born die. Saul not only watched his first born die, but he also experienced the same **physical pain** of death his son experienced in the battle against the Philistines.

GOD actually suffered **physical** pain as well as **emotional** pain through the life and death of Christ. This being a much overlooked fact. No, we did not say GOD died with Christ—GOD is eternal. We said, GOD suffered the same physical pain Christ suffered. GOD wants us to see King Saul and his "first born" son Jonathon, as a single individual with "one spirit within." Saul represented GOD'S spirit and Jonathon Saul's body. This parallels GOD inhabiting the body of Christ, the curtain of flesh that "suffered the pain of death" through which GOD came to all mankind. You have to view Jonathon's death, not as the death of a separate person, but simply as another painful situation experienced by Saul. Again, GOD uses the similarities in Bible stories to reveal "his character" and all truth. Saul was permanently connected to Jonathon from birth on. Like GOD, who is permanently connected to the life and the experiences of Christ, **from birth** throughout the rest of eternity. Basically, GOD **weaved** the natural experiences we face daily into HIS eternal make-up.

The Bible said -- HE redeemed *the world unto himself.* We will not go into great detail concerning the garments warn by the high priest during fellowship with GOD in the Old Testament Tabernacle. We suggest you look up these garments on the computer. We will tell you that these beautiful garments of Blue, Purple, Scarlet, and Gold threads **"woven"** throughout, represented the righteousness of GOD. The sash, wrapped around the waist of the high priest, ***bound*** the garment to his body. This sash represented GOD permanently binding the natural experiences of life to Himself. The body of the high priest represented the body of Christ. And the body of Christ was also represented by the Rock that GOD told Moses to strike in EXODUS. GOD clothed the high priest on the outside with righteous clothes, and on the inside with righteous thoughts while HE spoke to the priest in The Most Holy

Place. This paralleled GOD clothing Christ with righteous actions and thoughts. By clothing the high priest from without and within, GOD in a sense, made himself a part of that life. So it is with the body of Christ. GOD **alone** robed that body on the outside with righteous actions, and GOD **alone** filled that mind from within with righteous thoughts.

*²⁸Then said Jesus unto them, When ye have lifted up the Son of man, then shall ye know that <u>I am he, and that I do **nothing** of myself</u>; but as my Father hath taught me, I speak these things. ²⁹And he that sent me is with me: the Father hath not left me alone; <u>for I do **always** those things that please him</u>.* John 8:28-29. Think about the ABSOLUTE power of "nothing" and "always." Have you ever been told by your beloved spouse, "You remember **NOTHING** I tell you," or, "You **ALWAYS** <u>fail</u> to put anything in the dishwasher." Here is how I responded to those same accusations. "Baby Doll, <u>five days ago,</u> you saw ME put my <u>dirty fork</u> in that there dishwasher." Then I said, "You can no longer use those two words, because at least one **time** now, I have remembered and done what you have asked." That mind in Christ held **NOTHING** except what GOD almighty, our one and only heavenly Father allowed. Every action was **ALWAYS** in accordance with the Word. <u>These two words are reserved for GOD'S use only</u>. Because they are words of <u>absolute</u> perfection. You will "not" find a "ONE TIME" violation of GOD'S Word in the life of Christ Jesus. But in **JOHN 8:28-29,** we find those two words coming forth from the mouth of a man born of a woman, who used them to reveal his commitment to all things written in the Word. *In the beginning was the word, and the word was with God, and the word was God.* John 1:1. Every time that body of Christ was struck, our GOD, our heavenly Father felt the actual pain of that blow as we would have had it been us on the receiving end. It was GOD himself who suffered the indignation and pain through the body of Christ.

Look at the story of King Saul and his sons more closely. You will see the similarities that GOD gives in order to justify this comparison. For instance, besides Jonathon, two of his younger brothers also died in that same battle with the Philistines. Jonathon's name means the Lord has given. The second brother's name, Abinadab, means the Father is generous. The third brother's name, Malkishua, means my King saves. Three names or titles "manifesting" the character of GOD, which is exactly what the "three titles" of Father-Son-Holy Ghost manifest. In addition, the story said the <u>archers</u> **hit** Saul and that HE <u>took a</u> sword and <u>fell upon it</u>. It was the sword that took Saul's life. Through Christ, GOD suffered the **painful arrows** of rejection and indignation. HE suffered the same **pain** the body of Christ suffered at death. The <u>natural sword</u> took Saul's life. The <u>spiritual sword,</u> GOD'S Word, took the life of Christ for our benefit.

Remember, GOD told Moses in EXODUS—HE—would be on the Rock and that Moses was to strike the Rock. The Bible said that Rock was Christ. GOD being on that stone, meant the natural was going to become part of the supernatural. The experiences connected to that Rock, was going to become a part of GOD'S existence. Every painful experience from the day Christ was born has become a part of GOD, and they will remain a part of HIM throughout the rest of eternity. Saul's death, with his first born, is an example of the <u>complete</u> **pain** our heavenly Father suffered for us through the body of Christ.

The second story, which covers King David and the death of his first born, revealed the reason the Physical suffering of GOD has been somewhat overlooked. This began to go into obscurity about three to four hundred years after the church was started. At that time, the newly formed Roman church declared the Father—Son—<u>separate</u> individuals, yet coexistent coequal and coeternal. **Christ** <u>did not exist</u> until the day GOD over shadowed Mary.

In this story, GOD wants us to see David as representing HIM, and the child as representing Christ. He wants us, for just a moment, to look at them as two separate individuals. Yet both have a permanent family bond between the two like Saul and Jonathon, who also represented GOD and the body of Christ. However, since both David and his first born Child are seen as "separate" persons. Both are also seen as suffering "separate" levels of Pain. This is the attitude that lodges **"deep"** within our heart when one looks through the eyes, or the understanding promoted by the **definition** of the word—trinity—which means three separate and distinct individuals or things. David, who represented GOD, is seen as suffering emotional pain. And the child, who represented Christ, is seen suffering the physical Pain of death.

God the Father and Jesus Christ should be seen in a "singular" manner. The first name of Jesus and the last name of Christ represents GOD and **FLESH** momentarily bound together as one. As Saul did, so GOD also suffered both emotional and physical pain through the life and death of Christ. When we look through Trinitarian eyes we fail to see the physical pain GOD suffered. For example—have a Father and a Son stand side by side while holding hands. Then hit the Son gently across his back. Then ask the Father if he felt the blow? Naturally, the Father will say no. Even though they are close family members with the same spiritual connection flowing through their veins, and despite being joined together through the holding of hands. This is one of the problems with viewing GOD as being represented by three "separate" individuals. Again, trinity defined, means three **"separate"** and **"distinct"** individuals or things.

My little bird What has a question—how many scriptures in the Bible contain the word trinity? Answer—not one! I am not going try to explain the incomprehensible Trinity belief, which first popped on the scene in Rome about three hundred years after the church was formed. That you could look up on your computer. However, I will ask you to consider this question my other little bird asked. Why is Trinity not used by GOD in the entire Bible?

Answer—this word has the "unique ability" to **_drag_** our minds over to, and connect us with the word—Separate—a word GOD never will use in describing or defining Himself. Trinity means a GROUP of three people or things. We can discard the word—things—because the church world has clearly defined <u>one</u> as the Father, **one** as the Son, and **one** Holy Ghost as being the child's spirit. The word Trinity drives most minds into the spiritual parking lot of—I believe the Farther -Son - Holy Ghost to be three separate and distinct individuals. Because of this confusion, many <u>SEPARATED</u> and formed the group called the Oneness movement. The separating of believers is the devil's ambition, because it makes it easier to surround a group and nibble away, until that group crumbles. This is way GOD never used trinity, which "strongly promotes" the words <u>separate or separation.</u>

During meditation, GOD gave an example to help me understand the relationship between HIM and the body of Christ. Before I give you this earthly example, I want you not to be offended, or to think I am being disrespectful to GOD. The example is the relationship a ***ventriloquist*** has with its **puppet**. The puppet has no SPIRIT, no life or power of its own, and is under the <u>complete control</u> of the master *puppeteer.* He alone gives the puppet, what to the world seems to be a personality all its own. The puppet is a **<u>WINDOW</u>** through which the *puppeteer* reveals his <u>inner</u> character. The *puppeteer* is both outside and inside the puppet. The puppet has become the *<u>arm and hand</u>* of the *puppeteer.* The *puppet* and the *puppeteer* have become **one**. If you were to strike the *puppet,* you will be striking the *puppeteer.* It is the *puppeteer* who feels the pain of that blow. There is **<u>one spirit</u>** inside the puppet, and that is the *puppeteer* himself. The voice of the *puppeteer* seemingly comes from both the inside and outside of the <u>puppet.</u> Like in **LUKE 3:22,** *and a voice came from heaven.*

The very reason most of the Israelites rejected Jesus, was due to the fact that they saw Christ and GOD as <u>two separate</u> individuals. They knew there was only one GOD. They expected him to come in great power and defeat there enemies. Seeing GOD and Christ as two separate individuals is why they could not grasp the thought of Jesus, who humbled himself before all mankind, including Israel's enemies, was the one and only GOD Almighty. I guess one might say—GOD gave fellowship to mankind as an undercover boss, in disguise so to speak. You know, great leaders lead from the front, by example. Why, asked my little bird, would GOD put on such a ruse? Well, we all know one reason was—someone without sin had to pay the judgment price of death demanded by GOD'S Word, because all of us, had sinned.

The other reason is quite **beautiful,** and again, somewhat overlooked if you hold fast to the trinity belief of the three separate individuals. This being GOD'S humility. One cannot, including GOD, demand or teach humility unless that one is first humble himself. In order to allow the next group of recorded scriptures to have a chance to give their full impact on your hearts. We will not disrupt the flow by numbering the verses. **PHILIPPIANS 2:1-8,** *If there be any consolation in Christ, if any comfort of love, if any fellowship of spirit, if any bowls and mercies. Fulfill ye my joy, that ye be like minded, having the same love. being of one accord. of one mind. Let nothing be done through strife or vainglory; but in lowliness of mind let each esteem the other better than themselves. Look not every man on his own things, but every man also on the things of others.* **Let this mind be in you. which was also in Christ Jesus:** *Who, being in the form of* **God,** *thought it not robbery to be equal with God: But made himself of no reputation. and took upon him the form of a servant, and was made in the likeness of man: And being found in fashion as a man,* **he humbled himself,** *and became obedient unto death, even the death of the cross.* Notice! It said HE humbled **Himself.** But it did not say, they humbled themselves, or we humbled ourselves. Again, my little bird asked—What entity was it that humbled himself? It was GOD who humbled himself through Christ. Remember the words of Christ. [28] *Then said Jesus unto them, When ye have lifted up the*

Son of man, then shall ye know that I am he, and that <u>I do nothing of myself</u>; but as my Father hath taught me, I speak these things. ²⁹ And he that sent me is with me: the Father hath not left me alone; for I do always those things that please him. John 8:28-29. Remember ¹⁹ *To wit, that <u>God was in Christ, reconciling the world unto **himself**</u>, not imputing their trespasses unto them; and hath committed unto us the word of reconciliation.* 2 Cor. 5:19. That is right, it was GOD and HIM alone who suffered both the "emotional" and "physical" pain <u>in our behalf</u>.

Did you ever think how difficult it is for someone who is all powerful, all knowing, and the creator of all things to show forth his humble side? Especially during which time he had to administer correction and guidance such as witnessed in the Old Testament. I know it is hard for my kids to see my humble side, however few points of humility I may have that is. Especially after one of my many lectures. It is really hard to see my humility while I am standing on a chair crowing like an old rooster, announcing my victorious win in a game of dominoes. Jesus confirmed this difficulty of receiving honor in **MARK 6:4,** *a prophet is not without honor, <u>but</u> in <u>his own country</u>. and among his <u>own kin</u>, and in <u>his own house</u>.* GOD, through these two stories about Saul and David, is trying to help us see that we will miss so many **little points** in the Bible if we look at GOD through Trinitarian <u>eyes</u>.

There are stories told throughout the church world confirming this acceptance of the separation of physical pain between Christ and the Spirit of GOD. We will re-tell one of these as it was told by a man who definitely has a relationship with GOD. This young preacher is most assuredly saved. How can I say this with such confidence? Well, his speech, attitude, and actions run parallel with the Word. His heart is right with GOD. Yet, he did not view GOD and Christ in a singular manner. He viewed them as "separate" and "distinct" persons, which is what the definition of the word trinity promotes "deep" within our hearts.

The story goes like this. In the early part of the twentieth century. A father had to sacrifice his teenage son in order to save hundreds of lives. The father was the operator of a drawbridge which allowed passenger trains to cross a major water way. Apparently one day, the automatic warning system that informs the operator of approaching trains, had failed. The man's son, who happened to be playing at the water's edge, heard the train's whistle blow. The boy noticed the drawbridge had not begun to lower yet. He knew something was wrong due to his experience of being on the job with his father for many years. He knew his dad had not been alerted to the approaching train. The boy raced to engage the manual over-ride switch near the tracks which would lower the bridge. However, he slipped and fell into the gear mechanism that controlled the bridge at that same moment the father saw the approaching train. Just before the father lowered the bridge. He saw his son struggling to free himself. The train had already passed the point of no return. It could not be stopped in time before it got to that bridge. "The Father was high up in the control booth." So he did not have enough time to save both his Son and the hundred or more souls on that train. This guy new his Son would be crushed as soon as he engaged the draw bridge.

All those souls on the train arrived home safely that day. However, on that very same day there was one Father who suffered great emotional pain as he watched his Son die. Then the young preacher finished his sermon with—like the Father in this story who suffered as he watched his Son die, so it was with GOD who suffered as he watched his Son die on the cross. We can see this preacher's attitude concerning the relationship between GOD and his Son was—Christ experienced the physical pain of death, and GOD suffered the emotional pain of death. Notice, the key word in this story and sermon is, they watched both Sons die. You see how separating the Father—and the Son, caused this young dedicated preacher to miss part of the character and suffering of GOD?

One day the devil whispered in my ear—so GOD sent his Son to suffer did he? What kind of father would do that? Then the devil said—a real Father would have taken his son's place and sacrificed himself. At that moment I did not realize it was the devil whispering in my ear, promoting that train of thought in my mind. This attack on GOD'S character is what sparked my study into this subject. You know, the devil is not as smart as he thinks. Thanks to his attack on the character of GOD, I now **understand** who Jesus Christ really is.

GOD tested my understanding shortly after my study on this subject was completed. HE asked—how do I prefer to be addressed? Is it as," my Father," or is it as, "my GOD?" After a moment of thought, I said, "You prefer to be addressed by the name of *Jesus Christ."* Then GOD responded back with, "Why?" I then said, "The body of Christ paralleled the body of Adam. You took a rib from Adam's side to create Eve, his bride. You Lord used the body of Mary to create Christ, which is the body that became a **part of** You. From the side of this body came the spiritual rib from which You used to make your bride, the church. This spiritual rib from Your side is represented in **JOHN 19:34,** *but one of the soldiers with a spear pierced his side, and forthwith came there out blood and water.* The blood and water represented Your **spiritual rib** because it was **part** of You. The blood represented Your spirit and the water Your Word and Christ is the Word made flesh. As blood gives life to the body, so Your Spirit gives life to Your Word. From Your side GOD came a new creation and a beautiful bride, Your church. It was You GOD who moved that body step by step through the murky waters of pain and sorrow, which all mankind faces on a daily basis. Again I said, "It was You GOD, who on a daily basis filled that mind and opened the mouth of Christ, giving us the Words of wisdom understanding and power." Then I ended my answer with, "That life was Your greatest creation. You tied yourself to flesh and allowed yourself to be tempted. Then through much pain, You "permitted" that patch of flesh You had **woven** into your eternal makeup to be **torn** from You—**MARK 15:34,** *my GOD, my GOD, why hast thou <u>forsaken me</u>.* That torn flesh opened to all mankind the door of fellowship to You Lord. Through that body of Christ, You confirmed your reliability, humility, your absolute power, and Your love of all things good. GOD! Those eleven little letters, forming the name of ***<u>JESUS CHRIST, instantly</u>*** brings to mind all Your characteristics which makes you so great and wonderful. So thank You my GOD and my Savior for making this relationship so much more personal, through the giving of Yourself such a name to be addressed by."

Funny how we humans will accept things told to us as factual, without ever confirming them through intensive study. For example, at Christmas we always hear about the three wise men who brought gifts to the baby Jesus. However, there is not any mention of the number of wise men in the Bible. The Bible does state, only three types of valuable gifts were given. There could have been fifty wise men paying homage to the Lord that day. But someone assumed there was three, and their version permeates throughout the tradition of the birth of Christ to this day

My best friend, who was raised in a oneness church, believed that these words constituted an actual scripture. (GOD **robed** <u>himself in flesh and dealt among us</u>). However, and after a long search this friend realized, (GOD **robed** himself in flesh and dealt among us) was not a scripture at all. It was some preacher's personal interpretation of **JOHN 1:10,** *he was in the world, and the world was made by him, and the world knew him not.* This translation had permeated throughout that oneness organization for so long, that it finally was accepted by many as an actual scripture. There are several church organizations who call themselves Oneness. On one particular point, they all believe differently of what those who hold to the Trinity faith believe. They see GOD and Christ as one individual. The trinity somewhat separates the Father-Son-Holy Ghost into three separate individuals with GOD in contact to each one. Oneness believe the Father-Son-Holy Ghost is GOD manifesting himself to the world through three offices of authority. We want to make one point very clear before we go any farther. GOD does not acknowledge two separate groups called the "Trinitarians" or the "Oneness." GOD does acknowledge one group, called HIS Children.

Though I **agree** with the Father-Son-Holy Ghost being seen in a more singular manner, I have to disagree in using the interpretation of, (GOD **robed** himself in flesh and dealt among us). The problem is, it points toward the words enclosed and covered. As GOD would never use trinity to represent himself, because it points toward "separate" and distinct individuals. So GOD would never use in reference to himself, (**<u>robed</u>** in <u>flesh</u>), which points toward him being enclosed or covered. To be enclosed or covered means to surround and shut in something. GOD can never be surrounded nor can he be shut in. GOD will never accept partial truth that hints in any way toward HIM being covered or enclosed. GOD will always attempt to lead one through the cloud of incomplete understanding onward to complete understanding. If GOD would not accept this translation of (robed himself in flesh), then how can the Oneness people expect the Trinitarians to accept it? The proper translation is just the opposite. It should read, (GOD robed the flesh in righteous actions), which is a less restrictive statement. This is confirmed by the coat given to Joseph from Jacob his father, and by the beautiful clothes GOD had the body of the high priest covered with. **GENESIS** chapter **thirty- seven** said, Jacob, the father of the twelve tribes of Israel gave Joseph a *coat of many colors*. Most agree, that Joseph represented Christ, and the coat represented the righteousness of GOD.

As a kid, did you ever climb into a discarded box that a new washer or dryer came in? I remember how dark and spooky it was inside the box I climbed in. Let us use our imagination to climb back into another box. This will help us understand the **What** and **Why** in regard to the relationship between GOD, the body of Christ, and mankind.

First, get a three foot square piece of carpet. This three foot **area** is the 100 cubit by

50 cubit Old Tabernacle. The FIBERS of the carpet represent GOD. Now place a shoe box with the lid-side up in the center of the three foot square piece of carpet. Divide the box into two separate rooms with a piece of cardboard. Label one room The Holy Place (the Gihon River) which represented the Word, and the other room The Most Holy Place (the Pison River) which represented GOD'S spirit. All area of the carpet surrounding the shoe-box is the outer courtyard which represented the Tigris River. This is the area where all GOD'S creation lives and interacts with one-another. The outer-edge of the carpet is the Euphrates River. This is the doorway into life and the exit into eternity. All area beyond the carpet is endless eternity GOD alone inhabited. Both the cardboard and the Tent in the Old Tabernacle represents the sinful flesh. This spiritual separation between GOD and mankind is represented by the curtain dividing the two rooms, and the cardboard dividing the box into two areas.

For a moment, picture yourself down on your knees inside that box in total darkness, all the while you trying to touch the threads of that carpet. However, you cannot, because the box is in between you and the carpet. So it is when we are born into this world. Our box, our lives are in contact with GOD. But we cannot understand or fellowship the Lord because we cannot see or touch him. Our spirits are separated from GOD and able to go our own way. Just like the box, which can be slide across the threads of the carpet because it is not bound to the carpet.

The Holy Place was given this title because it represented the area where the spirit of GOD and the spirit of man had one point in common. That being—both for a short time were connected to an earthen vessel—the flesh. Mankind through birth, and GOD by choice through Christ. This is verified in EXODUS when Moses meet GOD at the burning bush. GOD called that area of meeting, **Holy** Ground. This is why GOD had Moses take off his shoes. So both Moses and the Bush would be in contact with the earth. **The Most Holy Place** was given this title because GOD—alone—occupied that

area of the tent. This was verified by the flame that—alone—occupied the bush. Moses and GOD fellowshipped, but yet they spiritually were separated by their natural dwellings, Moses <u>flesh</u> and the <u>bush</u> GOD spoke through. Both occupied dwellings that rose from the earth. This is why the first room in the tent was titled, **The Holy Place.** The Most Holy Place is from where the Word of GOD came to all mankind.

The two rooms of the Holy Tent, as was the spirit of man and the spirit of GOD, were separated. The tearing open of the curtain, (the death of Christ), allowed man's <u>spirit</u> and GOD'S <u>spirit</u> to become bound to one-another. Now, spiritually speaking, there is one room only. Now we can have with GOD a common bond in both <u>flesh</u> and <u>SPIRIT</u>. By a bond in flesh we mean—GOD endured and suffered the same daily experiences of life, (through Christ), as we do.

The Most Holy Place represented the body of Christ, an area <u>occupied by GOD alone</u>. To <u>occupy</u> means—to be the <u>established</u> <u>user</u> of a **place.** The boxes, (the two compartments of the tent), are separate from one-another and yet both are in contact with each other. The users of the first box, The Holy Place, is mankind. Because mankind uses this compartment, the Word, to connect with GOD. HE is the only established user of the second box, The Most Holy Place. Again, <u>the "fleshly" curtain of SIN separated the OCCUPANTS of the two compartments</u>. This kind of contact between the two is representative of the years GOD fellowshipped mankind through Christ.

Mankind constantly touched the flesh of Christ. However, until the death of Christ, that was as close to GOD as they could get. At that time, the two compartments became one because the dividing curtain was ripped open. Now, the individual **"who wants"** the spirit of GOD can become one with GOD.

The apostle John, whose writings continually point to the deity of Christ, understood better than anyone else who Jesus Christ really was. This is why John laid his head on the chest of Jesus at the last supper. It was simply John's attempt to get as close to GOD as possible.

You need to understand that the first room, The Holy Place, represented man attempting to fulfill the Word without the help of the spirit of GOD. This Word being the life of Christ. Again, the high priest delivering the Word he received from inside the second room, The Most Holy Place, represented the Word being delivered through the body of Christ to the world. The first room, The Holy Place, is mankind in fellowship with GOD through the Word alone. This is the Old Testament relationship mankind had with GOD.

However, having knowledge of GOD'S Word and trying to do the Word on your own is not enough. Because the Word, by it- self, does not have the power to change are nature. The Word brought death to us. It exposed the weakness and the depravity of the flesh. Our bodies came from the earth. It craves to please itself with whatever it sees, tastes, smells, hears, and touches. We needed **both,** a personal connection to the Word and to GOD'S Spirit. We need GOD'S personal assistance to bring the Word to life in our lives.

The dead body of Jesus, the Word, is represented in the first room called The Holy place. This room lies **between** the outer courtyard and The Most Holy Place. This again is why GOD chose the cross. GOD wanted to visually show his Word positioned between mankind and himself. GOD put forth great effort by coming through the fleshly curtain door from above. We must put forth great effort by **climbing up the tree** to meet with GOD. And where do we meet and fellowship with GOD? Answer— in the Word, The Holy Place, the first room where the dead body of Christ is represented. This Word, that was dead to us, was brought to life as soon as GOD stepped through that fleshly curtain door that separated the two rooms. This was confirmed by the resurrection of the body of Christ. Now, when we grasp hold of the Word, GOD brings it to life in us through faith in HIS ability.

Now do see the importance **of "picturing yourself '** as receiving GOD'S spirit? Faith is the acceptance of something your natural senses such as sight, taste, smell, hearing, and touch cannot perceive. BIG QUESTION—how can I see myself, or how can I be <u>**CONVINCED**</u> that I have received GOD'S indwelling spirit? ANSWER—you must accept the Bible as being ABSOLUTELY true. You must <u>understand</u> the **<u>necessary</u>** step by step procedure laid out by GOD in order to establish this faith. And you do it with an honest and sincere heart.

FAITH is like a big trophy bass. Hearing GOD'S Word for the first time is like setting the hook in this baby. Immediately the fight is on. You need confidence in your equipment and understanding in regards to their application in catching this big boy. After jumping to spit the hook, he heads deep to tangle the line in "debris" in order to brake it. Finally, you're in front of the camera wearing a big smile while holding this trophy. All because of persistence, and your <u>understanding</u> of the WHAT and WHY GOD placed this spiritual equipment in your hand.

Spiritually speaking, the debris the fish tried to tangle itself with in order to break the connection is the failures of people who claim to be Christians. You have to ignore those mistakes. That is why Jesus told Peter, "Do not worry about what they are doing, you follow ME."

Now back to the box and our Lord's dilemma. GOD had to address this Question: How to get inside mankind's box so that HE could connect with those individual spirits that are enclosed and kept in total darkness? Answer—<u>I **MYSELF** will become part of the box.</u> Then I shall allow the sinful forces of nature to rip a hole in the box. This will allow my spiritual light and strength into their lives. *[12] But as many as received him, <u>to them gave he</u> **power** <u>to become</u> the sons of God, even to them that believe on his name:* John 1:12.

Question—how would you go about the task of making the supernatural fibers of the carpet and the box one unit? Answer—We have to weave, or stitch the SUPERNATURAL threads of the carpet into the box. Woven thread binding two objects together is like stitching a wound closed. The stitch goes inside and outside the wound. GOD wove, or better yet, HE stitched into HIS eternal makeup the natural occurrences of life. Making those trials HE personally overcame a permanent part of Himself. This wisdom and strength to defeat the arrows of life he passes on to us, if we allow.

Now we have made the box and the carpet one single unit. So if you were to pull the box away from the carpet, you would tear the box open. This is exactly what HE is trying to show us. GOD'S first thread to be sown into the box, to bind HIMSELF to humanity, was through the body of Mary. Her body would be used to bring forth the house of flesh that GOD alone would occupy in order to connect to the spirit of mankind. GOD sowed more threads of his Word into humanity's box through Christ from birth to death. First, into Christ's mind—Secondly, out his mouth by way of the tongue and on into the ears of mankind. Like the ventriloquist, GOD alone occupied that body. Thus putting into that mind only what HE wanted the tongue to expose to mankind. HE was in 100% control of that life. No other spirit shared that body.

In the Tabernacle, from birth to the start of Christ's ministry, is represented by the distance in the open courtyard. It is the area from the entry gate to the Brazen Laver which is just before you entered the Holy Tent of Fellowship. The Brazen Laver represented Water Baptism. Jesus Christ **"officially"** started delivering the "Word" after being baptized by John the Baptist. This is why the first compartment of the tent represented the body of Christ, because it marked the official time the Word was openly revealed to the world. After Water Baptism, GOD began to publicly sow the threads of understanding throughout the box of humanity. Thus leading us in the right path, so we could eventually make our own personal connection to HIM.

Finally, GOD allowed the unrighteousness of this world to pull the box away from the carpet. This tore a hole in the box. This tearing open of the dividing curtain allowed spiritual light to pour into our lives through the Word. Let us do the math together: **<u>GOD</u>** + fleshly **<u>body</u>** = Jesus Christ. *²⁶And as they were eating, Jesus took bread, and blessed it, and brake it, and gave it to the disciples, and said, Take, eat; this is my body. ²⁷And he took the cup, and gave thanks, and gave it to them, saying, Drink ye all of it; ²⁸For this is my blood of the new testament, which is shed for many for the remission of sins.* Matt. 26:26-28. Notice! GOD, through Christ, said—my blood was shed for many. This means, not everyone is going to EMBRACE this gracious offering. That life, GOD'S Hand, was extended out to us by HIS arm. This Arm being HIS Word and Spirit. GOD gave a "piece" of himself because HE spiritually bound the natural to himself through the body of Christ. All those earthly experiences and victories of the life of Christ became his own, and can now become ours.

REALITY CHECK

"<u>Oneness</u>" groups have to let go of their (Elijah syndrome). This being—I am the only one attitude; which has the tendency to SEPARATE or to drive a <u>wedge</u> between themselves and others who are also the offspring of Jesus Christ. YES! WE mean Trinitarians, and YEP! This is a "rebuke" to those who continually holler out—**<u>WE have "THE" Truth.</u>** In reality, you have a <u>SIMPLIFIED</u> version of (**A**) truth, which I also IN PART happen to embrace. However, over time, some "oneness leaders" have pushed this version so hard that the acceptance of it has evolved into an absolute necessity to be saved. And this, I do not agree with. The Ethiopian eunuch, after being preached to by Philip, asked, *³⁶And as they went on their way, they came unto a certain water: and the eunuch said, See, here is water; what doth hinder me to be baptized? ³⁷And Philip said, If thou believest with all thine heart, thou mayest. And he answered and said, I believe that Jesus Christ is the Son of God.* Acts 8:36-37. Philip never said you have to accept Christ as being the one and only GOD, or to accept Jesus Christ in a singular fashion.

He only said you had to believe Christ came from GOD. Salvation "is not gained" and "maintained" if you embrace Trinity or Oneness.

REALITY CHECK

Trinitarians need to accept the more singular version of the Father-Son-Holy Ghost as well, because it ***simplifies*** our understanding of GOD. Anytime you simplify a spiritual subject, that in turn **shortens** the distance **between** the individual and GOD. Again, this is a relationship and not a salvation issue.

Things in this book are undeniable, just as **"SOME"** of the explanations from Trinitarians and Oneness are undeniable.

Not all Trinitarians or Oneness will be saved, but "MANY" out of both GROUPS will, because salvation hinges on a personal relationship with GOD. This being further advanced through the acceptance and application of small pieces to the large puzzle.

So please, knock down these spiritual dividing walls no matter how small they are, so we can grow and be one in spirit.

Speaking in Tongues

Speaking in tongues "as the spirit gives the utterance" is most definitely real. **ACTS 2:1-17,** *And when the day of Pentecost was fully come, they were all in one accord in one place. 2- And suddenly there came a sound from heaven as of a rushing mighty wind, and it filled all the house where they were sitting. 3- And there appeared unto them cloven tongues as of fire, and it set upon each of them. 4- And they were filled with the Holy Ghost, and began to speak with* **other tongues,** *as the spirit gave the utterance. 5- And there were dwelling at Jerusalem Jews, devout men, out of every nation under heaven. 6- Now when this was noised abroad, the multitude came together, and were* **confounded,** *because that every man heard them speak in his own language. 7-And they were all amazed and marveled, saying one to another, behold, are not all these which speak Galilaeans? 8- And now hear we every man in our own tongue, wherein we were born. 9- Parthians, and Medes, and Elamites, and the dwellers in Mesopotamia, and in Judea, and Cappadoca, in Fontus, and Asia. 10- Phrygia, and Pamphyia, in Egypt, and in the parts of Libya about Cyrene, and* **strangers** *of Rome, Jews and proselytes. 11- Cretes and Arabians, we do hear them speak in our own tongues the wonderful works of GOD. 12- And they were all amazed, and were* **in doubt,** *saying one to another, What meaneth this? 13- Others* **mocking** *said, these are full of new wine. 14- But Peter, standing up with the eleven, lifted up his voice, and said unto them, Ye men of Judea, and all ye that dwell at Jerusalem, be this known unto you, and hearken to my voice. 15- For these men are not drunken as ye suppose, seeing it is but the third hour of the day. 16- But this is that which was spoken by the prophet Joel. 17- And it came to pass in the last days, saith GOD, I will pour out my spirit upon* **all flesh**: *and your sons and your daughters shall prophesy, and your young men shall see visions, and your old men shall dream dreams.*

Just before the first stop on a guided tour of the city of Jerusalem. A man begun to speak loudly in tongues at the back of the bus. As the leader of the Americans was stepping off the bus, she noticed the Israeli driver looked awfully pale. Before the woman completed her exit, the driver gently grabbed her arm and pulled her aside and asked, who was that man that loudly spoke those words? She answered, "You mean George, the one in the back?" "YES, YES," said the driver," whose excited response revealed the adrenalin now pumping throughout his body. Then the bus driver asked the woman, "Where did that man learn to speak Hebrew?" The woman, being caught off guard, broke out into a big smile and said to the bus driver. George can barely read and write English, no way can he speak Hebrew. He is just an old country boy raised on the farm who recently gave his heart to GOD." Then out of curiosity the woman asked, "Can you tell me what George said?" The bus driver responded, "Fear not, for I have come to save my people from their sins, 'look to me.'" The driver then asked, "What do those words, 'look to me' mean?" The woman realized GOD had opened the door of opportunity to witness to this man. She said, "'Look to me' is telling you to receive Jesus Christ as your GOD and Savior." Well, the bus driver must have had some doubts still yet, because as George stepped back on the bus, the driver grabbed that country boy's arm and spoke to him in Hebrew. However, George politely responded back with, "Are you talking to me? Forgive me, I do not know what you are saying"

There is one purpose, and two ways GOD use tongues as an inspiration to accomplish it. The one purpose being, the uniting of all <u>mankind</u> under one <u>Tower</u>, Jesus Christ. The two ways HE uses diverse tongues to help accomplish this is: the wonderful <u>RUSH</u> of <u>JOYFUL</u> feeling and emotion, plus, the <u>MYSTERY</u> presented by the <u>unfamiliar words</u> coming out of a believer's mouth.

GENESIS 11:1-9, tells how all the people got together and said. <u>L</u>et us build a city and a <u>tower</u> that reaches to heaven and <u>make a name for ourselves</u>. This tower represented mankind's choice in how to establish and maintain a relationship with GOD. This attitude prompted GOD to confound their language. This insertion of DIVERSE TONGUES caused them to divide and scatter. GOD now uses DIVERSE TONGUES to unite us under the shadow of a strong new Tower, Jesus Christ, one built by GOD. This parallels the experience of Adam and Eve. Water of the Persian Gulf forced them out of GOD'S garden. And GOD uses Water Baptism to bring mankind back into HIS garden.

One of the two ways GOD uses diverse tongues is through public display. This we see in **ACTS** chapter two and in the story of the bus driver. Both stories reveal how DIVERSE TONGUES was used to draw attention to GOD. Both show how GOD penetrated the heart of those within hearing distance. The other use for diverse tongues is for personal use only. GOD uses the fantastic **Rush** of feeling and emotion in hope of generating a believer's interest in finding out more about this mysterious new language. Spiritual language is GOD'S thoughts and habits learned from the Word. This mystery is solved only by searching the Bible. This study will focus only on the personal use of tongues.

Paul said *¹⁸ I thank my God, I speak with tongues more than ye all:* 1 Cor. 14:18. Think about this for a moment. This guy gave us more "understanding" of the mind of GOD than anybody. *⁴ He that speaketh in an unknown tongue edifieth himself; but he that prophesieth edifieth the church.* 1 Cor. 14:4. In this scripture, to edify oneself means to improve one's **"knowledge"** of somebody. For a Christian, that somebody is GOD. Let us do another spiritual math equation. Paul + I speak in Tongues more than you all = greater understanding of the mind of GOD.

We have discussed how **Understanding the Word** is the dividing line between the saved and lost. We have revealed that one must first "read" the Bible, and secondly, one must "meditate" on what you read. Third point, is to have "total faith" in GOD'S ability to explain the scriptures. The first two points are easy steps to do. However, the third step, total faith in GOD'S ability is not so easy to come by. Quite frankly, it takes "practice" in giving one's trust to GOD. Here is where the ***gift*** of speaking in other tongues, *as the SPIRIT GIVES the UTTERANCE,* pays big dividends toward giving **<u>our</u>** *trust* to GOD.

The "gift' to speak in tongues should be accepted and embraced like a gift given to a newlywed couple. One of my little birds asked this question—Why do we give newlyweds gifts? Answer—to help make the "transition" from single life to married life <u>much</u> easier. So it is with the spiritual gift of speaking in other tongues. This gift, which ALL Christians can ENJOY at ANYTIME, **helps** in our "transition" from being single to being joined with GOD. The bible calls us his bride. To continually practice the use of this spiritual gift, **helps** in letting go of our self-reliance, and **helps** to place our dependence on the ability of GOD. It **helps** make the transition from natural to spiritual thinking much easier. It **helps** transform our natural <u>reflex</u> actions to the <u>reflex</u> actions of a spiritual man. For instance—hammer hits thumb—the reflex action of the natural man is to respond with bad language. The reflex action of the spiritually influenced man is to respond with good language, like—THANK GOD.

"Practice Makes Perfect" is the motto of a professional athlete. And so it is with a spiritual athlete. <u>The purpose of practice is to make your "responsive skills" automatic</u>. One of my daughters was recruited by several college softball teams. The one she choose had a highly respected softball program due to its many years of success. My daughter played catcher and third base and was recognized as having a powerful bat. She also was noted for being very quick, accurate, and having a rocket for an arm. However, on her first day of college practice, everything went wrong. Not one of those skills she was highly recruited for, showed up. This I saw for myself, because I was there hiding behind some stands. The head coach and the assistant head coach was standing very close, watching her every move as she caught for the team's top pitcher. My daughter's nightmarish practice started with the first ball she threw back to the pitcher. This ball sailed five feet over the head of the pitcher. The next ball she threw hit the dirt in front of the pitcher's mound and rolled on by. The third ball landed just two foot away from my daughter in front of home-plate, and never made it back to the pitcher. The fourth ball was carried, by my daughter, from home plate to the mound and deposited directly into the pitcher's hand. The coaches were shocked, they called her high-school coach and said something is wrong with her arm. To shorten this story, she went on to have a great college career.

The problem that held her in its clutches during the first day of practice was, "she was trying to control" every aspect involved in the **mechanics** of throwing the ball. In so doing, she dropped the ball, so to speak. Worry about the coaches watching her every move started that practice on a downward spiral. From that point on she tried to control, in her **mind,** every little detail involved in throwing a ball. In so doing, she had temporally lost the "instinctive" skills developed over time through much practice.

Instinctive means prompted by a **strong natural impulse.** Instinctive also means involuntary, which is spontaneous or automatic and not controlled or controllable by the mind. The moment worry entered her heart was the moment she began to—Drop The Ball—in her life. Worry should not be allowed to occupy your heart for very long, because it will rob you and dominate your life.

This same daughter won the national title game with her bat. On that day, I also enjoyed a moment of fame among the coaches and parents. I had predicted my daughter would hit the game winning home run before she ever got to the plate. The opposing pitcher through 65 to 70 MPH with good movement on the ball. Our team, including my daughter, could not touch her. We had a few sporadic hits and walks, but nothing together that could score a run. My daughter struck out her first three times as the fourth batter, hitting in the clean-up position. Now I know what you're thinking. All parents believe, or at least hope, their child is going to hit a home every time they get to the plate. Well on that day, I openly predicted to my wife and others, my daughter would strike out her first three at bats even before she got to the plate. You see, I know my daughter. I could tell she was <u>giving too much thought</u> to her swing and to the importance of the moment at hand. In addition, I could tell because of her yawning, looking around, and the extra-long time she took to get to the plate. You cannot react to a 70 MPH fast ball while thinking too much. <u>You have to **rely** on those **instinctive** reflexes **developed** through continual practice.</u>

It is the sixth inning and we were down by one. The leadoff batter walked and the two and three batters struck out. My daughter is in the on deck circle swinging a bat and warming up. The opposing team threw some insults at her. All of sudden, my girl turned and looked directly at their pitcher. She never took her eyes off the pitcher as she bent down to fill her hands with dirt. Here is where it looked like I had the super-power of clairvoyance. I knew my daughter was ticked as soon as I saw her grabbing the dirt while never taking her eyes off the pitcher. That is the moment I begun to clap and celebrate our victory. My wife and some the other parents looked at me with surprise. They asked, "What is with the celebrating?" I responded with, "Thanks to the other team, we just won the game—Hallelujah." I then said. "I do not care how fast the ball is thrown or where it is thrown, it is out of here."

She got to the plate so fast it would make your head spin. First pitch was a foot above the strike zone. Bang went the bat on the ball. It sounded like someone hit a church bell with a sludge hammer. The left-fielder did not bother to take one step toward retrieving that ball, as she could easily see the ball was gone.

The difference with that game winning hit was, she stop the **mind control** in regards to her "environment" and talent developed through much practice. Basically, my daughter took no thought on her situation or her swing. **She just went up to bat and hit the ball,** which turned out to be—a home run. **MATTHEW 6:25-34,** *therefore I say unto you,* take no thought *for your life, what ye shall eat, or what ye shall drink; nor yet for your body, what ye shall put on. Is not the life more than meat, and the body than raiment.* **MATTHEW 10:19,** *but when* **they deliver you up,** take "no thought" *now or* what ye shall speak: for it shall be given you in that same hour what ye shall speak. This I discovered at the turkey processing plant when GOD'S spirit would not allow me to cuss after losing my temper. Why! Because I trusted in GOD'S ability to give me the words that I would speak. Do you want to hit a home run? Then DON'T WORRY ABOUT "it"—because—the "it" becomes small when given into the hands of GOD. Job, with all his worry did not change anything. His life changed for the better when he gave GOD all his worries. So back to the question of, how can we give to GOD all those "valuable" worries that we do not want to turn loose of? It is not easy turning over to someone your most prized possessions, such as your worries. My little bird asked—Why worry when GOD offers peace and contentment?

Speaking in Tongues *as the spirit* **gives** *the utterance,* is the "continual" PRACTICE of allowing GOD to influence your thoughts, which will be reflected in the words that leave your tongue. It happens when you give GOD 100% trust in HIS ability to inspire your heart and mind. It is you being totally submerged in the spiritual river system where all understanding originates. In this river, according to GALATIANS 5:22-23, you will find—*love,* ***Joy,*** *peace, longsuffering, gentleness, goodness,* faith, *meekness, and temperance.* Excuse me, but did this scripture say FAITH is also found in this river? Included in this spiritual river are pure and perfect intentions. This is found in **ROMANS 8:28,** *and we know that* all things work "together" *for* ***good*** *to them that love God.* **If we allow,** this river will produce the proper verbal **reply** to any given situation. This is why understanding the two river systems, (the natural and spiritual), is so important. GOD'S children has access to both. New Christians have <u>way more practice</u> drinking from the natural river. From the natural comes bad attitudes, curses, hate, vengeance, envy, distress, confusion, depression, and <u>bad language</u>. Speaking in tongues immediately introduces us to the spiritual river by way of a powerful experience. Hey! Those people that came out of the upper room on the day of Pentecost were accused of being drunk. They were **<u>feeling</u>**—<u>Real Good</u>. Peter had to explain to all the people witnessing this event that they were not drunk on wine, but were under the **<u>influence</u>** of <u>GOD'S spirit.</u> This experience, at the get-go, clarifies what the spiritual river <u>feels</u> like. A **Rush** of **JOYFUL** <u>elation and pleasure.</u>

Inside that long scripture of **NEHEMIAH 8:10** it says, *eat the fat, and drink the **<u>sweet</u>**—for the **<u>joy of the Lord is your</u>** strength*. We need to CONSTANTLY experience this JOYFUL **Rush** of feeling and emotion in order to **remind** us how sweet this salvation is. GOD uses this experience to inspire us to jump back in time and time again. It feels clean and good as GOD'S spirit provides the <u>words</u> and inspires the <u>emotions.</u> The Bible teaches, we should strive toward trusting GOD with all of our heart, soul, mind, and body. The tongue is the most unruly member in the body. According to **MATTHEW 12:34,** It reveals what is in the heart. In addition, the entire third chapter in **JAMES** reveals the power of the tongue in regards to starting wars and destroying lives. Diverse Tongues is a confirmation that you, at that very moment, have completely given GOD influence over heart, mind, soul, and <u>body</u>. This GOD confirms with an <u>unbelievable,</u> and virtually impossible to contain, RUSH of feelings and emotions. The **"practiced"** use of this gift WILL help your "reactions" and "speech" to be quickened and more spiritual.

[2] *For he that speaketh in an unknown tongue speaketh not unto men, but unto God:*

*for **no man** understandeth him; howbeit in the spirit he speaketh mysteries.* 1 Cor. 14:2. The language of angels is one dialect new Christians do not **understand.** Question—what are the first things you need to start doing after permanently moving to a new country? Answer—begin to learn the **language** and the **customs** of the land. The customs of the natural land are bad, but the spiritual customs of this new land are joy, peace, kindness, forgiveness, and love without end. The language of the spirit is the Bible. Paul understood the purpose of speaking in tongues. GOD uses the **mystery** produced by unfamiliar words to inspire us to continually seek and find out what this new language is all about. Paul said, *¹⁴ For if I pray in an unknown tongue, **my** spirit prayeth, but **my** understanding is unfruitful. ¹⁵ What is it then? I will pray with the spirit, and I will pray with the understanding also: I will sing with the spirit, and I will sing with the understanding also.* 1 Cor. 14:14-15.

Whose spirit was Paul referring to? *⁹ But as it is written, Eye hath not seen, nor ear heard, neither have entered into the heart of man, the things which God hath prepared for them that love him. ¹⁰ But God hath revealed them unto us by his Spirit: for the Spirit searcheth all things, yea, the **deep** things of God. ¹¹ For what man knoweth the things of a man, save the spirit of man which is in him? even so the things of God knoweth no man, but the Spirit of God. ¹² Now we have received, not the spirit of the world, but the spirit which is of God; that we might **know** the things that are freely given to us of God. ¹³ Which things also we speak, not in the words which man's wisdom teacheth, but which the Holy Ghost teacheth; comparing spiritual things with spiritual. ¹⁴ But the natural man receiveth not the things of the Spirit of God: for they are foolishness unto him: neither can he know them, because they are **spiritually discerned**.* 1 Cor. 2:9-14. Many times I have SEEN wonderful things just after speaking in tongues *as the spirit gave the utterance.* In **JOB 38:1** and **40:6,** GOD answered him out of the Whirlwind. On many occasions I battled the urge to give up. And we all know who it was trying to sell that attitude to me. How did I shake it off? Answer—I did not—I let GOD shake it off for me through the personal experience of speaking in other tongues as the *spirit gave*—ME—*the utterance.* That feel—**OH-SO-GOOD**—of an experience, LIFTED me above and separated me from that earthly impulse.

Speaking of being Lifted. Have you considered **PSALM 103:5** and **ISAIAH 40:31?** Both tell how those who trust in GOD shall have their "strength renewed like eagles. Question—what LIFTS the eagle above the earth? Answer—the **RUSH** of WIND beneath its Wings. Elijah, in 2nd **KINGS 2:11,** was carried to Heaven by the *Whirlwind.* Some will say—it is the two wings that gives the eagle its strength. But wings hold no power without that RUSH of *Wind.*

Question—whose spirit is influencing our speech during this experience? HELLO—it is GOD'S spirit. This experience is GOD'S chosen way to CONSTANTLY inspire, strengthen, and communicate to the lost and saved. On the day of Pentecost, GOD used the tongues of the believers to speak easily understood words to the lost. The lost themselves were the translators of what was being said on that day, because what they heard was being said in each and everyone's native tongue.

However, what benefit is it to the believer to speak in an unknown tongue? Answer—none whatsoever—if you do not "understand" the language being spoken? The unknown language being spoken by the spirit, is an inspiration to the saved to SOLVE this mystery through the learning of the language. The definition of language is—the use of "spoken" or "written" words as a way of communicating. Question—What is the language of the spirit, or what is the language of angels? Answer—it is GOD'S Word. This Word holds **MYSTERIES,** the number of which cannot be counted. This is why diverse tongues will never cease to be used by GOD until we get to heaven, where we will not be hampered by these natural bodies. We will not have to struggle to find and receive every truth. We need to be constantly reminded that there are mysteries to be solved. *¹⁶And without controversy <u>great</u> is the mystery of godliness: <u>God</u> was manifest in the flesh, justified in the Spirit, seen of angels, preached unto the Gentiles, believed on in the world, received up into glory.* 1 Tim. 3:16.

Question—how does GOD reveal these mysteries? Answer—by having total influence in our hearts and minds, thus allowing HIM to <u>knit</u> together all scriptures. *² That their hearts might be comforted, being **<u>knit</u>** together in love, and unto all **<u>riches</u>** of the <u>full assurance</u> of <u>understanding</u>, to the <u>acknowledgement</u> of the **mystery** of <u>God</u>, and of the <u>Father</u>, and of <u>Christ</u>;* Col. 2:2. Question—What <u>gift</u> did GOD give us to inspire such trust? Answer—that wonderful FIRE and RUSH feeling we experience <u>every time</u> we allow GOD total influence over our heart, mind, soul, and body. That influence being revealed through the most uncontrollable member of the body, **our tongue.** This little guy is always the last member to submit to GOD'S influence. Question—Why does GOD use words unfamiliar as we speak in tongues? Answer—the mystery of the unknown promotes the desire to solve the mystery. If we allow, GOD will constantly RENEW and STRENGTHEN our spirit through the experience of the FIRE and RUSH. Thus inspiring us to read the Bible, where all mysteries are solved. *² And be not conformed to this world: but be ye <u>transformed by the **renewing of your mind**</u>, <u>that ye may **prove**</u> what is that good, and acceptable, and **<u>perfect</u>**, will of God.* Rom. 12:2.

Hey! We're not always in the perfect will of GOD—We—are constantly struggling to find HIS perfect will—We—constantly make mistakes—We—CONSTANTLY need forgiveness—We—CONSTANTLY need to be REMINDED that—We—are GOD'S *children.* This is why it is so important to "understand" the **spiritual mechanics involved** that qualifies us to receive GOD'S daily forgiveness and strength. GOD'S children need to understand why we—like David and Paul—

who were scoundrels at times get it and others do not. We need to "understand" what are the **spiritual mechanics involved** in order to keep it in our lives.

Look at the Bee and the BABY bear. Down the tree scampered baby bear all the while hollering—the Bee stung me the Bee stung me. Mother bear follows after him down the tree and gives her cub another taste of the Bee's honey. The sudden RUSH of SWEETNESS renewed in him the FIRE of desire. This wonderful feeling "stopped his playing around," and inspired him to "refocus" his attention back up the tree. He suddenly had the ENCOURAGEMENT and STRENGTH to again go through the Bee in order to get the Honey.

The **(Bee)** is the Bible. The STING of the **Bee** is the guilt or frustration we FEEL when the Bible exposes errors in our lives and any misunderstanding of scripture. We are the little bear who fled after receiving the BAD FEELING from the sting. No one likes to experience the BAD FEELING. So we have a tendency to back away from the **Bee,** the Bible. The bear cub again climbed up the tree and went through the Bee after mother bear renewed that GREAT FEELING in his mind and heart.

*² And be not conformed to this world: but be ye transformed by the renewing of your mind, that ye may **prove** what is that good, and acceptable, and **perfect**, will of God.* Rom. 12:2. That RUSH we feel as we allow GOD to speak through us is very important. That JOYFUL **Rush** of emotion from GOD'S spirit is the encouragement and strength we continually need. It helps us climb the tree through study of the Word. All Christians will be attacked by depression and anxiety.

GOD uses a language that we do not recognize because HE is trying to INSPIRE us to learn. For instance, have you ever asked yourself—I wish I understood what was being said after your one year old rattles off a bunch of jabber? Or, have you ever been around people talking and laughing in another language while staring directly at you? That unknown element of their conversation really bugs you. You find yourself wishing you could **understand** what is being said. GOD uses this same principal, hoping this unfamiliar tongue will inspire us to seek out the understanding of what is being said in the Bible. It did. Paul said, *¹⁴ For if I pray in an unknown tongue, my spirit prayeth, but <u>**my** understanding is unfruitful</u>. ¹⁵ What is it then? I will pray with the spirit, and <u>I will pray with the understanding also</u>: I will sing with the spirit, and I will sing with the understanding also.* 1 Cor. 14:14-15. Question—Where does this understanding come from? Answer—from between the lines of scripture in the <u>Old</u> and <u>Ne</u>w Testaments, which happens to also represent the two wings of the eagle and the wings of the two Cherubs covering the Ark of the Covenant. The <u>WIND</u> under the wings of those **two Cherubs** was represented inside the Ark of the Covenant. That being items representing GOD'S active presence.

HE is hoping that we will be inspired to read the Word, due to experiencing the **Rush** felt as GOD'S Spirit **Fires** through our souls, and due to the **Mystery** of the unknown tongue. This experience is a GIFT given to all Christians to be used at **"anytime"** to provide strength and inspiration. *⁵ Not by works of righteousness which we have done, but <u>according to his mercy</u> he saved us, by the <u>washing</u> of <u>regeneration</u>, and <u>renewing</u> of the Holy Ghost;* Tit. 3:5.

Think about this—the tongue only speaks what is in the heart. *³⁴ for out of the abundance of the heart the mouth speaketh.* Mat. 12:34b. The tongue is the most unruly member of the body. It is small in size, yet it has the power to start wars and to destroy lives. The poor tongue gets the blame for reporting what is in the heart of mankind. Totally placing your trust in GOD'S ability to bring the next word to the surface, <u>as you begin to speak,</u> is when you will speak in other tongues. In addition, you will begin to see deeper into the Word because of the more time spent under GOD'S *total* influence. You talk about a rush. It's like going from 0 to 100 in under one second. Why? Because it is God promoting the emotions felt, plus those words in your heart and mind. You do not have to be in a hipped up frenzy to experience this. While in a calm state of mind, I look to GOD to inspire the next set of words that leaves my tongue, and that is when I get that—WOW—WHAT A RUSH. It's like the children of Israel crossing the Red Sea. They stepped and GOD parted the waters. And so, I begin to speak and GOD inspires the words to be spoken. Again, the **practiced** use of this gift builds trust in GOD'S ability, and it *helps* in transforming our lives from the natural to the spiritual.

⁵But as one was felling a beam, the axe head fell into the water: and he cried, and said, Alas, master! for it was borrowed. ⁶And the man of God said, Where fell it? And he shewed him the place. And he cut down a stick, and cast it in thither; and the iron did swim. ⁷Therefore said he, Take it up to thee. And he put out his hand, and took it. 2 Kings 6:5-7. Here again, we have scriptures confirming the need of GOD'S "active" involvement in our lives. This story tells us how the Word of GOD shall be made to surface in our lives and become a useful tool to help others. The how, is represented by the stick the man of GOD cutoff and threw in the water. This being Jesus Christ (the active presence of GOD bringing HIS Word to life), and the water is life's situations. The IRON AXE is the Word of GOD because it is a **heavy** tool used to cut and prune trees. The Israelites held GOD'S Word deep in their Hearts. However, they did not have the active presence of GOD at work in their hearts. They had no power within to make GOD'S Word surface in their lives. Many Christians are living like those in the Old Testament. They memorize the Word and carry it around in their hearts. However, they do not allow GOD the opportunity to bring it to the surface during critical situations.

Hey! Did you notice the valuable AXE head was—borrowed? The Water is the situations and arrows that life fires at us daily. The borrowed AXE is like borrowed answers. Neither are able to solve the problem. Like the one who lost the Axe, we also have to ask GOD "personally" to give us the understanding and the victory. Faith in

GOD'S ability is the key.

My little bird What asked this question—How can we keep our tongues from speaking a bad word during a painful situation, such as the smashing of a finger with a hammer? Answer—You have to totally trust in GOD'S ability to bring, from the Depths of your Heart, that appropriate word or words to be said.

*[11] Not that which goeth into the mouth defileth a man; but that which **cometh out of the mouth**, this defileth a man.* Matt. 15:11. You have to let GOD bring those words to the surface.

This kind of faith is born through understanding and much practice. This life altering faith can be broken down into two parts. First—fill your heart, (your bag), with the Word of GOD. Second—Believe beyond any doubt that you are part of a righteous tree. For instance, an olive tree will only bare olives. So it is with those that have embraced Jesus. You are a limb of the Righteous Tree and "you will" bear righteous fruit. However, you have to **Fully Believe** that you are a limb of the righteous tree before the fruit can be seen budding forth. You have to understand that you cannot, through mind control, produce this righteous fruit. It is the nutriment— the **knowledge** of the Word and the **spirit** of GOD flowing inside the branch that produces the righteous fruit. As GOD said to the Israelites through Moses, *[13] And Moses said unto the people, Fear ye not, stand still, and **see** the salvation of the LORD, which he will shew to you to day: for the Egyptians whom ye have seen to day, ye shall see them again no more for ever.* Exod. 14:13. *[13] For it is God which worketh in you both to will and to do of his good pleasure.* Phil 2:13.

Question—does speaking in tongues guarantee that you will never do or say anything wrong? Answer—**NO**—it does not. Remember, *[32]the spirits of the prophets are subject to the prophets.* 1 Cor. 14:32. This is why you will see some misguided abuse of this gift. Somebody who claims this gift may offend you in some manner. Salvation is an on-going process. Like practice is the process by which an athlete masters his sport. So it is with spiritual athletes, who also masters there calling through much practice. Speaking in Tongues, as the Spirit gives the utterance, <u>is a **spiritual gift** that **helps** in this process</u>. There are some who mimic, and some that try to counterfeit this experience. But only things of great value are worthy to be counterfeited. However, all these cannot diminish the power of this gift.

There is another point we want you to remember. Speaking while under the influence of **GOD'S** spirit does not mean you will always speak an unfamiliar language. Remember, when you place 100% trust in GOD'S ability as you pray, that places you in *HIS* <u>spiritual river.</u> This means—you may experience moments of overwhelming grief, not for yourself but for others, because it is GOD'S emotion you're experiencing. Such a powerful experience may show up only as a groan leaving that body of ours. His love for the lost may also result in tears flowing from our eyes, as witnessed in the shortest scripture in the Bible. **JOHN 11:35**, *Jesus wept.* In this river flows these fruits—love, joy, peace, patience, <u>forgiveness,</u> kindness, inspiration, <u>compassion,</u> understanding, strength, good and perfect intentions, direction of travel one should take in life's journey, and <u>*faith.*</u> Question—is there anything in this river you would not want to catch?

All these are ours for the taking. We just have to relax and **LET** GOD have total access. We need FAITH that GOD will influence our minds and the direction we take in life. We need FAITH that GOD will set in-motion a plan of correction if we step in the wrong direction, as in the lives of Jonah and Elijah. We need FAITH that GOD will influence our speech and actions when confronted by situations that life **"suddenly"** throws us into. What, along with the Word, cultivates this FAITH? It is that WHIRLWIND experience of you SPEAKING in TONGUES as GOD INSPIRES the UTTERANCE.

Notice! Whirlwind means a **"sudden"** experience. I have gone into prayer with my mind in a state of total confusion, floundering in nothing but negative thoughts: Only to come out of prayer LAUGHING my head off. Why, because the source of my confusion got confused themselves and had to leave. I could not remember why I got so up-set in the first place.

But as for me, my feet were almost gone; my steps had well nigh slipped. **3,** *For I was envious at the foolish, when I saw the prosperity of the wicked.* **16,** *When I thought to know this, it was too painful for me.* **17,** *Until I went into the **sanctuary of God**; then understood I their end.* Psalm 73:2 & 3 &16-17. **Sanctuary** means a safe place, which spiritually is GOD. So where is that WHIRLWIND that changes our outlook on life found? In the presence of the All MIGHTY, our SANCTUARY, our GOD.

Many Roads to Choose

Many roads have more than one highway traveling the same asphalt or concrete pathway at the same time. For instance—while traveling, you see a sign that says Inter-State 44, and on the same sign-post you will see highway 66. Both high-ways use that particular stretch of road to get travelers to different destinations. At some point they will divide and go their separate ways.

Spiritually speaking, our lives follow the same pattern. For instance—a <u>fear</u> or a complete and <u>partial</u> misunderstanding of scripture may be carried deep in our hearts for years, even after we commit our lives to GOD. Our hearts is the asphalt or concrete road that more than one highway uses. That fear, or those partial truths which are attached to your commitment to GOD, are the highways using your heart to travel on at that particular time in your life. Fear and confusion's destination is failure, and partial truth's destination is victory. At some point these highways separate and go their own way. The questions are—which highways will we go on when they part? Will we follow fear and confusion? Will we follow GOD from partial truth to complete truth?

Remember my story of how GOD **<u>permanently</u>** separated me from that deep-rooted fear—GOD, do you love Me – Me? That question has never again come up in my heart because it just is not there anymore. I know beyond a shadow of a doubt GOD loves—Me—personally. That highway of fear went East away from GOD, and I went on the highway of commitment West with GOD. That question finally surfaced in my heart due to some bad times experienced. This same question will confront ALL Christians in these last days as the wickedness of this world grows worse. This fear traveled with me for years. I managed to push it deep within my heart and hide it from everyone. Well, almost everyone—[39]*give to every man according to his ways, <u>whose heart</u>* **thou**

knowest*; (for thou, even thou only, knowest the hearts of all the children of men;)* 1 Kings 8:39b. We, like Elijah and Job, have fears and character flaws we do not see or we simply try to ignore and hide them. We even justify them to ourselves. GOD has to separate us from those fears and correct our thinking in order to fulfill in our lives a passage in John. *[10] I am come that they <u>might have life</u>, and that they might have it <u>**more abundantly**</u>.* John 10:10b.

Abraham, like all of us when we first come to GOD, had many highways using the same road, (his heart), to travel on. He had along with his commitment to GOD, worldly interest such as doubts fears and acceptance of partial truth. GENESIS 12:10-20 tells how he talked his wife into lying to Pharaoh the King of Egypt. Sarah was to say, "I am Abraham's sister," because she was one good-looking woman and Abraham thought the King would have him killed in order to have his wife. *[15] The princes also of Pharaoh saw her, and commended her before Pharaoh: and the woman was taken into Pharaoh's house. [16] And he entreated Abram well for her sake: and he had sheep, and oxen, and he asses, and menservants, and maidservants, and she asses, and camels.* Gen. 12:15-16. Basically, Abraham was willing to give his own wife to save his hide. Fear is a strong enemy to face by yourself. Abraham, in this instance, choose to follow the high-way of fear. Fortunately, Abraham was not alone. God set Pharaoh straight real quick. This story took place at the start of Abraham's and GOD'S relationship together. However, and later in Abraham's life, we find him telling the same lie. *[2] And Abraham said of Sarah his wife, She is my sister: and Abimelech king of Gerar sent, and took Sarah.* Gen. 20:2. God plagued the house of Abimelech as HE did Pharaoh's house.

The difference in these two stories is, Abraham admitted his wrong and come clean to king Abimelech; whereas, he did not with Pharaoh. *[11] And Abraham said, Because <u>I thought</u>, Surely the fear of God <u>**is not**</u> in this place; and they will slay me for my wife's sake. [12] <u>And yet indeed she is my</u> sister; she is the daughter of my father, but not the *daughter of my mother; and she became my wife.* Gen. 20:11-12. So it was not a total lie; it was partially true. Abraham finally choose to follow the highway of commitment to GOD through trust and change. This being, the "giving up" of that partial truth he clung to.

Later in the life of Isaac, Abraham's son. We find this partial truth migrating into a full blown LIE, after the situations of **life** again applied **extreme pressure.** In chapter twenty-six, we find Isaac living in the same land that was under the control of a king with the same name of Abimelech. Isaac carried the same fear of being killed because of his wife as Abraham did. So he told the same lie, that his beautiful wife Rebekah was his sister and not his wife. *⁷And the men of the place asked him of his wife; and he said, She is my sister: for he feared to say, She is my wife; lest, said he, the men of the place should kill me for Rebekah; because she was fair to look upon.* Gen. 26:7. Here, in Abraham's house, we have an example of two directions partial truth can take a person. In Abraham's case it led to the full truth, but in Isaac's case, it led to a complete lie, because Rebekah his wife was not his sister. Abraham' and Isaac's story shows how all lives, connected to both the partial truth and the complete lie, was disrupted by confusion and division. Partial understanding of truth is strongly connected to mankind's thoughts. This being our natural ability to reason and deduce the outcome of a situation. Look at the following passage. *¹¹And Abraham said, Because **I thought**, Surely the fear of God is not in this place; and they will slay me for my wife's sake.* Gen. 20:11. It was his "own" power of reason that led him to accept and cling to partial truth as his means of deliverance. Notice the scripture said—*I thought,* and what was this thought of Abraham's? Answer—*God **is not** in this place.* He did not think GOD was involved in his life at that particular moment. He judged his situation through the natural, what he saw and heard, without the input of GOD. Spiritually speaking—Abraham did not realize GOD was involved in his fearful situation, trying to change his life for the better by getting rid of a fear he held in his heart for years. Abraham finally "admitted to himself" and "others" that he had been clinging to a partial truth. High-way 6 points toward man's thoughts, and high-way 7 points toward GOD'S thoughts. After many years of traveling the same concrete pathway, the two roads parted and Abraham chose high-way 7. Notice how Abraham was confronted with the same situation until he choose the right highway to follow.

GOD is constantly trying to align the thinking of all church organizations into agreement with one-another, because the Book of Matthew says, *²⁵ Every kingdom divided against itself is brought to desolation; and every **city** or **house** divided against itself shall not stand:* Matt. 12:25b. Confusion in an individual's life concerning GOD'S Word equals a **city** divided, and every **house** represents every church organization. GOD'S children, the Bible says, will be greatly challenged in these last days and the love of many will grow cold. This is why it is so important **not to** brush-off any information that challenges any particular truth you hold so dear.

Being separated by denominational fences allows our enemy more maneuverability. It says in chapter one, rule 23 of Sun Tzu the Art Of War—if your enemy is united, separate him. How important is the rules handed down through centuries from Sun Tzu? All countries who violated these rules of warfare eventually lost the war, including the United States in Vietnam. This is why some church organizations have gay ministers. And others have become lifeless and boring through repetitious rituals. And why others worship statues, dead saints, and other objects.

I have also seen GOD-loving churches adhere to ways so outdated that they scare away many, especially the youth. The growth of these churches have slowed to a snail's pace. Without youth, the church has limited potential. YES! With young people comes music and habits hard to endure for the elder Christian. It may take years of tolerance and patience before the Word grabs their hearts. These churches need to look over the top of their fences once in while so they can pick-up this attitude <u>I discovered in another church</u>. **I will do anything just <u>short of sin</u> to get the Word of GOD out to the lost.** QUESTION—what is the first step necessary in establishing a relationship with GOD? ANSWER—*¹⁷So then faith cometh by hearing, and hearing by the word of God.* Rom. 10:17. People cannot **hear** if they do not come to church. Granted, most that come to church will never make that spiritual connection to the Lord. However, the more that comes translates into more that will.

Some churches, through the years, have shifted their focus to the <u>does</u> and the <u>don'ts</u> and the <u>who's</u> that bring the Word. We creatures of habit sometimes forget the power of the Word and remember only the power of our position. This attitude causes a premature deliverance of our personal views to the new converts in regards to music, dress, and habits. These personal views generally cause more confusion and distraction in a new Christian's life. We cannot forget, it is the Word and its understanding that will lead to a union with GOD, and this spiritual union will provide the inspiration to change. The apostle Paul did not forget what was most important. **PHILIPPIANS 1:12-18** explains how some preached from a pure heart while others preached out of envy and rivalry, and some preached out of selfish ambition. But here is what I like about Paul. He was not too concerned over the does and the don'ts of why those men preached. Paul only wanted the Gospel of Christ to get out, because he knew the power of the Word. I like how the NIV version of the Bible put it—**the gospel has its objectivity and validity <u>apart from those who proclaim it;</u> the message is more <u>than the medium</u>.**

The attitude of separation is why many individuals and church organizations consider themselves on a higher spiritual plain than all the rest. Remember, Elijah's high-minded opinion of himself momentarily separated him from all others who were faithful to GOD. That separation lead to his downward spiral. Many have chosen to travel Route 6, (man's choice), the Politically Correct high-way.

We know there is a legitimate fear one has to deal with when it comes to accepting a change in thinking, and that is the fear of being wrong. But GOD attacks this fear through these five scriptures. *⁷Ask, and it shall be given you; seek, and ye shall find; knock, and it shall be opened unto you: ⁸For every one that asketh receiveth; and he that seeketh findeth; and to him that knocketh it shall be opened. ⁹Or what man is there of you, whom if his son ask bread, will he give him a stone? ¹⁰Or if he ask a fish, will he give him a serpent? ¹¹If ye then, being evil, know **how to** give good gifts unto your children, how much more shall your Father which is in heaven give good things to them that ask him?* Matt. 7:7-11. The words **"how to"** means—GOD knows the best actions to take in regards to changing our thoughts and our lives. And one action I know HE takes, is by "continually confronting us with information through angels unawares, which may conflict with thoughts we hold so dear. *¹⁵And if in any thing ye be otherwise minded, God shall reveal even this unto you.* Phil 3:15b. Again, GOD will bring the same subject to your attention time and time again. However, it is still up to you to receive and travel the new highway of thought.

Look! There are so many inherit characteristics with being human that makes accepting change in our lives difficult. It makes us uncomfortable and insecure until we settle in and fully accept that change. We also hate to let go of things handed down from generation to generation. In the case of many, we are a little lazy and do not want to research the subject in question through study, prayer, and meditation. All preachers, teachers of the Word, church leaders, and individuals should not be afraid of change. But, all should devote the time necessary through study and prayer to facilitate it.

²⁶Whose voice then shook the earth: but now he hath promised, saying, Yet once more I shake not the earth only, but also <u>heaven</u>. ²⁷And this word, Yet once more, signifieth the removing of those things that are shaken, as of things that are made, that those things *which cannot be shaken may remain.* Heb. 12:26-27. These scriptures tell us—any lie or partial truth established through the reasoning power of man will fail under **"extreme"** pressure. GOD, in these last days, is strongly promoting the idea of non-denominational churches. HE is pushing open the gate to allow more information to flow into the hearts of his children.

Many church organizations, through the years, have collected some good information beneficial to a child of GOD. The gathering of this information by these individual church organizations has served a good purpose. The very reason these groups came into existence was due to the discovery of a new highway of thought from GOD. However, in those same groups, you will find partial truths and partial truths that has migrated into full blown lies. The problem is, it is hard to penetrate that fence of protection put up by many of these denominational churches. This fence is like a barricade blocking the flow of traffic into the city. The traffic being vital information, and the city being the individual child of GOD.

[12] Verily, verily, I say unto you, He that believeth on me, the works that I do shall he do also; and greater works than these shall he do; because I go unto my Father. John 14:12. Miracles are wonderful, but that is not the *greater works* that is most important to GOD. Bringing to the world the understanding of GOD'S Word is. Read the rest of that chapter, and you will see he was taking about us receiving the spirit of **truth**. Question—what was the *"work"* that Christ did, and what is the *"greater work"* that we shall do. Answer—Christ delivered the "understanding" of the Word more perfectly to many, but we shall deliver **greater** "understanding" of the Word to **"many more"** than Christ. We can do this because of our great numbers, who, as individuals have GOD'S spirit, and collectively been given more time and in-roads into our lives to accumulate and disperse vital information. For instance, besides the Bible, hundreds of books have been written by individuals who have received

enlightenment on one or more subjects. However, we sometimes push this information aside due to our lack of **open-hearted** research, through study prayer and meditation. Denominational organizations have served their purpose. They were formed because of information received by individuals from GOD, which was rejected by their peers. But now it is time for all leaders, preachers, teachers, and individuals of the church to test what they believe through study, meditation, prayer, and by "crossing the fence of fellowship" with one-another. We can no longer ignore information that constantly challenges what we have accepted as truth all of our lives. Because it may be GOD using an angel unaware to fulfill that last half of **PHILIPPIANS 3:15;** *and if in anything ye be otherwise minded, God shall reveal even this unto you.*

Warning

Make sure you're connected with GOD as you dig through the field of information. You have to KNOW and BELIEVE beyond a **shadow of doubt** that you are GOD'S child. Because complete trust in GOD'S ability is required to put your heart and mind on the right highway.

Picking what to believe out of this vast field of available information is like picking your future wife out of the vast number of available women. Question—why do some marriages fail and others last a life time. Answer—either the man or the woman choose the wrong partner to live with. Many a woman and man choose through the natural selection process. Meaning, because of the outward appearance and according to what they thought they wanted in a partner. Now I cannot tell you why other marriages worked or failed. But I can tell you why my marriage of over 42 years has worked. **QUESTIONS**—What led me to, and Why did I partner up with the greatest woman I have ever known?

I was 23 and looking forward to start my own family. However, I was scared due to the high rate of failed marriages. Like all of us, I wanted someone who looked beautiful on the outside and was beautiful on the inside. So I needed some way to put the odds of choice in my favor. Like a Wall Street Trader, I needed someone on the **inside** to help me make the right investment. **Someone** who had vital information, concerning my future partner in question, that no one else had. That someone was GOD. I prayed, "Lord, bring us together, and please do not let me pass her by, whether or not "she is hid in a crowd or standing alone." About two weeks later I was at our church organization's general conference. I was standing amidst thousands, when all of a sudden the sea of people parted and I saw her for the **first time.** She was a beautiful 4' 11" specimen of womanhood. Even though I had never seen her before, I knew within myself she was the one GOD was pointing at. Look, I know human nature will say—all men think she is the one. But in this case, GOD confirmed my choice. One month earlier, during a diner party at our pastor's house, his wife said, "I know the perfect woman for you, she goes to the Collinsville church about 50 miles away and her name is Beverly." Guess who the woman was I connected with at that general conference amidst the thousands of people? YEP! Her name was Beverly, and yes, she lived in Collinsville. Coincidence you say—out of more than four thousand people—Right. Now God did not have any influence in me falling in love with my wife. All GOD did was to point her out, but the rest HE left up to me. Bev and I put the effort into getting to know each other, and that is how we fell in love. Oh by the way! My wife thought I WAS A BIG JERK AT FIRST. To those that know me—Can you imagine that? Uh! Don't answer that.

Many times GOD will bring us in contact with information that we reject simply because we did not set aside enough time to get to know it better. The more I learned about my future bride, the more I was pulled to her. Information from GOD is like a magnet. Once you begin to "really" touch it through study prayer and meditation, you will not be able to let go of it. Truth will constantly pop-up and haunt your thoughts, causing you to throw a little water, (GOD'S Word), in your face. Just like the thoughts surrounding my future bride caused me, on occasion, to throw a little water in my face; in order to cool my spirit and give me some temporary peace of mind so I could get some sleep.

Look again at Abraham and his son's story. Both the *partial truth* and Isaac's *total lie* had some outward beauty, which was represented by their gorgeous wives. To us, in this story, those <u>beautiful</u> wives represented lies and partial truths that we choose to be our permanent partners. However, when the **"extreme"** pressures of life <u>went after those partners</u>. Confusion, fear, and separation soon followed in the lives of those connected to their stories.

Here are some facts concerning partial truth. It stands for partial success. Like Adam and Eve, a person who embraces it might be more tempted to withdraw when it is challenged. This happened many times when Jesus challenged the priest's understanding of scripture. This withdrawal of those that hold it may reveal itself as anger, or through an extremely argumentative response. Partial truth affects a part or parts, but not the whole. This is why many fail in their relationship with GOD. They simply "stop short" of having enough understanding of the Word in order to change their outcome. Here are some facts concerning truth. It corresponds to fact or reality, and it is <u>consistent</u> or in <u>agreement</u> with something else. It is <u>similar</u> and <u>equivalent</u> to something. It is <u>conscientious</u> in its support of somebody or something. Now regardless of your opinion—**<u>INFORMATION</u> must be accepted, once it makes a connection to an idea and it proves itself not to be contradictory.** This word contradictory means—either inconsistent within itself or in relationship to others. So then, once information crosses your path and turns your attention to run parallel to the Word, it must be accepted.

My **<u>SEVEN LAYER DIP</u>** was sitting on the counter. I just finished making it as one of my three son-in-law's walked in the kitchen. He said, "Man that looks good, can I have some?" I said, "Here is a spoon, help yourself." After tasting it he said, "Ooh that is perfect." After gorging himself full with chips and dip he asked, "Could you teach me how to make it?" I said, "Sure, I would be happy to." I then said, "It is really simple to make."

"You start by mixing together ½ to ¾ cup of chopped jalapeno peppers, 2 to *2-1/2* cups of chopped white onion, and a large can of refried beans. You spread this mix evenly into a normal cake-pan approximately 9 inches wide and 13 inches long and *2-1/2* inches deep. Then you spread approximately an eight-inch layer of sour cream on top. Next, you chop a full can of pitted black olives and evenly spread those on top of the sour cream. Now you cover the entire area with a layer of lightly salted, very small tomatoes cut in half. You now cut a bunch of long stem green onions into *1/4* to *1/2* inch pieces and completely cover all the tomatoes, using only the green stems of the onions. Finally, you cover all the area of the pan with finely shredded mild cheddar cheese, until you can no longer see the green of the onion stems."

Several times my son-in-law called me on the phone saying, "It does not taste or look the same as the original." During each call, **we had to go back to the beginning,** and I had to explain in greater detail each step and **WHY** each step was important. For instance, in order to speed things up, he relied on the LABOR of something else. He used a machine to chop the tomatoes and the onions, which is what many Christians do. They rely on the LABOR of someone else to tell them what they should believe. But these two items needed the LABOR from his own hands to "personally" *cut* through them. Otherwise, the entire dip turns to mush, because all the "good" juice is forced out of both the onions and the tomatoes due to the pressure applied by the machine.

Spiritually speaking, the good juice is thought changing information that enters our hearts. And the pressure of the machine is the organized denomination itself. The "pressure" of the "organizational machine" **sometimes"** forces the thought changing information out of our hearts.

I had to explain to my son-in-law, that <u>**you**</u> cross cut the onion in one-eighth to one-quarter of an inch slices and <u>you</u> turn the onion and cut down through those slices. This will produce small pieces of onion. Then take very small tomatoes and <u>**you**</u> cut them in half and place the halves on the olives with the cut <u>side up,</u> completely covering the entire area. This personal hands-on method keeps the juice in the onions and tomatoes, ready to burst all their flavor in your mouth as you bite down.

Even though he knew <u>**WHAT**</u> ingredients made up this dip, he still only had partial understanding of **WHY** <u>you should maintain the order of placement given</u> as you make the dip. For example, the chopped green onion stems has to be between the tomatoes and the shredded cheese. The stems kept the juice in the tomatoes, and, from soaking into the cheese. This, as I explained to him, is one of "two" reasons my dip stays firm and fresh for one to two weeks even if there is only one serving left in the pan. Notice—I said **one** of <u>**two**</u> reasons. My son-in-law did two things all Christians should learn to do. He listened intently, and he <u>caught a **SMALL** detail</u>. This being the other thing I do in order to keep the dip fresh and firm. <u>Then he "asked" **what** that little detail was</u>. I explained, "Before you put the layer of sour cream on, you "drop" the pan several times at a distance of one to two feet onto a "firm" but <u>cushioned surface</u>. This "forces" all the air out of the mix. It makes a good compacted high-way for any residual fluid to flow out into the open end of the pan, where the dip has already been removed. Then before you put the dip back in the fridge. You can take a paper towel and wipe up the little bit of residual fluid out of the open area of the pan. This keeps the dip uniform, neat in appearance, and firm."

Finally, and after several attempts I thought he had it, but I was wrong. My son-in-law called one last time and said, "I <u>have</u> <u>followed all the instructions to the letter,</u> but still yet the flavor is not equal to the original?" So <u>once more</u> **we** <u>went over every little detail</u>. Then I asked him one last question. "Did you use El Paso refried beans?" He said to me, "NO." "Aw," I said, "That is your problem." I said, "After umpteen tries, I found that I could only trust the flavor of EL Paso beans because they are the best." Now my son-in-law's dip is as good, and seemingly better than the original. Due to his "persistent effort, he now owns the dip, it is his. Finding truth, and holding on to it, runs parallel to my son-in- law's discovery and his attempt to reproduce and permanently make the dip his own. His first encounter with the dip, through sight and taste, was as a finished product. But in order to "consistently" REPRODUCE or to RENEW the pleasurable taste <u>he suddenly</u> experienced <u>from within the dip,</u> he would have to understand how it is made.

This is like all who <u>suddenly</u> experience their first <u>DIP</u> in the spiritual river. In order to improve or consistently RENEW this spiritual rush of delightful flavor, from which comes continual strength and focus, one will have to understand how it is made. As there is a certain order of procedure in making the dip, so it is in establishing and maintaining a spiritual relationship with GOD. All Christians first experience salvation as a finished product. [30] When Jesus therefore had received the vinegar, he said, **It is finished**: and he bowed his head, and gave up the ghost. John 19:30. My son- in-law, on several occasions, had to revisit the directions from start to finish before that dip became his own.

Partial truth is partial success—it affects a part or parts but not the **whole.** TRUTH is something that is equal too, or runs parallel to something else. Though my son-in-law kept improving the dip through research, <u>it still did not match the *flavor*</u> of the original until he applied that last bit of information. The moment he put his trust in the right brand of refried beans is when **his** <u>**dip**</u> became equal and ran parallel to the original. Once he accepted and applied that last bit of information, the **whole** flavor of the dip changed and became consistent with the original.

QUESTION—why are so many Christians unhappy and constantly complaining or unable to overcome a particular addiction? ANSWER—"<u>*deep*</u> within their hearts", they are "uncertain" whether or not they are GOD'S child. Even though my son-in-law had all the ingredients and the order of placement was correct, he still would not present the dip to his friends. <u>He</u> was not **<u>satisfied</u>** with the taste. <u>It did not meet his expectations.</u> This caused him to back away from presenting the dip as his own. But he did what many Christians fail to do. That being, he **continued** his search by asking the creator of the dip one more question. The last answer he received finally changed the **<u>whole</u>** dip, which caused it to meet his expectations. This gave him the confidence to claim the dip as his own. <u>He now presents it proudly to his friends.</u>

I have seen so many people seeking satisfaction from GOD give up, and when their answer might have been just one request away? There is always a <u>line to cross</u> when seeking something from GOD. That line is, satisfaction. In order to cross that line—you must BELIEVE you will receive. You must also apply a much overlooked ingredient—HONESTY to YOURSELF.

There I was, crying out to GOD, needing change and satisfaction in my life. All of sudden, this question from one of the many people surrounding me penetrated my hearing—ARE YOU SATISFIED YET? I stopped praying at that time. Then, while total silence had engulfed us all, I looked at the group surrounding me. After a long moment of thought, and because of my extreme emotional stress, I answered loudly—NO—I WANT MORE. With eyes closed, back to prayer I went.

I was sitting Indian-style with legs crossed when it happened. Suddenly, I felt the passionate embrace from within as <u>my spirit</u> was lifted skyward. It felt like I had suddenly been given the ***wings of an eagle*** and a supernatural ***WIND*** was beneath those wings, causing ME to soar higher-higher and higher. The experience was so joyously great that I thought I would burst. The people around me said—I lit up with a glow as a smile engulfed my entire face. No one again asked if I was satisfied, because that big-stupid- glowing-grin said it all. The ***WIND*** was GOD himself lifting me up, fulfilling the promise of victory found in the Bible.

The ***wings of an eagle*** is the Two Testaments that provide the promises. They also reveal the effort it takes on our part to receive them. For example, both Testaments teach this principal found in **MATTHEW** 7:7, *Ask, and it <u>will</u> be given <u>you</u>; Seek, and <u>ye</u> shall find; Knock, and <u>it shall</u> be opened unto <u>you</u>.* This scripture says nothing about stopping short of receiving your answer. Question—have you ever noticed that GOD'S favorite number is 7? And HE put this absolutely PERFECT PROMISE in the numbered sequence of—<u>7</u>:<u>7</u>. I think GOD wants us to ware this scripture as a necklace around our necks, so we do not forget and stop short of receiving the promised answer to **all** our requests.

The toughest thing for us to do is to ***CROSS THE LINE.*** In every question or problem that grips our lives, there is an invisible line drawn between dissatisfaction and satisfaction. My son-in- law's goal was to recreate the dip and make it his own. It took several attempts and a <u>persistent asking for help</u> before he was <u>completely</u> satisfied. Before he reached this goal of satisfaction, he encountered bits of information, (partial truths). These, once applied changed the structure and looks of the dip, but it did not change the flavor. In other words, these partial truths changed a part or parts of the dip, but they did not change the whole. The flavor <u>of the dip</u> crossed the line from dissatisfaction to satisfaction after the last bit of information was applied. Whether or not you are a new Christian or an old-timer seeking GOD, do not stop short and stay in the land of dissatisfaction.

PEOPLE-PEOPLE-PEOPLE—it is not that hard to receive spiritual satisfaction from GOD! There are only <u>TWO</u> ingredients **we** have to provide and put into this spiritual dip. And that is, Faith & Honesty. But an important fact overlooked is, the proper order in which these two ingredients are applied. Many put Faith before Honesty. But Honesty should always be applied before Faith. Otherwise, your <u>*DIP*</u> into the <u>*SPIRITUAL*</u> might turn to mush and not last. Example—when I was crying out to GOD in prayer for change and satisfaction in my life, a question was asked—**<u>are you satisfied yet</u>**? During my momentary pause in prayer. Many negative thoughts went through my mind of why I should stop at that point. One was—it is okay for you to stop, because you feel a **little better** <u>now that you have repented</u>. Another was—you can stop now, because these people around you have seen your act of commitment to GOD. However, the one thought I choose to follow, **<u>be HONEST with YOURSELF,</u>** "forced" me to shout out—NO—I WANT MORE. Because at that particular moment, I was not **FULLY** satisfied. We can have faith in GOD. But if we are not HONEST with ourselves, that dishonesty can cause us to stop short of satisfaction. Confidence and strength is the offspring of spiritual satisfaction. "Uncertainty" and "weakness" is the offspring of spiritual dissatisfaction.

Many people make that initial commitment to GOD by repenting and being baptized in water. However, they stop short of fully experiencing spiritual satisfaction. Like the bean dip, the spiritual dip has specific ingredients and an order in which they should be added. The FLAVOR of the DIP did not satisfy my son- in-law because he did not use the right brand of refried beans.

HONESTY is the right brand. It is—absolutely—a necessary ingredient in the spiritual dip called salvation. The **right brand** of beans should have been the first <u>ingredient</u> used. HONESTY should be the first ingredient applied in everyone's search for GOD. This is verified by the thief that was crucified with Christ. [41] *And we* *indeed justly; <u>for we receive the due reward of our deeds</u>: but this man hath done nothing amiss. ⁴² And he said unto Jesus, Lord, remember me when thou comest into thy kingdom. ⁴³ And Jesus said unto him, Verily I say unto thee, Today shalt thou be with me in paradise.* Luke 23:41-43.

Many people who first come to GOD, through repentance and water baptism, <u>are told by others</u>—you are now saved. The first words a new born Christian should hear from the church is not an answer, but QUESTIONS—**<u>Are you satisfied yet—does the flavor of this spiritual experience exceed your expectations—did you feel the "RUSH" that comes from the spirit of GOD</u>??????** A new Christian should be encouraged to be HONEST to themselves in answering. Do not let them stop short of experiencing the complete power of salvation as stated in **PHILIPPIANS 2:13** -- *For it is **<u>God</u>** which **<u>worketh in you</u>** both **<u>to will</u>** and **<u>to do</u>** of his good pleasure.*

Riding the Rails of Truth

Many "fail" to apply this principal as they search for truth. **Data** showing a relationship and showing that it runs parallel in a conscientious support of a specific subject, must be accepted and applied to that subject. Disregard of this principal encourages this disorientating question to lodge in our hearts. How can I know what is truth when everyone has their own interpretation? We need to understand the "spiritual mechanics involved" in recognizing Truth. Information providing a tread of connection to GOD'S character or thoughts will always run parallel in consistent support of each other. More pennies worth of facts collected, makes Truth more visible. More Truth understood closes the distance between US and GOD.

Lies or Partial Truth is confirmed by disagreements, which happens when two opinions flow in opposite directions. Partial truth means—we DO NOT HAVE, or we HAVE NOT ACCEPTED enough DATA. This is the spiritual mechanics involved in the production of arguments, confusion, and division. We all fight, and rightfully so, the urge to accept facts that does not fit what we have been taught. However, we should apply the energy found within that FIGHTING SPIRIT to the research of those facts. The mechanics involved in seeing or the understanding of a single Truth runs parallel to the mechanics needed to see and interrupt the picture held within a puzzle. Many little pieces will have to be applied before the picture within a puzzle becomes recognizable. How many pieces may differ in regard to the spiritual ability of the individual? Personally—I am so slow that the whole puzzle is required, and then I still need GOD'S help to determine what is in the picture. For example—I am honking the horn—I am in a hurry—the arrow is green—why will they not make the turn? My wife said, "Maybe their car died." I said, "No way. **I can see** the two talking to each other. They're just not paying attention." I missed that light—now I am mad. So I get out and stormed up to their car and said, "WHAT IS THE DEAL?" The elderly lady looked up at me with tears in her eyes, and said in a quivering voice, "My car will not start." As I walked to my car I asked myself, "How did I win the BIG JERK of the day award?"

Answer—I rejected **data** given by an angel unaware, (my wife), that was given for the purpose of changing my mind. It could have caused my mind to run parallel to the TRUTH that lay within this situation. Instead, my opinion, or truth I choose to cling too was formed on limited-info. The spiritual mechanics involved in the production of my wrong opinion was, LIMITED DATA due to the **REJECTION** of NEW DATA. Look— I **saw** the light turn green, and I saw the car in front of me was not moving. That information was easy to interpret. But the dead engine HIDDEN under the hood of the car was not as easy to see. This made it harder to interpret it as being part of the situation. I rejected data which did not fit my attitude "I felt justified" in having. Partial Truth affects a part or parts, but not the whole. The actual TRUTH of the situation was not revealed, nor did my opinion change, until I accepted and applied this **fact**—their car engine had died.

GOD gave us, in **GENESIS 28:12,** Jacob's ladder as a visual reminder of three things we need to understand in regard to finding truth. **First**—where is Truth found? Answer—It is found between the Old and the New testaments, which are the two main rails of the spiritual ladder. **Second**—how do we receive it? Answer—Truth is received and confirmed through GOD'S personal intervention, initiated by our request. This is represented by the ascending angels (our requests), and the descending angels (our answers). **Third**—how do we recognize truth? Answer—Truth corresponds to fact or reality and is consistent or in agreement to something else. Truth is conscientious in its support of somebody or something. So far, we have discussed the first and second points in regard to finding truth. However, we have not looked closely enough into the <u>spiritual mechanics</u> of the third part, **<u>recognizing</u>** truth. Understanding the LADDER and all the connecting threads of similarities will help.

[12] *Work out <u>your own</u> salvation with fear and trembling.* Phil. 2:12b.

[15] <u>*Study to* **shew thyself**</u> *approved unto God, a workman that needeth not to be ashamed,* **<u>*rightly dividing*</u>** *the word of <u>truth</u>.* 2 Tim. 2:15. In regard to spiritual things, I am not an advocate of living my life simply because someone said I was supposed to live that way. Eve got her definition of Truth from Adam and not GOD, and we all know what that led to. This life-style is like the baby bear who grows up in captivity. Once he is let back into the wilderness to fend for himself, he will die. He has no experience in feeding or fighting for himself, and so it is with many children of GOD. They die spiritually because they do not have a basic understanding in regard to the <u>mechanics</u> of the SPIRITUAL LADDER. Notice how most Bible scholars call it—**<u>Jacob's</u>** ladder. GOD wants you to have your own ladder. HE also wants you to understand the principals involved in the construction of this ladder, and how to apply them. Again, understanding is the key to spiritual growth. Preachers, teachers, and angels unaware are included in those descending angels on Jacob's ladder. They bring spiritual information into our lives. They are a BIG part of GOD intervening into our lives. But many forget that the information they deliver should <u>only</u> be the <u>catalyst</u> which inspires us to search for ourselves, the subjects presented by them.

There are several "threads" tying Jacob's Ladder to the crosses that held the two thieves and Christ. A ladder has two rails and a cross has two rails. A ladder's **steps** connects those two rails, which in turn supports our weight as we climb. Spiritual Steps is the **<u>understanding</u>** procured from GOD'S **Word.** This understanding supports our weight. They give us a place to rest, until we gather strength to make the next step upward.

Jesus Christ, being attached to both rails of the cross, supports the fact that he was both man and GOD. In other words—that life was subject to the Word as well. In addition, the cross presented a visual representation of a spiritual ladder at its worst. The two rails are not parallel to one another, but cross each other going in opposite directions. Christ's body was attached to the rail pointing upward, directing our attention towards GOD'S thoughts and actions. Christ hands were attached to the horizontal rail. This pointed toward mankind's thoughts and actions. Mankind is represented by the two thieves crucified to the left and right of Jesus. All Christians start with the same broken ladder. *³Can two walk together, except they be agreed?* Amos 3:3. Our task, is to allow GOD to realign our thoughts and actions to run parallel to HIS. We have to, spiritually, build a new ladder. The cross is meant to be more than an emotional experience. It is also a tool GOD uses to teach us many things. GOD is not only the great CREATOR and SAVIOR, but HE is also our great TEACHER.

We continuingly fail to apply the **REVERSE** PRINCIPAL to subjects we have been introduced to, through reading or from preachers and teachers. The Bible confirms this principal. *¹⁰I was in the Spirit on the Lord's day, and* heard **behind me** a great voice, *as of a trumpet,* Rev. 1:10. This means—to understand the present, one must look in the past. Another way to word this is—GOD'S "LAST" suggestion was to look again at the "FIRST" things he taught. All Christians get their start in the New Testament. But in order to fully understand, we have to "walk with GOD" back through the Old Testament. *¹⁶So the last shall be first, and the first last: for many be called, but few chosen.* Matt. 20:16. Yes! We know, for many are called and few are chosen, is referring to the lives of Israelites and Gentiles. But the last shall be first and the first shall be last applies, in general, to all categories. This being the beauty of GOD'S brilliant Word.

Question—how can a **thief** profit from someone else's invention? Answer—he would have to <u>acquire one,</u> and then, **reverse engineer it** so the item could be reproduced and sold as his own. We, all mankind, are the two thieves on the cross. **LUKE 23:39-43** tells us, only one thief repented. He took the cross and made it his own. One thief profited from the cross and one did not. **MATTHEW 6:20,** But lay up for yourselves treasures in heaven. HEY! To become RICH SPIRITUALLY, one must first acquire the life changing experience of the cross. Part of our spiritual treasure comes from selling others on the power of the Cross. But before you can efficiently sell the experience of the cross as your own. You will have to understand why it was made, what teachings are hid within its structure, and how it can be used to enhance life. Now the only way to fully understand the Cross, is to **reverse engineer it.** Take it apart piece by piece and put it back together: SO LET'S DO IT.

The three crosses together paralleled Jacob's ladder. In your mind, see only the upright rails that held the bodies of the two thieves. You're facing the thieves, looking straight into their **eyes**, the Two **WINDOWS** into the Soul of GOD. The rail to the left represented the Old Testament. It is the—**view**—we get through the WINDOW labeled the Father. This WINDOW first shed the light of GOD, <u>revealing mankind's sinful nature</u> and our inability <u>to fulfill the Word</u>. The position of the Candlestick to the left in the Holy place confirms this analogy. It provided the light as the Word does in our lives. The rail to the right represented the New Testament. It is the—**<u>view</u>**—we get through the WINDOW labeled the Son. It revealed a life that **<u>due to the power of GOD, fulfilled the Word</u>**. This analogy is confirmed by the table of manna positioned to the right in the Holy Place. This manna represented the life of Jesus Christ.

At this point in your imagination, you should only have two beams running parallel from the earth upward. Now in this picture, insert the cross of Christ in between the two rails that held the thieves. Question—what is in this picture? Answer—It is the first step in—your—spiritual ladder. <u>ALL</u> ladders that make the connection to GOD will have the same first step—HONESTY to ONE'S SELF. This step is confirmed by the thief who said—we deserve our punishment because we are sinful. His honesty propelled him onward to repentance and eventually on into paradise.

In your mind, please look slowly and very closely at the cross of Christ. If it will help you, draw the THREE crosses on a piece of paper. The cross rail holding the hands of Jesus represented the first step in our spiritual ladder. Those hands our pointing toward mankind's two decisions to make. The life of Jesus, positioned between the two thieves, is the separating line between a life full of dissatisfaction and a life **full** of satisfaction. Here, within this picture of the three crosses, is the question GOD wants us to answer. What is the first step in crossing this invisible line? Answer -- **honesty to one's self**. This being confirmed by the thief who went to paradise. Now do you—really—see the sadness in the story of the two thieves? This tiny little word—**honesty**—is all that separated the two. And by the way, **everybody cries** uncontrollably when they pull, and I repeat, PULL this HONESTY from their hearts and present it to GOD. Do not let embarrassment, due to your pride, be the one word that keeps you from crossing the line into the land of satisfaction.

GOD used the word (ladder) because it is a recognizable tool used by all cultures and nations to conquer an objective. Both rails of Jacob's ladder and the rails holding the two thieves parallels one another. Both sets represent the Old and New Testaments. They are our guides to live by and tools to be used in conquering. Mankind's permanent responsibility to the Word is represented by the attachment of the two thieves to those rails. The Golden Candlestick, beaten into shape out of a "single piece" of gold, confirms this. The six branches coming out of the main shaft is mankind. The Gold it is made from represented the Word.

Both the DESCENDING ANGEL on Jacobs's ladder and JESUS CHRIST on the cross, represented GOD'S personal involvement in changing our thoughts and actions.

The design of the Old Tabernacle supports this analogy of the three crosses. The open area of the courtyard, on all sides of the Holy Tent, represented mankind's existence. The <u>area within the Holy Tent</u> represented the two Testaments and the tent walls themselves represented flesh, the dividing line between the natural and the spiritual. The <u>Candlestick</u> and the <u>Manna</u> represented the Word that all mankind is JUDGED by. These two items, being positioned up against the **<u>South</u>** and the **<u>North</u>** walls, parallels the two thieves being up against those two crosses. Those crosses represented mankind's situation. We all owe the debt of death because we cannot satisfy the demands of GOD revealed to us. Our nature itself is evil, PARTLY due to the flesh. Notice! We said, PARTLY, because some would choose evil regardless. The devil has no natural influences such as the flesh to deal with, but yet, choose evil. We need help! So, GOD paid our debt, and HE will personally strengthen our spirits **<u>if we allow</u>**. The spiritual dividing line between the two walls, or the two Testaments, is <u>the</u> cross of Christ. Remember, the **<u>invisible</u>** image of his cross ran from the Altar of Burnt Offering—up through the Holy Tent—and stopped at the Ark of the Covenant in The Most Holy Place.

Again—In order for you to profit from someone else's invention, you have to get one and **<u>reverse engineer it.</u>** So it is with the Cross that carries salvation into our lives. We, by faith, purchased it from GOD as a finished product. But in order to present it to the world as our own. We need to understand its construction from the ground up.

To better understand the mechanics of truth. Let us look at another closely related example of the ladder. A Railroad Track provides a way to move much needed commodities. This track consists of two RAILS held consistently parallel to one another by supporting cross beams. Question—what if both, the railroad track and GOD'S Word was not in **"<u>perfect</u>"** alignment with themselves? Answer—both would be unreliable, and that would render them useless. Both sets of rails must run parallel to themselves, otherwise they would eventually cross and go away from each other in opposite directions. For example—lay two sticks a foot apart, equal in distance from each other at the top and bottom. Now shorten the distance at the top by six inches. What do you have? You have two sticks out of alignment that will eventually CROSS each other. This is a picture of the mechanics of a total lie or partial truth in action. They may have one point in common? But after that initial contact, they move in opposite directions. They do not run parallel in **constant** support of one another? The Cross + is a symbol of disunity, a picture of disharmony no peace and no consistency. Jacob's ladder—II—is a symbol of unity, a picture of harmony peace and consistency, because both rails travel together in the same direction. *³Can two walk together, except they be agreed?* Amos 3:3.

By now, you have probably realized the first <u>**Tabernacle**</u> is the most important subject to study and understand in the Bible. LOOK! All things concerning <u>GOD'S</u> nature and the reversal of mankind's fortune, from death to life, centered **"around"** and **"through"** that Tabernacle. EXODUS through DEUTERONOMY explained its <u>intricately</u> detailed construction—how to maintain it—how to enter it—how to leave it—It held the ten commandments—GOD spoke through it—it directed the Israelites movement—and it is a magnifying glass. It helps us to recognize truth because it connects to all things spiritually pertinent. On top of that, the Israelites spent over forty-years encamped around it. It is a tool of confirmation used to keep our minds running parallel with, and consistent with, and in agreement with, the thoughts and actions of GOD.

For example—many unbelievers claim the Bible is incomplete, therefore rendering it unreliable. They say—many books were left out by those who put it together due to selfish political motives. But the total number of 66 Bowls Knops and Flowers on the Golden Candlestick shafts, CONFIRMS the number of 66 books in the Bible. GOD'S will shall be done regardless of the attitudes of the participants. The only time GOD disrupts the natural flow of everyday life, without being asked to do so, is when he is making sure HIS Word is fulfilled.

Are you beginning to understand why we have looked at the small details of some widely accepted subjects? Why we have glanced, *at different angles,* the same subjects in other chapters? It is to get us in the habit of looking more closely at the truths we hold so dear. Because they may only be partially true and subject to failure under **"extreme"** pressure, like Abraham, who clung to partial truth as his means of deliverance. Yes! Abraham, at first, profited from this partial truth he clung to. This being represented by the gifts of wealth given him by Pharaoh the King of Egypt. But even though that partial truth looked pretty and it worked for a time, it failed in the end due to extreme pressure.

It is the **SMALL** pieces of the puzzle that brings **TRUTH** into focus. In these last days, the spiritual tree is being shaken. People clinging to partial truth may fall—backward—toward earthly things as Lot's wife did. Life dealt her one nasty situation which exposed what she loved and put her faith in, and it was not GOD.

You cannot spiritually overcome and prosper due to someone else's relationship with GOD. *²And Joash did that which was right in the sight of the L*ORD *all the days of Jehoiada the priest.* 2 Chron. 24:2. *¹⁷Now after the death of Jehoiada came the princes of Judah, and made obeisance to the king. Then the king hearkened unto them. ¹⁸ And they left the house of the L*ORD *God of their fathers, and served groves and idols: and wrath came upon Judah and Jerusalem for this their trespass.* 2 Chron. 24:17-18. The king left GOD as soon as he was separated from the influence of the man of GOD, because he lacked a strong *"personal"* relationship with the Lord.

Looking at the penny's worth of small details will help align are thoughts with GOD'S. Data having any connecting treads to a subject regardless of how small those threads may be, will always run parallel to each other if they are in TRUTH a part of that puzzle. Truth is consistent or in agreement with something else—it is similar and equivalent to something—and it is **conscientious** in its support of somebody or something.

Data from this book may have brought you to a (+cross road +) in regards to some of your beliefs. The questions are—will you allow your thinking to be slightly adjusted? Will you throw away a piece of the puzzle just because it does not fit what others have taught you? Will you apply an open-heart, and the energy necessary to thoroughly dig into the information presented?

Newton's explanation of gravity was widely accepted for over 250 years. He understood that the apple was being pulled to the ground. However, he <u>suspected</u> there was a force pushing the apple downward as well, and that, he could not explain. Newton had a part, but he did not have enough pieces to recognize the whole picture presented in the puzzle of gravity. Then "centuries later," along came Einstein who said, "I want to know GOD'S THOUGHTS in an equation—I want an equation that will encapsulate the power of the universe—I want an equation that explains the physical laws of nature that was set in motion by GOD." It took 10 years of **trial** and **error,** but in 1915 the General Theory of Relativity was born. This equation basically says -- <u>Space and Time tells Matter and Energy where to go, and Matter and Energy tells Space and Time how to look.</u> Oh by the way! Einstein had **rejected** this same equation three years earlier because he first thought it to radical, because of its <u>***simplicity.***</u>

We know you're asking, "How does this theory benefit my life?" Answer—without its application, Global Positioning System would be several miles off. Without the <u>understanding</u> provided by Einstein's theory, we would be lost if stuck in the wilderness. Understanding GOD'S Ladder Theory pinpoints truth and our spiritual position.

WHOA BABY-WHOA BABY-WHOA! You're ready to VISIBLY SEE things in the Old Tabernacle never seen before. *Spiritual Stuff* so **<u>SIMPLE,</u>** which made me feel so stupid because it took ME soooo long to see. Excuse me! I've got to take a moment to PRAISE our Lord before we look. And I am going to use a word used by snowboarders to describe *excellence* and *brilliance*—***SICK***—GOD is ***SICK***. HE makes many things so **simple** it is hard for us smart guys, who knows everything, to see. Nobody traverses down the "slippery" slopes-of-life like GOD.

This illustration shows there is two rivers making the NATURAL and two the SPIRITUAL. The outer wall surrounding the Tabernacle compound is the **Euphrates,** the beginning of all creation. Beyond that wall is eternity that GOD alone inhabited.

Within that wall, surrounding the Holy Tent, is the Tigris River, where all creation, both seen and unseen interacts with one another. It is daily life, from where all those ARROWS of DESPAIR are shot from. These are the two that form the Natural River. The two rooms of the Holy Tent are *GIHON the* WORD, *and PISON the* Spirit, which is GOD himself who enforces that WORD. These two form the Spiritual River which all mankind is subject to.

SEE TABLE ONE at end of book.

TABLE TWO shows the Three WINDOWS of opportunity used to CAPTURE all truth: PERSONALLY built into the church by GOD; providing us with *three* ANGLES of VIEW from which to get a good look at ALL things. These being the Old Testament (FATHER), the New Testament (SON), and GOD'S personal assessment of ALL information collected, the (HOLY GHOST); the spiritual BAPTISM received on the day of Pentecost in the upper room.

SEE TABLE TWO at end of book.

TABLE THREE reveals the first FIVE books in the Old Testament represented the ENTRANCE into, and the FOUR surrounding walls of the Tabernacle. Genesis is the entrance—Exodus—Leviticus—Numbers—Deuteronomy are the four surrounding walls. *Genesis* is "foundational" in understanding the Old Testament, because it is the beginning. *Genesis is also the base of the Golden Candle Stick.* Exodus thru Deuteronomy introduced GOD'S laws—our need to repent—the reward for obedience—and the promise of salvation to come. The open courtyard surrounding the Holy Tent represented the rest of the Old Testament, because those books basically confirmed what was first revealed in Genesis thru Deuteronomy in regard to daily life.

The Old Testament gave us the BIG PICTURE, and like our modem G.P.S. systems, the Holy Tent gives us a ZOOMED-IN look. The Tabernacle was Israel's Jesus. It VISUALLY exposed the mind of GOD.

SEE TABLE THREE at end of book.

When searching for answers, one must approach each on an individual basis. This will cause you to continually go thru the Old Tabernacle from start to finish and back again. While answering one question, you will gather little "TREADS" of information which will be used to solve future issues. The tabernacle provides us with **visual images** confirming anything pertinent to connecting and maintaining a relationship with GOD. Some pictures become visible only after we connect the dots. The *<u>arrow</u>*, in 2nd KINGS 13:17 Elisha and King Joash shot thru the <u>East </u>window, becomes visible after connecting the Candlestick-the Table holding the Manna-and the Alter of Burnt Offering. Plus, **ISAIAH 49:2** calls Christ, *a polished shaft hid in a quiver.* The side walls of The Holy Place is the two extra arrows shot by King Joash; (Mankind's <u>imperfect </u>interpretation), but still yet acceptable to GOD. GOD'S chosen weapon used to PENETRATE <u>mankind's heart,</u> because an arrow can travel a great distance.

SEE TABLE FOUR at end of book.

The illustration showing the ARROW answers that age-old question—what about the thief who repented and was saved, he was never baptized in water? Remember, the first room of the Holy Tent represented the New Testament and the outer courtyard the Old Testament, and both being TWO time periods. The tip of the arrow is the short transition of time connecting the two.

Question—where, in the arrow illustration, will we find the thief on the cross that repented. Answer—at the point or tip of the arrow, at the Alter of Burnt Offering. The ARROW, GOD'S **wisdom** and **power,** brought us in from the Old to the New. It TRAVELED a great distance in connecting us spiritually to GOD.

Remember this—there are only TWO AREAS within the Old Tabernacle representing a Spiritual <u>Relationship</u> with GOD, that being, inside the Tent and "within the boundary" of the Arrowhead itself. **All area** within the Tent and Arrow-Head represented the MERCY-FORGIVENESS-and POWER of GOD. <u>His power</u> took the repented thief to paradise. The AREA within the THREE SIDES that form the boundary of the Arrow Head represented the "will" of GOD. The "area" between the walls of The Holy Place and the Arrow-Head itself, represented "mercy" and forgiveness in regard to HIS **children's** weaknesses that is contrary to GOD'S will. Inside the Tent represented GOD'S power and mercy.

Jesus, upon his return after the cross, reminded his followers <u>they will have to receive this same power</u>. This HE said in **ACTS 1:4-5,** stay in Jerusalem and *wait for the promise of the Father. 5, for John truly baptized with water, but ye shall be baptized with the Holy Ghost.* This power will eventually lead us into paradise, not only after death but in our daily lives as well. **JOHN 10:10,** *I am come that <u>they might have life</u> and that they might have it more <u>abundantly</u>*. Ten (10), because of the Ten Commandments, represented government; which is "someone" with "authority" to bring order to a chaotic situation. In other words—*ONE* with AUTHORITY to CLEAN UP a MESS, <u>that being our lives</u>. And here we have a scripture numbered **10:10,** promising us a more abundant life if we receive this powerful experience the believers received on the day of Pentecost. This being the **whirlwind** experience which caused them to speck with other tongues as the *spirit gave them the utterance.*

GOD'S reason for designing the Holy Tent with four walls is; HE wanted an area to show his tolerance in regard to some of our weaknesses while in pursuit of HIS perfection. This area is between the ARROW and the WALLS of the Tent, an area representing his children. I do not think we "fully" understand, that GOD took on the responsibility for our sins—and—the responsibility, <u>if we allow</u>, to defeat those sins. GENESIS 6:6, *And it <u>repented</u> the Lord that he made man on the earth, and it <u>grieved</u> him at his heart.* GOD hates the brutality of mankind.

The bottom line is—GOD (himself) REPENTED, because HE created mankind. Thus, HE (personally) took on the RESPONSIBILITY of "OUR" SINS. HE has suffered GREATLY, from the day when Cain killed Abel on through <u>HIS</u> suffering through the body of Christ. GOD'S personal sacrifice has created a <u>place in his heart,</u> where HE **tolerates** "some" weaknesses of those that have **repented** and **grasped** HIS Hand in fellowship while in pursuit of perfection. It is the area covered by HIS BLOOD, HIS SACRIFICE. **Questions to be answered**—Are YOU greater than GOD, who took on the responsibility of HIS creation's failure? Will you admit to, and accept your responsibility in regard to your failures? Will you accept GOD'S offer of Mercy-Forgiveness-and Power which gives one LIFE more ABUNDANTLY? Or will you <u>condemn yourself</u> to an eternity of misery, by SLAPPING HIS HAND of fellowship away?

Some say—what kind of GOD would allow children to be abused? Answer—ONE—Mad—GOD. Had it not been for a couple of good things HE found in the heart of Noah, none of us would be here. Mankind would have been washed away in the flood. All those innocent children who passed thru the door of death, AS ALL MUST DO, are "permanently safe" in the hands of a loving GOD. But WOE to the ones responsible for that passage. [7] *Woe unto the world because of offences! for it must needs be that offences come; but <u>woe</u> to that man by whom the offence cometh!* Matt.

18:7. If **"Pictures"** speak louder than a thousand words, then put this one in your head—GOD bites HIS clenched fist as HE patiently waits for the "appointed" Day of Judgment.

Table Five shows the interior area of the "first" room in the Holy Tent. It shows three Windows, (Old and New Testaments plus GOD'S personal assessment) HIS CHILDREN look through to capture and reveal all things. We are represented outside the arrow-head, in between the four walls of the The Holy Place and the THREE outer edges of the arrow-head itself. It is the place of FORGIVENESS and MERCY that GOD has created within Himself, because the BLOOD of Christ fills that area. Remember! GOD came through one door and we go through the other. And where do WE and GOD meet? In The Holy Place: In the Word. *He must increase and I must decrease.* John 3:30.

SEE TABLE FIVE at end of book.

YOU hard core Oneness, those believing people are lost who are baptized in the titles Father-Son-Holy Ghost verses Jesus name, have to LET-GO of your attitude. Because, ***both*** these titles and Jesus name are found within the boundaries of the ARROW-HEAD. This area represented what was ***acceptable*** to GOD.

YOU Trinitarians, those calling Oneness heretics and crazy, have to LET-GO of your attitude. Because, on this "ONE" particular truth of applying the name of JESUS to the one being baptized in water, is MORE accurate. Why? Because Father-Son- Holy Ghost form the outer-edge of the arrow-head, but Jesus Christ, who is the shaft the arrow-head is attached to, is at the CENTER, the HEART of the arrow so to speak.

You Oneness have to let go of the, I am the only one attitude that Elijah overcame.

SEE TABLE SIX at end of book.

GOD'S WILL is within the border of the ARROW-HEAD. And HIS children, find and understand HIS will while looking thru the THREE WINDOWS of authority. These being, Old Testament (Father)—New Testament (Son)—Spiritual Baptism (Holy Ghost), which is GOD'S personal assessment of all information collected. It is GOD'S voice in the mind of HIS children, *"trying"* to—RIGHTLY—divide the Word of Truth.

GOD had another use for the FOUR walls. They confirm the LADDER as representing the SPIRITUAL MECHANICS involved in finding **Truth.** The Old and New Testaments, the two rails, is represented by the two 100-cubit long North and South outer walls of the Tabernacle. (GOD descends) and (WE climb) this spiritual latter. The connecting rungs or steps used to support ones CLIMB, is represented by the 50-cubit long West and East walls. These steps, which support our weight as we climb, is the ***understanding*** received out of both Testaments do to GOD'S personal assistance.

Without the story of Jacob's Ladder, we would have never recognized the perimeter of the Tabernacle as representing "one small section" of the ladder. Nor would we have seen and acknowledged The Holy Tent as representing the SPIRITUAL activity seen taking place on Jacob's ladder. This being the interaction between mankind and GOD; we ask HE gives; we seek HE helps us to find; we knock and HE opens. HE ANSWERS!

SEE TABLE SEVEN at end of book.

Table Eight shows the four perimeter walls and the entry curtain into The Holy Tent, represented GENESIS—MATTHEW—MARK—LUKE—JOHN. GENESIS is *"foundational"* in understanding **both** Testaments, because it chronicled the natural origin of Christ, which was repeated in MATTHEW. Again, GENESIS is the base and the four Gospels reveal Jesus Christ, the promise which was first given in the first five books of the Old Testament.

The area within the Tent represented ACTS thru REVELATIONS, which also covered a Christian's daily life.

SEE TABLE EIGHT at end of book.

GOD approaches all solutions as we do. How do I know that you ask? Well! **GENESIS 1:26** said, *let us make man in our image, after our likeness.* GOD picks the *goal,* and then develops the solution to reach that *goal.* HE started by developing a basic principal, which in the case of salvation is a THREE-PRONG ATTACK. HE saw this as being the simplest way to arrive at a solution. These three angles of approach being—Father-Son-Holy Ghost, three offices that all mankind can relate to. Most have been parents, all have been offspring, and all know they will give up the Ghost eventually.

GOD first introduced this three-prong attack in Genesis. *¹ And the **LORD** appeared unto him in the plains of Mamre: and he sat in the tent door in the heat of the day; ² And he lift up his eyes and looked, and, lo, **three** men stood by him: and when he saw them, he ran to meet them from the tent door, and bowed himself toward the ground,* Gen. 18:1-2. Note! Abraham saw and connected with **"GOD"** as he LOOKED at *three sources,* or as he looked thru three *WINDOWS* of opportunity, which is represented by the three men. Note! Abraham saw ONE Lord thru three extensions of one substance, the (flesh); or better yet, three **BRANCHES** of the ONE spiritual TREE. Father-SON-Holy Ghost was revealed through ONE fleshly body, that being Jesus Christ. This is why in **JOHN 14:9** Jesus said – *if you have seen me you have seen the father.*

GOD used a tree to represent Himself because it has many limbs extending from it, helping us to see all those extensions as ONE substance. These three men, or angels, or sources, would later be represented by the STAFF—BRANCH—ROD. These all being the extension of the tree. The Staff was introduced in **GENESIS 32:10,** the Branch in **GENESIS 49:11,** and the Rod in **EXODUS 21:20.** All three are the same in substance, wood. All three can be used to support one's steps, to meet out correction, and be used in measurement.

The three angels that told Abraham Sarah was going to have a son and revealed the future destruction of Sodom and Gomorrah, were "indistinguishable" from one another. And so it is with the Staff-Rod-Branch. All are used in *walking, discipline,* and *measurement*. Their only distinguishable by the titles applied, and so it is with Father-Son-Holy Ghost. As the titles staff-rod-branch bring forward to our attention certain characteristics of the stick, which is an extension of the tree; so does Father-Son-Holy Ghost bring forward certain characteristics of GOD. They give three angles of view in which to better understand the abilities of both the natural and spiritual Tree of origin. Remember when Elijah fled to the mountain of GOD in fear of his life. He did not make a spiritual connection to GOD until he encountered all THREE MANIFESTATIONS of GOD, which was the Wind-Earthquake-Fire. Each alone was not sufficient enough to give him the understanding necessary to make that spiritual connection. Elijah only heard the voice of GOD after he encountered all three.

The point is—salvation (is not) dependent on seeing Father-Son-Holy Ghost as **three separate individuals** revealing GOD, as the definition of Trinity promotes. Salvation (is not) dependent on accepting the Oneness version of Father-Son-Holy Ghost, which is **three offices of "authority"** that reveal GOD. Salvation (IS) dependent on *"accepting"* our LOST status situation—*"understanding"* the steps necessary in approaching and connecting spiritually with GOD—and *"believing"* in those STEPS.

Many Trinitarians and Oneness have a great relationship with GOD. However, this one point (separates) GOD'S children. And remember, separation (is not) GOD'S will, it cannot be found within HIS Arrow. The very reason Trinity cannot be found in the Bible, is it promotes the word (separation) by presenting Father-Son-Holy Ghost as three _**distinct**_ persons. And this word <u>distinct</u> means -- _<u>distinguishable</u>_ characteristics that <u>separate</u> the Father—Son—Holy Ghost from each other. However, the teaching of the (three men) or angels that came to Abraham, along with the three sticks (Staff-Rod-Branch), go in a different direction. There are NO (distinct or distinguishable) separating characteristics within both groups. The only distinguishable characteristic is the name or title applied.

Example—take THREE identical pencils, all having graphite, wood, and an eraser. Lay them side by side with some space in between running parallel with one another. Then put labels with the words Branch on one, Staff on the other, and Rod on the last one. Hey! I can switch the labels because all are indistinguishable from one another. Even I, who switched labels, cannot tell the difference between the three. All have an eraser, graphite, and wood. All can be used to accomplish the same goal.

The angels that came to Abraham had one voice with NO characteristics that distinguished them one from the other. Father—Son—Holy Ghost can be applied to anyone of the three. Why, because there are NO distinct characteristics between the three.

Some would argue—(Ha-Ha! the Son had flesh, so there is your difference). But remember, GOD said in **JOHN 1: 1&14**—*In the beginning was the Word, and the Word was with God, and the Word was God. 14: And the Word was made flesh.* So we can apply these titles of Father-WORD-Holy Ghost to the angels and still be within the arrow-head of GOD'S will. Father and Son are titles, identifying two recognizable offices of authority we can look thru to better understand GOD. Oneness and Trinitarians should bind themselves together as one group, because both interpretations are somewhat promoted within many scriptures. These being represented within the boundaries of the Arrow-Head, which includes things <u>ACCEPTABLE</u> to GOD and not necessarily the

PERFECT will of **GOD**.

There are TWO advantages gained in seeing the Father-Son-Holy Ghost in a more singular manner. First—it allows you to receive out of some scriptures things others might have missed, like the physical pain GOD suffered we discussed in this book. Second—if you bind the three pencils together they become stronger and can support more weight. They become harder to brake. Presenting Father-Son-Holy Ghost together under the ONE heading of Jesus Christ makes a much STRONGER presentation to the world, because you have *simplified* a truth.

Consider this complicated machine that comes in many pieces we use to transport ourselves from one point to another? We call it an automobile, car, or vehicle. This machine is useless, and we do not call it a car until all those little parts are put together and covered with an outer layer of skin? Only then can it be seen as one single unit. When showing our new car to a friend, we do not say, "Look at my new brake-pad, transmission, or oil pan." No! We say, "Look at my new **Car**."

Many feel "they have to" present each individual request to the Father, and the Son, and the Holy Ghost before they feel comfortable that their prayers have been heard. This stems from a "deep" rooted acceptance of Father-Son-Holy Ghost as being three distinct or distinguishable individuals who represent God. This is the result of the "definition" of Trinity promoted throughout the centuries. Many, not all, pray in this manner to cover their bases because of the uncertainty or confusion that lays within the depths of their hearts. When a person or church **feels the "need"** to present their requests with—in the name of the Father-Son -Holy Ghost, they are acknowledging each has their **own "*individual* power.** If l only used Jesus to address our creator, not using Father or Holy Ghost, would that be acceptable? YES, it would! Because **I know** that NAME covers all of GOD'S attributes; such as, Father-Creator-Savior-Teacher--Holy Ghost-my strength-my hope-my joy-my peace-my Friend. That NAME of JESUS says it all. Using that name "shortens the distance" I have to travel in each prayer when connecting with GOD. _Understanding_ who Jesus Christ is benefits us, because it simply SHORTENS that spiritual distance of travel we should be making each day. It makes no difference in regard to salvation, whether you adhere to Trinity or Oneness: Because both interpretations can be found within the boundary of the Arrow-Head, which is what represented the "acceptable" WILL of GOD. It is a relationship and not a salvation issue. So please, knock down this dividing wall of pride.

I challenged **GOD'S** explanation, in regard to the three sticks HE used as an inspiration to create this Triangular three _window_ approach. I asked, "Should not the perimeter of the Tabernacle form a triangle instead of a rectangle, because YOU used only three sticks as YOUR starting inspiration?"

GOD'S response was—I did stay within the boundary of the three stick principal; however, _one,_ I broke in-half. I needed four walls to enclose the Arrow-Head, because they would carry additional "information" which would help in revealing MY _spiritual arrow._ Plus, it will provide an area identifying the position of the lost, and the area "I" CREATED within "MY" heart where the redeemed is found. This being the area in the room called The Holy Place, in between the outer edges of the spiritual _Arrow-Head_ and the walls of the Holy Tent. Then GOD said—look again at **JOHN 10:10** - _The thief cometh not, but to steal, and to kill, and to destroy: I **am** come that they might have life. And that they might have it more abundantly._

I can picture GOD, just after the fall of man, laying "three sticks" on the ground and thinking—three angles of view would be the **simplest** way to expose _my mind._ Yes, three _spiritual_ windows to look thru that could "surround" and "attack" all issues. These three could also be used to form the outline of an Arrow-Head, a weapon already identifiable by mankind. But because of the amount of information needed to VISUALLY introduce this arrow, I will need a structure with four walls. Then I could use the four walls to represent those four original rivers in order to expose this *spiritual arrow*. But I will have to change the Hiddekel to the Tigris River, because Tigris in Hebrew means Arrow.

Knowing GOD is consistent, and that he chose to base all things off those three sticks, is why I asked, "How did you get four walls out of three sticks?" After GOD'S explanation, I understood that two sticks represented the two 100 cubit North and South perimeter walls. And the 100 cubit long area in between, which included the Holy Tent, was the third stick. I recognized the two 50 cubit East and West perimeter walls equaled 100 cubits, if you turned them to run parallel with the other two.

GOD confirmed the breaking of this stick in the design of the Holy Tent. *The Most Holy Place* was ONE-HALF the size of the first room called the *The Holy Place,* where GOD connected spiritually to mankind. However, one point of our conversation left me a little disoriented. GOD repeatedly said—LOOK—at **JOHN 10:10,** which is what confused me. So I finely listened to my little bird's advice and *asked,* **"Why?"**

Every solution, or truth, has a starting point. I did not realize GOD was confirming a truth to me on a molecular scale. This was one molecule of information pointing me someplace; but where? To the Old Tabernacle as I finely discovered. GOD was confirming, by example, the spiritual mechanics I recently discovered in regards to finding and accepting truth. All information regarding salvation, no matter how insignificant it might seem, will be confirmed not only in the New Testament but in the design of the Old Tabernacle as well. All of our personal opinions we consider to be GOD'S acceptable will, should run parallel, being consistently supported in both Testaments.

Sometimes GOD will attach one individual scripture to a truth in a *unique* way to help you receive the importance of said scripture. Example—(7) represented completeness;

in short, it *"shall"* be done, finished, completed. Now behold how GOD put the emphasis on one scripture that holds this promise. **MATTHEW** (7:7)—*Ask, and it shall be given you; seek, and ye shall find; knock, and it shall be opened unto you.* GOD doubled up on SEVENS to better help us in accepting this promise; which is, the *completion* of your prayer request or your spiritual search.

JOHN 10:10 is no different. There was some teeny-weenie bit of information that GOD wanted to show me. I am taking about info the size of a molecule. It was just for my enjoyment only, because most are argumentative and would justify a different opinion. Tiny little fun stuff GOD gives to those who like to go spelunking, spiritually. Something that would thrill my soul. For you see, and as my wife would testify to, I love to jump up and down in celebration of HIS *"brilliance"* as the mind of GOD unfolds. And GOD is **SICK** with it. HE knew I would recognize the direct link between JOHN 10:10-the King James Bible-and GOD'S personal *room* in the Tabernacle, called *The Most Holy* Place. And here is a question I hope all of you ask. Why did GOD think you were ready to see JOHN 10:10 in this manner? ANSWER—because I now UNDERSTOOD the mechanics of the SPIRITUAL latter; all info will run parallel, being supported by the design of the Old Tabernacle and both Testaments. GOD is SICK-SICK-SICK with **BRILLIANCE.**

TEN (10), as we said before, is a number representing government because that number is connected to the 10 Commandments. This number represented ONE that has the AUTHORITY and the POWER to bring order. We are going to quickly disassemble **JOHN 10:10** and put it back together. Look at the last *(half)* of that scripture, where it said—**I am** *come that they might have life, and they might have it more abundantly.*

Moses first introduced Israel to GOD as the great I am. The one with the authority and power to save and bring order into their lives. This promise being extended to all mankind. Now for the fun part. **JOHN 10:10** is GOD'S *unique* way of confirming to the world that HE, not only was the authority behind the creation of the Old Testament Tabernacle; but was also responsible for creating the KING JAMES Bible. Look at **JOHN 10:10** along with this truth—The <u>dimensions</u> of the room called <u>The Most Holy Place,</u> that represented the great <u>I am,</u> were <u>**10**</u> by <u>**10**</u> by <u>**10**</u> by <u>**10**</u>. GOD, the great I **am** alone has the "authority" and "power" to fulfill **JOHN 10:10,** *I <u>am</u> come that they might have life, and have it more abundantly.* **MATTHEW** 7:7 and **JOHN 10:10** are two of many scriptures confirming the King James Bible as the inspired Word, due to their unique relationship to the Old Tabernacle through their numbering and wording. If you need a little more confirmation, then look at the 47 men who "brought" it to the public. It took them from <u>1604</u> to 1611 to "complete" the King James Bible. Excuse me! It took 7 YEARS to **COMPLETE.** Is that a—coincidence—or what? Is it another coincidence that 54 were originally ask, but only 47 participated? Since 7 was "separated" from the 54; is this GOD'S way of suggesting, in order to see something, we separate 7 from 40? Then 40 can be seen as **10+10+10+10.** And 7, as the stamp of a COMPLETED work.

One more little molecule to consider is; JOHN 10:10 is cut in half. **First half**—*The thief cometh not but to steal, and to kill, and to destroy.* **Second half**—*I <u>am</u> come that they might have life, and that they might have it more abundantly.*

This is the stick that was cut in half. The "first half "is the Old Testament. It revealed the devil as our adversary and our terrible situation. The "second half (the New Testament), <u>fully</u> revealed how GOD (the great I am) will save us. Can you see JOHN 10:10 casting two shadows, 10 is one-half and 10 is the other half? One is the South wall and one is the North wall of the room called The Most Holy Place. The two dot colon in between 10:10 is the West and East walls.

GOD uniquely attached JOHN 10:10 to the Old Tabernacle through the "numbers" and its "wording" to help confirm the King James Bible as HIS chosen vehicle;

bringing salvation to the world.

I know this is deep and down to bedrock stuff. But come on now! GOD is meticulous, and in his hands HIS word becomes so versatile; always maintaining a flow in the same direction. There are no coincidences when it comes to HIS thoughts. Some say—the original documents the 47 men used to create the Bible cannot be trusted. But again, the Golden Candle Stick in the Old Tabernacle confirms there are 66 books, and the King James Bible has 66 books. GOD *shall* have HIS way regardless of the people involved. Some would say—these are mighty small threads. But remember, GOD uses many small threads to complete a garment. It is the gathering of little pieces that reveals the picture in a huge puzzle.

Some say—the King James cannot be trusted because words were added by those 47. But remember, GOD gives HIS children the right to participate in HIS creative process if their input does not change the polarity of HIS Word. Like in the creation of What and Why, "my" two imaginary birds. GOD allowed "me" to pick the color of their eyes. GOD, thru Christ, constantly asked HIS disciples to give their input.

Hey! What do you see in ROMANS **10:20**? *I revealed **my-self** to those who did not seek me.* Is this another coincidence that the Holy Tent consisted of two rooms, one being **10** cubits long and the other **20** cubits long? Is it another coincidence that GOD, who is the great *I am, revealed* Himself to all mankind in ROMANS **10:20** and thru those two **10** and **20** cubit rooms in the Tabernacle. Look at how this scripture is worded along with its numbering of **10:20.**

Hey! I can fill a book with these coincidences in regard to the King James Bible.

Miracles

Throughout my life, GOD has allowed me to participate in a few of "his" spectacular moments. These left me in AWE of "his" love and power. I personally did not want to write this chapter. Not that these events your about to hear are not true, but simply because of <u>two</u> reasons. **First**—I feel undeserving to be associated with such greatness. **Second**—GOD wanted my FAILURE as well as my victories revealed. This you will find in the next chapter, "The Prodigal Son's Return."

YES! I am a prodigal-son, which in my opinion is the greatest miracle of all. I am an ordinary guy who has experienced many ups and downs throughout my life. But the Lord reminded me that it is not the ups and downs that matters, but what does, is how you finish. Some of these miracles took place "before" and "after" a twenty-year period, from 1980 to 2000, in which I turned my back to GOD and ran.

You see, I love to talk about the victories GOD has accomplished in my life. However, attached to the inspiration to record these miracles, was also the inspiration to write about MY failure and rejection of GOD. Here, the Lord used on me the same principal many politicians use to slip their bill through Congress. They attach it to a major bill that most likely will pass through our legislative system. After prayer and meditation, I realized why GOD wanted my failure recorded. His purpose was to lead us into the greatest prodigal son story in the Bible. A story that is somewhat obscure and overlooked. Both my return and his return is recorded in the next Chapter.

I absolutely love to talk about—my victories—or better yet, <u>HIS</u> miracles preformed in my life. So if you are a BELIEVER, please give this book to someone who has failed GOD, and tell them to read the thirteenth and fourteenth chapter. GOD wants **<u>all</u>** his children to <u>forget about their failures,</u> and "again" be ready to experience the supernatural events that will take place as we tag-along with him. This includes those who feel insignificant and the individuals that, (because of their failure), consider themselves unworthy. All people "connected" to GOD, at any time, **will** experience an event or events that will leave us speechless and in awe. The world will call it a coincidence. But we that experienced them know better. We are giving you a few of those miraculous moments. We hope you will be inspired to forget about your frailties, short comings, and failures. We want you to look only at the limitless power and knowledge of GOD **you will** experience, regardless of those ups and downs. Because the greatest of GOD'S achievements, through my life, came on the second time around.

It is October 1972, I am a twenty-two year old just discharged from the Air Force. I am sitting in church, surrounded by 300 people I have only know for a few months, and wondering—"Where do I go from here?" Then this unfamiliar man comes to the pulpit and says, "Your pastor suddenly became sick and asked me to preach Sunday's service." He came 90 miles to deliver today's message. He started his message with—where do I go from here, and followed it up with—GO, for GOD will get you there. When the twenty or so young people I was sitting with heard this, all eyes shifted to me. Because the night before, I told them—I did not know where to go from here, except maybe to Oklahoma where my aunt lived. She was the only one I knew of in my family that had a connection to GOD. So I bought a sleeping bag, small tent, rain gear, a water canteen, several cans of beans, corn, spam, and I hit the road toward Oklahoma with a twenty dollar-bill in my pocket.

During my trek across the States an unbelievable occurrence happened in Barstow California. Back in **1972**, it was the last town before you crossed the desert. It was raining hard, and there were about ten of us hitch-hikers huddled under the bridge of Inter-State 40 at about midnight. Suddenly the rain let up a little. Since I had rain gear on, I decided to weather the storm. So I went and stood under the light at the bottom of the Inter-State off-ramp. You cannot hitch-hike on an Inter-State. You can only thumb a ride on the on or off ramps. Two other guys came and stood under that street light with me. Suddenly the rain intensified to such a degree, that you could not see your hand in front of your face. It came down so hard it actually hurt. All three of us decided, at the same time, to go back under the bridge. However, before I took my first step, these words **"loudly"** went through my mind. Wait under the light, I have a ride coming for you. So I stood and waited while the others disappeared under the bridge. The torrential rain, that kept all other hitch-hikers under the bridge, pounded me for another ten to fifteen minutes. Then this man stopped, rolled down his window and asked, "Where are you headed?" I answered back, "Wherever you're headed is fine." Because the chill in my bones from that October rain was so intense, I did not care where he was going, I just wanted to be warm and dry.

This guy was a well-to-do chef headed to his brother's funeral in Indiana. He was driving because he hated to fly. He paid for all my meals. He even gave me a hundred dollars for helping him drive just before we parted company in Tulsa. During our journey, I asked him why he pulled off the Inter-State where he picked me up, because there was no gas station there that I saw. He said to me, "I got so sleepy as I approached the off ramp, that is when I saw you standing under that light, and decided **I just had to** have someone help me drive." I then asked him, "How could you even see me, because you were driving 70 miles per hour in heavy rain at midnight, plus, the light pole is at least three hundred feet from that exit?" He said, "That brilliant light surrounding you, allowed me to see you clearly, even before I got off the ramp." Then he said, "You know, I was so tired and it happened so fast, I did not have time to think about it—but now, looking back, that was an unusually bright light."

WARNING—do not hitch-hike, because it is extremely dangerous. Two situations I encountered during my trip could have easily taken my life. Yes, how GOD delivered me to my destination was a miracle. But understand this, it was not GOD'S means of travel that I chose. It was the second option I chose, meaning, MY way. The first option, (GOD'S WAY), was **ask for help** from GOD'S people. The church would have bought me a one-way ticket to fly, but I chose my own way due to my stubborn pride.

Because of that choice, it took me a little over three days to get to Oklahoma. Like Jonah, I spent <u>three days</u> in the belly of the whale. Had I taken option number one, GOD'S choice, I would have made the entire journey in three <u>hours</u> vs. three <u>days.</u> You're probably asking yourself, "What does he mean by—I spent three days in the belly of the whale?" Answer—it was the worst **three days** of travel I have ever experienced. Like Jonah in the whale, I was surrounded by water, because it **rained** every step of the way. And I could never rest due to the dangerous situations that, at any moment, could <u>**swallow-up**</u> a hitch-hiker.

One Saturday morning I said to my wife, "I **just have to** go fishing." She said to me, "It is 105 degrees out. What fish would be dumb enough to swim around in this heat?" You know, I had to agree with her. No fish in his right mind would bite in this heat. But like the man who stopped and picked me up and delivered me to my destination—<u>**I just had to.**</u> I got to the dam, threw out my line and sat in that heat for about 30 minutes. Finally, I said to myself, "This is ridiculous, I am the only one here, and I am going home." A car pulled up and a man got out as I was putting my gear in the truck. I had just started my truck when these words entered my mind—go over and introduce yourself to that man. Well, I fought off this urge by saying to myself, "He will think I am a wacko." That twenty minute drive back to my house was one unpleasant experience. I was in tears because I knew I had missed the call of the Lord. GOD told Philip in Acts, *[29] Then the Spirit said unto Philip, Go near, and join thyself to this chariot.* Acts 8:29. This man from Ethiopia was about to read some scripture. GOD wanted Philip there ready to explain what the man read. By the time I got home, I realized that GOD had some purpose concerning this man. My wife, seeing that I was upset, said, "Go back, for if GOD is involved, he will keep him there." I found the man sitting on a big rock looking at the river below. As Philip did, I too ran up to the man and said, "GOD told me to talk to you." The man began to weep and said, "I came out here intending to commit suicide." Thankfully, I was able to direct him to a reliable minister near his home.

It was just before the start of Sunday morning's service. And the pastor was greeting people in the foyer. I walked up and gave him this message. "In tonight's service, be prepared, a group from another church is coming to check us out." Well, I got the look of doubt and surprise I anticipated. I was only **delivering** information I had received from GOD during a wonderful time of prayer that took place between 5 a.m. and 7 a.m. that Sunday morning. That Sunday night, sure enough, a large group of ladies from another church came to check us out.

One morning, a peculiar prayer begin to fire through my soul. This is what was said—Lord, speak to the one at the convenience store from across the street, and let him find himself coming to church though he does not understand why or how he got here. For at least three months this prayer would continually gush forth. Then one Sunday morning, just after service started, a man entered into the foyer of the church. I noticed him nervously standing there while he was looking around. I went into the foyer and said, "Hello, can I help you?" After a moment of silence, he said, "I know this sounds strange, but I do not know how I got here—one minute I was pumping gas across the street and next minute I am walking through the door." After talking to him, I found out that his marriage was on the rocks. He was so upset and discouraged with life. He had no peace, and it was all he could think about. His state of mind was probably the reason he did not remember crossing the street and coming to church.

Look, while in prayer, many of **GOD'S** plans involving the lives of other will reveal themselves through our verbal request; even though we do not understand at that time the reason behind the prayer itself. Sometimes we receive warning of future events, such as Jesus telling John that Judas was the one who would betray him. All these come from your connection to the spiritual river, because that river is GOD who knows all and sees all.

It is August of 1976 and we are sitting in the living room of our very first home. It was a little 950 sq.-ft. three bedroom mansion, or so we thought. I am in the recliner reading, which was positioned next to the four-foot open area leading into our tiny kitchen. The wife was on the couch across the room from me. Suddenly, we heard the words—pop-pop—coming from the kitchen. As I looked up from my book, I saw my fourteen month old girl struggling to carry one of those old heavy two quart <u>all glass</u> pop bottles. I knew it was hot and under a lot of pressure, because we just came from the store. So I slowly eased out of the recliner, not wanting to startle her and cause her to drop the bottle. However, as I got to my feet, she dropped it anyway. I was three feet from her when a good size piece of glass hit my knee so hard, it spun me to the floor. Several pieces embedded into the sheetrock throughout the living room. Now here is the miracle. After I got back up on my feet, my wife and I washed the sticky pop off our little girl's body. We checked every inch of her. Guess what we found, even though that bottle EXPLODED at her feet? Notta—nothing—zip—not even a scratch. I, on the other hand, was given a memento to remember this special occasion. A nice little scar left by the glass that embedded into my knee. A reminder to me, of how GOD can take care of my family.

There I was, lying on the living-room floor, <u>thinking</u>, "I need to commit more time to the study of the Word and take on more responsibility in the local church. At that particular moment however, I could hardly move without hollering in pain. The shots given by the doctor to relieve my back pain did not work. I had not been to church in two weeks because I could hardly standup. So I prayed, "Lord, if I am to commit to the study of the Word and take on more responsibility in the church, then I will need you to touch my back." Prior to having this flare-up, my only involvement for two years was through daily prayer at the church. My pastor constantly encouraged me to move from the back of church to the front, and take on more responsibility. For instance, he wanted me to lead opening prayer and possibly take on some other leadership role, such as the hospital ministry. However, I would come up with some excuse of why I could not. I just did not want any responsibility concerning people's lives. I was happy just spending my two, to some times four hours in prayer each morning in fellowship with GOD, during which, I witnessed many of those requests come to pass, and learned many wonderful things about GOD. However, there I was, lying on the living room floor thinking—I need to give more time to the study of the Word, and take on more responsibility. My back begun to improve immediately after I prayed that next Sunday evening. During this time my wife was at church, from which I now had been absent for three weeks. So I picked up the Bible and dove in.

Here is the MIRACLE in this story. Early that next Monday morning at about 3 A.M.—I awoke with a detailed message pouring into my mind. Then, during prayer, I got the strangest of requests from the Lord. HE said—**go tell** your pastor that you have been given a message to give at Wednesday night's service. Here is my wife's lengthy response after I told her. "GOD said your to do—WHAT—did you hit your head on something and knock yourself silly?—think about this, you have not been to church in THREE WEEKS—and you have never been asked to teach as of yet." However, I knew the command came from GOD. I thought to myself, "The worst that could happen is, I look stupid and windup at the back of the church, forever; which is where I prefer to be anyway; out of sight and out of mind with no responsibilities." So I called and made an appointment to meet the pastor at noon. Again I said to myself, "I will lay the ball in his court." I did not even sit down when we meet, because I was in and out real quick. All I said was, "Pastor, GOD gave me a message to give this coming Wednesday night." I then thanked him for meeting with me and left. As I hastily left his office, his response was, "Ooookay." I felt good. **I did what GOD said to do.** And so I forgot about it until about 4 A.M. Wednesday morning. That is when GOD again woke me, and renewed the same message in my mind I had first received early Monday morning. After I again studied the message, I went back to bed. Before I fell to sleep, the phone rang. At that time, we did not have caller identification on our phone. GOD, at that very moment when the phone rang, told me it was my preacher. So, I went into the other room to answer the call. I picked up the phone, and before he spoke and identified himself, I said, "Pastor, do not worry about the message tonight, because GOD renewed it in my mind this morning." I could tell he was in a little bit of a shock, because it took him almost a minute before he spoke. He said, "Go ahead and teach tonight, because my wife and I are sick with a stomach virus. We cannot even stand up." I almost forgot to tell you. His wife was also a licensed minister and the co-pastor of the church. The pastor told me later that for both of them to be unable to preach at the same time had never happened before.

I took over the hospital ministry shortly after filling in for my pastor in that Wednesday night service. Yep! I finely agreed to take on some responsibilities. But I did not know this new road of commitment would lead to an almost unbelievable experience in GOD'S healing power. It still leaves me in awe and speechless every time I think about it. This woman in our church asked me to visit their friend's twelve year old daughter, who had now been in the hospital for about three weeks. This extremely sick girl and her family did not attend our church. A bacterial infection caused her lungs to collapse, putting her into a coma. She had been on life support for several weeks. As I drove to the hospital, GOD <u>clearly</u> spoke these words into my mind—I will heal the girl but not immediately, for there is a problem amidst their family that must be settled. I knew nothing about this family. So when we meet, I introduced myself and asked to see their little girl. But due to the seriousness of her condition, only the parents were allowed in her room. So I sat with the mother and the two grandmothers. The mother had been living and sleeping in the hospital. The situation was bad, and all three women was in tears as we talked. That is when I gently took the mother's hand and said, "Do not worry, GOD promised to heal your daughter shortly." Then I said, "But first, there is a problem amidst your family HE is trying to settle." I asked the three women, "Is there a problem that we together can pray about?" Suddenly, the grandmother on the father's side got up and left the room. I asked the mother, "Did I say something wrong?" The mother hesitated, and said, "No, it was not anything you said." She revealed that her and her husband were separating and were in a nasty custody battle over the girl. The father of the girl was a real piece work. He really did not want his daughter. He just did not want to pay child support. This girl was in the hospital fighting to stay alive for weeks. During her entire stay in that hospital. The father showed up a couple of times. He did not even show-up on the day they cut her off of life support. Here, as I discovered, was the problem GOD was working toward changing. The father's mother was backing her son's attempt to win full custody of the girl. Eventually, she accepted the fact that her son did not care about anybody but himself. So she switched her support to her daughter-in-law.

Now back to my first attempt to visit the little girl. Since I was not allowed to see the girl, and after we discussed the situation, I prayed with them. Then gave them my phone number and went home. Three days later the mother called. While fighting back the tears, the mother said, "She is not responding to any treatment—the doctors said we need to seek an alternative form of healing." The mother said to me, "Please come and pray for her for the doctors will let you see her now." This was my second time to see the family. As the mother and the two grandmothers stood by the daughter's bed, I prayed this simple prayer. "Lord, thank you for your involvement in this family's situation, and thank you for the healing **you will** bring into this child's body." So we all hugged one another, and then I left. About four days later, the girl's mother again called me on the phone. She was panic stricken and said, "Please come and be with us, for they are going to take her off life support and she is still in a coma with collapsed lungs, and they do not expect them to work." This was my third trip to the hospital. Before we four, the mother, the two grandmothers and myself went into the girl's room, I said, "Expect a miracle." because GOD again renewed that promise to me on the way to the hospital. I will be honest, it was the scariest situation I ever faced, and that includes my year in Vietnam. I do not know why they had to take her off life support. It could have been due to no insurance, or the fact that she was not responding to any treatment. But there we were, watching as the doctor cut the life support. Just after the doctor cut the equipment off, I noticed the grim expression on his face started to change. A smile begin to appear, and was soon followed with these words—WOULD YOU LOOK AT THAT. The mother frantically asked, "What do you mean doctor?" He responded back to the mother, "One of her lungs is beginning to work." All hearts immediately went to joyful anticipation. After we all happily embraced, I went back home.

Now this story had one more twist. Because of the massive amount scar-tissue caused by the bacteria, she was scheduled for a lung transplant. Her mother called me one last time and said, "They have canceled the surgery, both lungs are working and the scar tissue is gone and she is going to be fine."

I will be honest, had I not been prepared by GOD through prior experiences, I would have never had the courage or the confidence to deliver to this family GOD'S promise. Earlier experiences taught me how to Identify GOD'S VOICE, and the victory that comes from obeying. Like David of old, we must first tackle and defeat the bear and the lion before were able to defeat a problem presented by a situation the size of a—Goliath. Oh by the way! I do not go around delivering words of absolute healing to all that are sick. By the time I met the girl's family, I was very familiar with GOD'S voice. One must be careful. And one must know beyond the shadow of doubt, it is GOD'S Word you are delivering.

Yes—You're right! I did not need to be there for the girl to be healed. It was because of GOD'S love for his children that HE allows any of us to participate and to witness first-hand, HIS miracles.

The Prodigal Son's Return

GOD wanted my failure and return recorded so HE could introduce the greatest **turn around** in the Bible. It is, in my opinion, the greatest prodigal son story of all time. Yet, this story rarely receives the notice it deserves, due to its dispersal throughout 2nd KINGS. Several chapters, which covers several years, lays between this servant's rejection and his renewal to glory. Plus, we have to allow GOD to take us in between the lines. Because HE uses the New Testament to confirm parts of this servant's story. We will keep my personal failure and return brief as possible.

It is September 1980, and I am lying in my hospital bed, thinking, "What am I going to do? It has been almost two weeks since my surgery, and I have no clue?" I had just been informed that the company I worked for closed down. Plus, the church organization I was involved with has ignored my situation and forgotten about me and my family. My parents "temporally" turned their backs on me, because earlier, I chose not to move my family from Oklahoma to Chicago Illinois in order to live near them. Sitting next to my hospital bed was our five year old and my wife holding our newborn. She, due to complications, just got out of the hospital with our second girl. After pondering on my situation, I said to myself, "That is it, I give up." Then I prayed my **last** <u>sincere</u> prayer to GOD. "Lord, forgive me; I do not blame you or anybody else; I blame myself; I just do not **<u>understand</u>** why I have been so unhappy with religion these past several years; please Lord COME AND GET ME AGAIN." Well, twenty years later, in 2000, HE did.

Here is how I arrived at this juncture in life. I am lying in my bunk at DA Nang Vietnam in 1970. I just awoke in a cold sweat, due to a dream everybody warns you about. Yep! It was the old tunnel of light dream. Only at the end of this tunnel was a hand beckoning me to come through it. To this day, I vividly remember that dream.

Two years later, on a day in July 1972 near Castle Air Force base California, I realized it was GOD'S hand all along prepping my heart to meet HIM. On that July evening, I needed "a lot" of drinks. I was headed to an old bar just off base that I had not been to in a couple of weeks. However, instead of walking into a bar, I had walked into a *spiritual* **Bee-Hive.** A local church had purchased the bar and turned it into an outreach center. Two guys come up to me like sharks to a wounded seal and asked, "Do you want to pray and meet Jesus?" I turned, and with a pace just short of a run, got out of that place. The sting of those BEES, gave me—**the bad feeling.** Like Elvis Presley's song said—Hey-Hey-I'm All Shook Up. I got about two hundred feet when these words stopped me in my tracks—you're miserable, what do you have to lose, why not go back and give Jesus a try? The problem was, my foolish pride would not allow it. I wanted to, but I could not. I needed help just to turn my body around in order to go back. So I decided to walk down the irrigation canal that was just in front of me in order to get away from the road. It was dark and no one would be able to see me kneeling. I then prayed, "GOD, if you are real, I need your help because I cannot get myself to go back to that place." Now only those who have experienced GOD'S intervention can appreciate what happened to me next. Suddenly a power came, either into me or around me, I really could not say which. What I can say for sure is, I found myself headed back to that place faster than I left it. A few months after connecting with GOD, I was on the road headed to Oklahoma. However, a little over seven years later, in 1980, I find myself in a hospital bed. With a wife; two babies; no money; no home; no job; no church organization or parents to give support to my situation; and no faith or hope left in my heart. One week out of the hospital, and while we were living with the wife's parents, I received a six thousand dollar settlement due to my back injury. My wife's parents were rich in love but poor economically. They wanted to give us part of their two and a half acre plot. However, we made them take 2500 dollars, and we used the rest as a down payment on a house-trailer. In 1986, we built a house where the trailer used to set. We still live in the same place to this day, which happened to be just nine miles from the church we were originally married in.

For years we would not attend any church. But in the year 2000 that would change. That is when my wife started back to a recently-built church six-miles down the road from us. Two weird points concerning this new church. **First point was**—since the first day it was built, I hated to drive by it. Yep, they stuck that building next to the road I used to get to my place of employment. Sometimes I would be so convicted that I got teary-eyed as I drove by. Other churches gave me no trouble. But this newly-built church tugged at my heart every time I drove by.

Only after my wife started going did we discover the reason, which is the **Second point.** This was the same church my wife grow up in. And it was the church that we were married in 26 years earlier. The elders got a great deal on ten acres. So they sold their old building and moved three miles and built at the new location. Many of our old friends still went there. My wife and I did not know who went there, because we no longer associated with the church world.

Here is a fact GOD revealed later on as our fellowship again blossomed. HE used this church because we still had friends in attendance there, hoping they might make our return easier. GOD is so thoughtful when it comes to our lives. My wife was the first to start back. I on the other hand still would not go. My attitude begin to change the day we closed the refinancing on our home. The woman doing the closing **"just happened"** to go to that church. Hey! GOD IS SLICKER THAN ICE and I AM NOT LYING. From the start of the closing to the finish, all she could talk about was the wonderful things happening in their church. I have to admit, it stirred my soul.

Finally, on Saturday night after the closing and after the family was in bed, I prayed, "GOD, **show me where** I <u>**belong."**</u> After prayer, I made to myself a commitment to go to that church Sunday morning. That morning, a young minister came to the pulpit and said, "Our pastor, at the last minute, came down sick and so he asked me to preach. Then he presented the title of his message—**You <u>Belong</u> Here.** Again, I will repeat—GOD IS SLICKER THAN ICE and I AM NOT LYING. The Lord had duplicated my situation I first faced in California in 1972, when I asked GOD, "**Where do I go from here?**" Both ministers in 1972 and 2000 were, due to sickness, replaced at the last minute by other preachers. This THREAD of SIMILARITY along with, it was the same church we were married in, convinced me that GOD stilled loved us. It took a lot of planning, time, and effort on GOD'S part to pull this off. This second time around has been great. I am full of faith. I know the voice of GOD. Depression and doubt does not abide in my heart and mind. I continually swim in that beautiful river of GOD, of which, constantly reveals the deep and wonderful things hidden in the Word. Due to my dependency on GOD'S ability, I am no longer subject to the spiritual failures of friends, ministers, or churches. I can <u>glean</u> that which is true and reject what is false, regardless of the ministry or church organization I am visiting with. Question—Why did I fail the first time? The Answer is seen in my departing prayer from my hospital bed in 1980. "Lord, forgive me; I do not blame you or anybody else; I blame myself. I just do not **<u>UNDERSTAND</u>** why I have been so unhappy with religion these past several years."

This book is dedicated to <u>FIVE</u> goals. <u>ONE</u>—to convince you of the *"absolute"* importance of *"seeing"* yourself as having GOD'S power within. TWO—to show the *procedure GOD laid out* in order to establish this kind of Faith. <u>THREE</u>—to clearly expose that **<u>invisible line</u>** SEPARATING Mustard-Seed-Faith from Growing-Faith. Which also is the same line that SEPARATES spiritual satisfaction—from dissatisfaction. FOUR—to reveal spiritual tools and how they are used in order to cross that line. FIVE—to break down denominational walls, so the church will have a better opportunity to be perfectly aligned to the thoughts and actions of GOD; through making individuals into strong towers of knowledge and understanding; so the church can BETTER sell the world on the greatness of this salvation.

The greatest "prodigal son" story is recorded in 2nd KINGS chapters four five and eight. Elisha, who represented GOD, had an assistant named Gehazi who allowed himself to be separated from his master due to greed. This separation took place when the great general Naaman of Aram came to Israel, hoping Elisha would heal his leprosy. Naaman was so thankful after being healed, that he tried to give Elisha and Gehazi great wealth. However, Elisha would not allow the general to give them anything. Shortly after the general left to return to his own country, Gehazi snuck out and caught up with Naaman. He, under false pretense, took some of the wealth the general offered and tried to hide it when he returned home. But GOD revealed this treachery long before the return of Gehazi. So Elisha said, *²⁷ The leprosy therefore of Naaman shall cleave unto thee, and unto thy seed for ever. And he went out from his presence a leper as white as snow.* 2 Kings 5:27.

Later on in Chapter-Six, it tells how Syria laid siege to Israel, causing a terrible famine. When the King heard reports of cannibalism, he went to kill Elisha. The King blamed GOD for his situation, and so, went after the Lord's prophet. *³³ behold, the messenger came down unto him: and he said, Behold, this evil is of the LORD; what should I wait for the LORD any longer?* 2 Kings 6:33b.

When they met in 2nd KINGS, *¹Then Elisha said, Hear ye the word of the LORD; Thus saith the LORD, To morrow about this time shall a measure of fine flour be sold for a shekel, and two measures of barley for a shekel, in the gate of Samaria.* 2 Kings 7:1. Then the King's right hand man mocked the prophet. He basically said—ain't no way; maybe if the Lord opened the windows of Heaven, HA-HA. Then Elisha responded to this guy's mockery. *² Behold, thou shalt see it with thine eyes, but shalt not eat thereof.* 2 Kings 7:2b. This came to pass a little later. *²⁰ And so it fell out unto him: for the people trode upon him in the gate, and he died.* 2 Kings 7:20. This happened at the end of the famine, when food was first brought though the gate of the city. He was crushed under the mob of people rushing to get it. His demise would open up the highest paying job opportunity in the kingdom of Israel, which eventually was filled by a guy that <u>was,</u> at one time, the poorest, sickliest, and down trodden individual in all of Israel. YEP! You guessed it, a man who had been totally healed of his leprosy by the name of Gehazi. Question—how did he get healed of leprosy? Question—how did he end up in the King's palace as his advisor in such a rich and powerful position?

2nd KINGS chapter seven, tells how four <u>leprous</u> men were outside the starving city talking to one another, saying—*why sit we here until we die?* They said—let us go to the enemy's camp, and maybe we can get some scraps, and if they kill us, so be it, we're dead anyway. When they got there, the camp was empty. GOD made the Syrians hear the noise of chariots, horses, and a great host coming against them. The enemy thought the King of Israel had hired the Hittites and Egyptians to help defeat them. So they fled, leaving all their food clothes silver and gold behind.

As the four lepers ate, drink, and grabbed <u>up the silver and</u> gold. One of them said—guys, we are not doing well. We need to go tell the others. So they came and stood outside the city gate, and out of the <u>night's darkness,</u> called unto the porter of the city. They told how they found the camp empty, and everything they needed was there for the taking. When their story was confirmed, and food was brought into the city, all the people rushed to the gate. That is when the King's advisor was trampled and killed.

Apparently, out of gratitude, the King made Gehazi his new personal advisor. Because in **2nd KINGS 8:4,** we see the <u>King asking Gehazi to tell him of the great things Elisha the prophet did</u>. This question was asked while the King, from his castle throne, settled local disputes. This is how we know Gehazi got the job vacated by the guy who had earlier mocked the prophet. This is also how we know Gehazi's leprosy was healed.

Which had to have taken place somewhere between the **night** the lepers delivered the lifesaving news to the city, to his being by the King's side in the castle. One with the fearful disease of Leprosy would never be found in the castle next to the King in such a powerful advisory position, no matter how grateful the King was.

Many will ask—how can you assume Gehazi was healed of his leprosy? Answer—two reasons—ONE, is him being the King's new advisor—Secondly, is a precedent confirmed in the New Testament, involving ten lepers being healed as <u>they</u>—*went.* *¹⁴And when he saw them, he said unto them, Go shew yourselves unto the priests. And it came to pass, that, as <u>they</u>* **<u>went</u>**, *they <u>were cleansed</u>.* Luke 17:14. After these ten asked for pity, Jesus said—*go shew yourselves unto the priests.* While in the **process** of fulfilling the Lord's command, they were <u>*healed*</u> somewhere in between. Gehazi was <u>*healed*</u> as he **went.** This took place while he was in the **"process"** of fulfilling GOD'S second most important commandment. *⁸If ye fulfil the royal law according to the scripture, Thou shalt love thy neighbour as thyself,* **ye do well***:* James 2:8. Look what conversation pop-up as the four lepers looted the camp *⁹ Then they said one to another,* **<u>We do not well</u>**: *this day is a day of good tidings, and we hold our peace: <u>if we tarry till the morning light, some</u>* **<u>mischief</u>** <u>*will come upon us: now therefore come, that we may go and tell the king's household.*</u> 2 Kings 7:9. We underlined the last part of this verse. Because this response, due to their situation, hints of a person who experienced a similar situation in the past. A PERSON WHO—*PREVIOUSLY*—TRIED TO HIDE THE **<u>WEALTH</u>** FOR HIS OWN PERSONAL GAIN and GOT IN TROUBLE. It most likely was Gehazi influencing this unselfish attitude and the conversation concerning their next step they should take. This being, the sharing of their good fortune with those in the starving city. Again, Gehazi being rewarded with the position of being the king's advisor confirms this. Also, someone saying—**we do not well,** as they gathered the treasure up for themselves, reminds us of how Gehazi came down with leprosy to begin with. That being, his selfish greed.

Due to his change of heart and because of his close relationship with Elisha, who represented GOD, he is an-example of a prodigal son at the highest level of Christianity. Gehazi's story is GOD'S attempt to help encourage fallen ministers and teachers of the Word, to again come back to him. Because those who fail and fall away, that held prominent positions in the church, generally carry greater condemnation. It is hard for them to forgive <u>themselves,</u> and to again capture that elusive critter called—Faith. Without which, you cannot connect with GOD.

Gehazi's story can be applied to anyone at every level in Christianity, from the beginner on up to the top. This again is why GOD included his story in the Bible. Because Gehazi best represented a preacher's life, one who is at the top of the spiritual hierarchy. A minister delivers GOD'S lifesaving commandments to people. Gehazi delivered, from Elisha, the commandment to general Naaman to wash in the dirty Jordan River, which eventually saved the General's life. And later, after he **understood** his error, we find him again delivering <u>information</u> concerning <u>his</u> master's great accomplishments while being the KING'S <u>personal servant.</u> *⁴And the king talked with <u>Gehazi</u> the <u>servant of the man of God</u>, saying, <u>Tell me,</u> I pray thee, all the <u>great things</u> <u>that Elisha hath done</u>.* 2 Kings 8:4. GEHAZI the PREACHER was back, and in a BIG-BIG WAY.

Repentance and **Obedience** to GOD'S Word, that teaches to put others first, led to the healing of Gehazi's leprosy. Elisha, like GOD, was invisible to Naaman. So the message of healing was given to Gehazi to deliver to the General. This again is why we can put Gehazi in the position as representing a preacher. *⁹So Naaman came with his horses and with his chariot, and <u>stood at the door</u> of the house of Elisha. ¹⁰And <u>Elisha</u> <u>sent a messenger</u> unto him, saying, Go and wash in Jordan seven times, and thy flesh shall come again to thee, and thou shalt be clean.* 2 Kings 5:9-10.

These are those threads of similarities identifying Gehazi as a <u>PREACHER</u>. Who, due to his selfish love for power and wealth, failed and was separated from GOD. Through he may not have realized it at the time of his failure, GREED was his FIRST LOVE, and his "<u>second</u>" love was people. You cannot find lasting peace and contentment when you put your own personal satisfaction ahead of others. Gehazi finally, while gathering up all that wealth in the enemy's camp, **<u>understood</u>** why he got separated from his Master. That being—he lost **faith** in Elisha, and through his own power and craftiness tried to change his personal life. After General Naaman was healed, he returned to bless Elisha and Gehazi with great wealth. However, the prophet said no. *[16] But he said, As the LORD liveth, before whom I stand, I will receive none. And he urged him to take it; but he refused.* 2 Kings 5:16. This refusal caused Gehazi to lose **"<u>faith</u>"** in Elisha's ability to change his life style and status. He <u>lost</u> the **<u>handle</u>** of the <u>spiritual sword</u>. He lost his faith in his master's ABILITY.

Gehazi's leprosy began to heal as he **"went"** from the enemy's camp to the starving people. Because he finally <u>understood</u> what was reaffirmed in the Book of 3rd John. *[2] Beloved, I wish above all things that* **thou mayest prosper** *and* **be in health**, *even as* **thy soul prospereth**. 3rd John 1:2. <u>Gehazi did not get what he wanted when he thought he should of got it. And so, he gave up and tried to get it through his own ability</u>. Bottom line, GOD new he was not ready to handle such wealth and power. Gehazi finally learned—serving others is a greater wealth than gathering riches for yourself. Life begun to improve the moment he understood and accepted this change of attitude into his heart. It took more time and ugly situations than Gehazi cared to experience. But in the end, look what happened. He became the *"King's"* **<u>close</u>** and personal servant, with **MORE** <u>influence</u> and <u>wealth</u> than he could have ever gotten through his own conniving ways. **3rd JOHN 1:2** basically said—First, *let your soul prosper,* then, your <u>everyday life</u> will <u>prosper</u> as well. GOD wants to be the one that inspires change and brings prosperity, because HE knows in what increments it should come. Otherwise, it could do more harm than good.

While working at a pipe-yard, I constantly tried everything possible to worm my way into the position of fork-lift operator. This was a massive machine with heat and air. After a year of trying every trick I could think of, I gave up. From that day on, I <u>went about doing the best I could at whatever task committed to my trust</u>. I did not think about getting that position for over a year. Then one day, out of the blue, the boss stepped out of his office and **tracked me down** in the pipe-yard. He said to me—old Gus failed his eye exam. Can YOU drive that fork-lift? Many that had seniority wanted the job, but it fell to me. I got the job because of GOD'S effort, not mine. <u>All I did was go about my daily business as best I could</u> and "<u>not worry</u>" about what I wanted or what I did not have. Jesus said, *²⁵ Therefore I say unto you, Take no thought for your life, what ye shall eat, or what ye shall drink; nor yet for your body, what ye shall put on. Is not the life more than meat, and the body than raiment? ²⁶ Behold the fowls of the air: for they sow not, neither do they reap, nor gather into barns; yet your heavenly Father feedeth them. Are ye not much better than they? ²⁷ Which of you by taking thought can add one cubit unto his stature? ²⁸ And why take ye thought for raiment? Consider the lilies of the field, how they grow; they toil not, neither do they spin: ²⁹ And yet I say unto you, That even Solomon in all his glory was not arrayed like one of these. ³⁰ Wherefore, if God so clothe the grass of the field, which to day is, and to morrow is cast into the oven, shall he not much more clothe you, O ye of little faith? ³¹ Therefore take no thought, saying, What shall we eat? or, What shall we drink? or, Wherewithal shall we be clothed? ³² (For after all these things do the Gentiles seek:) for your heavenly Father knoweth that ye have need of all these things.* ³³ <u>*But seek ye first the kingdom of God, and his righteousness; and all these things shall be added unto you.*</u> ³⁴ <u>*Take therefore no thought*</u> *for the morrow: for the morrow shall take thought for the things of itself. Sufficient unto the day* *is the evil thereof.* Matt. 6:25-34.

Question—What is the greatest treasure of all? The Answer comes from King Solomon, who was the wisest man of all t i m e .

⁹ Give therefore thy servant an <u>understanding heart</u> to judge. 1 Kings 3:9a—YES! We did not finish this scripture because we want you to finish it with—Lord, give me an UNDERSTANDING HEART **to judge** ("<u>not</u>" **myself** <u>unworthy of another chance</u>). Apostle Paul said, *³But with me it is a very small thing that I should be judged of you, or of man's judgment: yea, <u>I judge not mine own self</u>.* 1 Cor. 4:3. He left that in hands of GOD. So the question is—how does GOD judge those prodigal sons who have run away? Answer—with OPEN ARMS.

LUKE 15:11-32, tells us a man had two sons, one being faithful and the other unfaithful. This son took all the riches given him by his father and spent it satisfying his own lusts. Then when he was "totally broke" and all his so-called friends left him, he ended up slopping hogs for someone else. After he <u>came</u> to his <u>senses</u> he said to himself, *¹⁷How many hired servants of my father's have bread enough and to spare, and I perish with hunger! ¹⁸I will arise and go to my father, and will say unto him, Father, <u>I have sinned</u> against heaven, and before thee,* Luke 15:17-18. LOOK at the father's response after he saw his son still yet a great distance away. *²⁰And he arose, and came to his father. But when he was yet a great way off, his father saw him, and had compassion, and **ran**, and <u>fell on his neck, and kissed him</u>.* Luke 15:20.

You that have lost your faith and have fallen away—FORGET ABOUT IT—Because that was yesterday and today is a new day. **You do not have the right to judge yourself unworthy of a new and greater relationship with GOD than you have ever had before.**

Now You're Ready to Solve the Confusion

¹Brethren, my heart's desire and prayer to God for Israel is, that they might be saved. ² For I bear them record that <u>they have a zeal of God</u>, but <u>not according to knowledge.</u> ³ For they being ignorant of God's righteousness, and <u>going about to establish their own righteousness,</u> have not submitted themselves unto the righteousness of God. Rom. 10:1-3. Faith allows GOD'S righteousness to be produced in us through trust in HIS ability. Paul was saying—my fellow Israelites do not get it, they just "do not" UNDERSTAND.

Question—What happens when our bodies give out in this life, if the all-powerful all-knowing and <u>eternal</u> spirit of GOD is "actively" at work in us? This includes all situations after death, when we, like the angels Michael and Gabriel deliver the will of GOD to other creative wonders? For instance, the angel Gabriel attempted to deliver **GOD'S** answer to Daniel's prayer request for understanding in regard to a vision concerning the future. After that initial contact, the angel said, *¹² Then said he unto me, Fear not, Daniel: <u>for from the first day that thou didst set thine heart to understand,</u> and to chasten thyself before thy **God, thy words were heard**, and I am come <u>for thy words</u>. ¹³ But the prince of the kingdom of Persia withstood me one and twenty days: but, lo, Michael, one of the chief princes, came to help me; and I remained there with the kings of Persia. ¹⁴ Now I am <u>come to make thee understand</u> what shall befall thy people in the latter days: for yet the vision is for <u>many</u> days.* Dan. 10:12-14. GOD'S strength remains with us forever. Constantly brushing aside anything contrary to HIS nature as in the case of Gabriel, who needed help to fulfill GOD'S will, keeping us *forever more* in line running <u>parallel</u> with HIS Word. *¹¹ But if the <u>Spirit of him</u> that raised up Jesus from the dead <u>dwell in you</u>, he that raised up Christ from the dead shall also <u>quicken</u> your mortal bodies by <u>his Spirit</u>*

that dwelleth in you. Rom. 8:11. GOD'S quickening power continues to work in us throughout eternity.

Look! We are not going to set on our hind-ends in heaven. We, with our new indestructible and eternal body, will be GOD'S extended arm to all future created wonders produced by HIM. We might even be the first of our kind, or maybe the second? Scientists tell us our Earth is fairly young, and that the universe is expanding at ever increasing rate of speed.

Question—Why is it **absolutely necessary** to LET this binding of your spirit with GOD'S take place before you die? ANSWER—We have only been given this short TIME of life to FREELY choose or to REJECT this spiritual union. It has been proven that no creation can resist evil without GOD'S personal assistance. Both the devil and mankind were without sin to begin with. Both were given the ability to choose their own way. However, both eventually succumbed to evil, because neither had a "spiritual connection" to GOD. Whether it took one year or a billion years, neither had the strength to resist evil as time rolled by. The flood in Noah's day reminds us of mankind's degenerative nature. Our eternal spirit being temporarily bonded to the natural, the flesh, was our chance to prove we could be righteous. However, we also failed. Note! The devil had no fleshly weaknesses to deal with, and yet in the end, he too turned totally evil. GOD will not allow any such creation to permanently inhabit eternity. HE will, at some point in time, isolate those who have rejected HIS plan. They will be "forever" alone, kept in total darkness without the ability to move about, which is similar to being kept in a coffin.

*13 Then said the king to the servants, Bind him **hand** and foot, and take him away, and cast him into outer darkness, there shall be **weeping** and **gnashing** of teeth.* Matt. 22:13. One will never be able to sleep or move, always nagged by thoughts and desires you cannot satisfy. *44 Where their worm dieth not, and the fire is not quenched.* Mark 9:44.

The WORM is "your" individual desires and memories you gathered in this life. And the FIRE is the pain of not being able to satisfy those desires, along with this nagging thought—I could have had it all, but I refused it.

*²³ And in hell <u>he lift up his eyes</u>, being in **torments** (plural) and seeth Abraham afar off, and Lazarus in his bosom. ²⁴ And he cried and said, Father Abraham, have mercy on me, and send Lazarus, <u>that he may dip the tip of his finger in **water**, and cool my tongue;</u> for **I am tormented** in this flame. ²⁵ But Abraham said, Son, remember that thou in thy lifetime receivedst thy good things, and likewise Lazarus evil things: but now he is comforted, and thou art tormented. ²⁶ And beside all this, between us and you there is a **great gulf fixed**: so that they which would pass from hence to you <u>cannot; neither can they pass to us</u>, that would come from thence.* Luke 16:23-26. It is like being stuck in a coffin with 10,000 mosquitoes. However, that buzzing they make will always be heard, and you will not be able keep them from biting. Nor will you be able to scratch those itches caused by those bites in order to relieve the pain they produce. This will go on FOREVER—FOREVER—FOREVER.

The reason for this separation, is so they will be unable to interfere with any future created wonders. The individual puts himself in that horrible place, not GOD. HE has extended out HIS HAND to all mankind. Giving us a plan to **FOREVER** obtain FORGIVENESS—MERCY—and HIS ETERNAL STRENGTH. All we have to do is to GRASP HOLD of it. Those that used their power of FREE WILL and CHOOSE to accept and follow GOD'S plan, are going to be an active part of all GOD'S creative efforts from then on. Able to freely move throughout eternity. Questions—are you going to be the one who **SLAPS** HIS HAND away, or the one who **EMBRACES** HIS **HAND** in fellowship?

² Do ye not know that the <u>saints shall judge the world</u>? and if the world shall be judged by you, are ye unworthy to judge the smallest matters? ³ <u>Know ye not that we shall judge *angels? how much more things that pertain to this life?* 1 Cor. 6:2-3. In the Bible, there are only three angels given identifying names. Two angels were given a single identifying name each, Gabriel and Michael. Both names point to the redeemed as being an extension of GOD'S helping hand to all present and future creations. Michael's name means—who is like GOD. Gabriel's means—man of GOD, and GOD is my WARRIOR. We, the born again, will be the ACTIVE extension of GOD'S hand to any and all creations to come. The third angel, (the devil), was given several descriptive names which points towards his declining character. <u>Lucifer</u> the Morning Star as recorded in ISAIAH 14:12 means the shining one, because in the beginning he was pure and beautiful. <u>Satan</u> as recorded in many scriptures means the accuser. Abaddon/Apollyon, only found recorded together in REVELATION the 9 chapter and the eleventh verse, means Destroyer. So Lucifer went from being pure, to the accuser, and finally to the destroyer. GOD will never allow evil to go unchecked. The devil could not stop, from within, the growth of selfishness, greed, hate, revenge, and lust. These being first formed in his heart, and eventually passed on to all GOD'S creation.

There are only two ways to conquer disease. One is to <u>remove the source.</u> And two, is to <u>build a resistance from within</u> through inoculation of antibodies. The nature of this disease fighting antibody becomes a part of the body. The natural instincts and actions of the antibody defeats the enemy when confronted. If GOD'S spirit dwells in you? His nature will rise-up and "eventually" defeat anything contrary to that nature throughout all eternity to come. Now in this life, some things may take a little more time to defeat than others. But in the end, those weaknesses will surrender to GOD'S effort if we through faith allow him to do so. Consider the <u>entire</u> Bible the syringe because it carries within, from GENESIS to REVELATION, the power of GOD. HE is the lifesaving, life changing, and evil destroying

ANTIBODY. The pain delivered by the needle through which this *spiritual antibody* flows, is the natural situations that arise in everyday life, along with the Word. These two is what **"pricks"** our heart. This **_needle_** of life's situations plus GOD'S Word opens up a little hole in us as to allow the lifesaving antibody, *GOD'S Spirit,* to FLOW into our hearts and become a part of our lives. Spiritually, it becomes the force that NATURALLY fights against any evil that comes against a child of GOD.

No one can be saved after death. If you die without GOD in this life, you will forever be lost. *³…and if the tree fall toward the* **south**, *or toward the* **north**, *in the place where the tree falleth,* there it shall be. Ecc. 11:3b. Mankind, throughout the Bible, is constantly compared to a tree. In other words, if you die without GOD you forever remain without GOD. Remember, the thief's cross to the **South,** the left wall in The Holy Place, represented those who died without GOD and were lost. And the thief to the **North,** who went with GOD, represented those that will be saved. Now look again at **ECCLESIASTES 11:3.** Remember the spiritual mechanics in regard to finding truth. Information must be accepted and applied if it runs parallel===in agreement with, in support of, and equal to.

No one can stand in and accept salvation for you after you die, and there is no conversion possible after death. Remember ²⁶ *And beside all this,* **between us and you there is a great gulf fixed**. Luke 16:26a. Praying to dead saints for their help is spiritually a waste of your time. Praying for GOD to forgive and change the dead is a waste of your time. QUESTION—when is the time one must be saved? *² (For he saith, I have heard thee in a time* accepted, *and in the* day *of salvation have I succoured thee: behold,* **now** *is the* accepted time; *behold,* **now** *is the* day *of salvation.)* 1 Cor. 6:2.

Purgatory is supposedly a place after death which much of the world has been **DUPED** to believe in. It is supposed to be a place where one can, after death—atone for wrongdoing—make amends—show remorse—or suffer punishment for wrongdoing and then go into heaven. Purgatory is not found in the Bible. The origin of Purgatory is found in one of the four history books of the Maccabees. These books were written several hundred years before Christ, and centered on Jewish history. Two of these books were declared to be God's inspired word by "ONE" of the early church leaders. Later, due to **his** influence, it was accepted into **their** faith by the rest that group. Then it became one of the seven additional books the Roman Catholic Church added to their Bible.

Question—if I am Catholic, WHY should I "challenge" some, if not all my beliefs? ANSWER—only 66 books are confirmed by the Golden Candlestick as being GOD'S chosen Word, and not the 73 that make-up the Catholic bible. Remember, Gold the Candlestick was made from represented GOD'S Word. That Candlestick was Beaten into shape out of a SINGLE piece of *GOLD*. Incorporated into that SINGLE piece of GOLD was the total sum of **66** *bowls, knops,* and *flowers*. These, GOD used to confirm the number of books HE choose. If the origin of some your beliefs are from those unauthorized books not accepted by GOD? Then where does that put you in regard to what you have put your trust in? It may have outward beauty like Abraham's wife. But behind that outward beauty hides an ugly lie. Remember the mechanics of truth. If threads of similarities do not run parallel in support of one another, they must be rejected. If they run parallel in support of one another, they must be accepted and applied as being part of the equation. Again, the purpose of the Old Testament Tabernacle is to confirm or deny PERTINENT spiritual information. Question—what about all those Dead Sea Scrolls? Answer—GOD did not have them destroyed, HE simply allowed them to be hide at the **"DEAD"** Sea—GET THE "DRIFT."

I once presented this information to a well read, highly educated individual who believed those added seven books, in "his" bible, were God's inspired word. Every time I asked him about the Golden Candlestick, he would respond with—BUT, followed by a long highly intelligent answer which <u>ran away from</u> the question. His response was filled with so many big words that I actually got lost along the way? So I would again ask him about the Candlestick. Again he responded with—BUT, followed by another confusing answer that went away in the <u>opposite direction</u> from the "simple" question. Contradictions began to show their ugly heads within his own answers. Finally, he got <u>mad</u> and told me to leave him alone and walked off. Moses could not enter the promise land with the rest of Israel because he rejected <u>A</u> truth that GOD had given him, which was, speak to the rock and not hit the rock as he did. Moses choose his own truth through his own logic. Likewise, this gentlemen could not HANDLE the <u>question</u> generated by the Candlestick. He could not enter that specific area of the promised land of GOD'S Word, because it did not fit what he was told to believe. As did Moses, he choose to follow his own logic. He rejected a piece of the puzzle, which in turn brought frustration and confusion into his life. This being revealed when he got mad and "blew" his stack. Every time I asked about the Candlestick. His response was—BUT-BUT-BUT-BUT-BUT. To me, it started to sound like—putt-putt-putt-putt-putt, reminding me of a little train STRUGGLING to run on rails that ran un-parallel to one another. Which in the end, caused it to run-off crash and explode. All "threads" of information, in regard to a specific subject, will run parallel==in constant support of one another if they truly are a part of that subject. This being the mechanics of finding TRUTH represented by the Spiritual Ladder. Information in regard to a subject that +crosses+ and runs away from each other, will always produce frustration confusion and in the end, loss of temper and bitter arguments. These are the mechanics represented on the +cross+, mankind's thoughts—vs.—GOD'S thoughts.

Now back to the origin of this overwhelming desire Paul experienced in ROMANS. [1]*I say the truth <u>in Christ</u>, I lie not, my conscience also bearing me witness in the Holy*

Ghost, ²That I have great heaviness and continual sorrow in my heart. ³For I could wish that myself were **<u>accursed from Christ</u>** *for my <u>brethren</u>, my kinsmen according to the flesh:* Rom. 9:1-3. These scriptures are basically saying—I would cut *off my* **right arm,** if this <u>ONE ACT</u> on my part would save my kinsmen. Notice the scripture said, *I say the truth in Christ.* <u>Paul was under the</u> influence of that spiritual river we have talked so much about. Where these fruits abide, <u>faith,</u> joy, peace, longsuffering, gentleness, goodness, meekness, temperance, <u>understanding,</u> and the greatest of all—***Love*** . Yes! Paul was expressing a willingness to give-up his relationship with GOD, if that <u>single act</u> would save the Israelites, his kinsmen.

WOW! Here is a deep thought, which could have only come after we understood the relationship between GOD and the body of Christ. Paul was actually reflecting GOD'S loving attitude toward the Israelites and all mankind. It was GOD'S way of saying through Paul—I AM willing to cut-off MY RIGHT ARM, if that one act would make them righteous. This is "why" Paul said—*I say the truth in Christ, I lie not, my conscience also bearing me witness in the Holy Ghost.* The apostle Paul wanted us to know where those inspired words of "self-sacrifice" came from. GOD would sever his own right arm—Christ—from his existence. GOD was willing to disregard all his planning, time spent, and the pain HE endured through Christ, if that One Act would cause you and me to have a righteous nature. GOD is saying—I AM willing to step backwards to a place that I hated. That being, the COLD relationship HE endured with Adam and Eve.

But the truth is, there is no single or multitude of acts on ours or anyone else's part that can save us. We, as individuals, are saved by that ***<u>tether</u>*** of Faith. Believing is how WE **attach** ourselves to GOD'S promise of forgiveness and his ability to gradually change and keep us from evil. The Israelites claimed to be righteous because they were the natural born descendants of Abraham, and were first to be given the Word of GOD.

They thought the doing of the Word made them righteous. But in reality, that same Word convicted and condemned them and us to death, because we could not fulfill every little detail the LAW of GOD required. Claiming to be righteous because you do "some" good deeds, which happens to run parallel to GOD'S Law, is living by the Law. But if your claim to righteousness is the doing of good deeds proclaimed by that Law? Then ONE failure which testifies that you have "some" unrighteousness at work within, makes you subject to the penalty of that same law—which is spiritual death. People who say—GOD will not let me go to hell as long as I do good deeds, do not realize that they are putting themselves under the Law. They are basically saying to GOD—My many good deeds **PROCLAIMS** me righteous. Let us put it another way. My MANY good deeds confirms that my nature is perfect like GOD'S, who is without flaw. This is fine if you **never fail** to do what is right, and **all** that you do is in *"perfect'* harmony with GOD'S Law. Then after death, you can stand before GOD at the throne of judgment and "demand" entry into heaven. But what about the ONE TIME you just lose it and take your frustrations out on someone else? Or jealousy and hate grabs hold, causing you to say or do something bad to someone else. Remember, the Bible clearly teaches that the penalty for *sin* is death. That means, one mistake or one failure to fulfill any of GOD'S Law, proclaims that there is also unrighteousness at work **within** you. And the Bible clearly states—the unrighteous WILL NOT inherit the Kingdom of Heaven, but will be cast into outer darkness.(Will be) means—eventually.

Question—Why will GOD not allow any creation to inhabit eternity on their own authority and power with one lingering sin? The Answer is in GALATIANS. *⁹A little leaven leaveneth the whole lump.* Gal. 5:9. In other words—there is "nothing" to stop that one sin from growing. This again is confirmed by the only two creations of GOD we are familiar with. The devil, who is a fallen angel, and mankind. We got to have GOD'S eternal strength in us.

Here is an example how those will respond at the judgment seat of GOD that believe good works will get them into Heaven. John tells how the scribes and Pharisees brought to Jesus a woman who committed adultery. *⁵Now Moses in the law commanded us, that such should be stoned: but what sayest thou? ⁶This they said, tempting him, that they might have to accuse him. But Jesus stooped down, and with his finger wrote on the ground, as though he heard them not. ⁷So when they <u>continued asking him</u>, he lifted up himself, and said unto them, <u>He that is without sin among you, let him first cast a stone at her.</u>* John 8:5-7. Their reaction to this statement was, *⁹And they which heard it, being **convicted** by their own **conscience**, went out one by one, beginning at the eldest, even unto the last: and <u>Jesus was left alone</u>, and the woman standing in the midst.* John 8:9. The guilty conscience that caused them to separate themselves from Jesus will also keep us out of heaven. *²¹ The like figure whereunto even <u>baptism doth also now save us</u> (not the putting away of the filth of the flesh, but the <u>answer of a **good conscience** toward God</u>,) by the resurrection of Jesus Christ:* 1 Pet. 3:21. Unless one accepts and applies GOD'S PLAN in regard to connecting with HIM, you <u>will be</u> lost. You <u>will be</u> putting yourself in Hell simply because **you rejected** GOD'S plan. Or in other words—you SLAPPED HIS extended hand of fellowship away.

These next few paragraphs are real important to remember, because it summarizes the steps and why they are necessary in order to make that spiritual connection to GOD. Plus it tells how GOD verifies, in your heart, that connection.

*⁵Jesus answered, Verily, verily, I say unto thee, Except a man be **<u>born</u>** of <u>water</u> and of the <u>Spirit</u>, <u>he cannot **enter**</u> into the kingdom of God.* John 3:5. Remember! This spiritual water is GOD'S Word. John is saying—<u>in order to even connect with</u> GOD, you first have to believe the Word and then apply the step by step procedure laid out by the Word. This being repentance and water baptism. These two steps are GOD'S chosen way to clear one's conscience, in order to establish *faith* STRONG ENOUGH *to* make this *SPIRITUAL* connection. We also need to realize the proper way these two steps should be applied. This being through "honesty" and the "understanding" of the what and why we are doing these two steps. Because together, they alone have the power to *"open"* the door, allowing GOD who is the SPIRITUAL BAPTISM to become a part of our lives *forever.* GOD'S entry into our lives is being born of the spirit. Which is confirmed by that—WOW what a RUSH. It is that unbelievable feeling those experienced on the day of Pentecost. You know, the experience that left them drunk with **delight.** This RUSH **"solidifies"** our faith in GOD being a part of our life. This experience is so much more than the good feeling we get in just complying to GOD'S Word.

Complete faith in GOD'S ability is difficult to establish in our personal lives. Faith needs to be strong enough to carry us through those most terrifying moments life throws us into. This is why all new believers should be encouraged not to stop, until they experience this Spiritual Rush. This is the *satisfying* experience which "totally" convinces an individual that - OH YES—I GOT IT.

Justifying themselves because of many good deeds was the attitude most Israelites clung to. Paul was sad, because those kinsmen will be lost. And them being given the very Word that could lead one *into* eternal life, which is a spiritual union between GOD and us. They did not **understand** the concept of righteousness being attained through faith. This simply being, the acceptance of GOD'S NATURE into our lives through "HIS" wisdom and power. Notice! HIS wisdom came first, this being HIS instructive Word. And HIS power came second, this being those righteous characteristics operating in the life of Christ. Most Israelites did not understand that doing good deeds cannot STOP the growth of sin. Only GOD'S NATURE, who alone is without sin, can. So GOD gave us **HIS plan of mercy.** This being, his **continual** forgiveness and HIS **continual** strength to overcome sin. But WE have to take it. This freedom of choice separates us from being mindless robots. This freedom allows us to become children of GOD by Choice, which is exactly what GOD has desired all along. A creative wonder that loves righteousness as HE does. **GOD declares** those RIGHTEOUS who take HIS HAND. GOD accepts the responsibility of our sins, and, their defeat.

This spiritual union does not eradicate all sin and mistakes overnight. Salvation is a ***progressive*** change gradually brought about by the "ACTIVE" influence of GOD. The reason spiritual change from mistakes to perfection is not 100% immediate, is because of our attachment to this nasty old body. To all you Dudes and Dudettes! We will feel the "STING" daily because we are in a "BEE" fight—ouch—*to bee,* or *not to bee.* This is where GOD applies HIS daily *MERCY, FORGIVENESS.* and *STRENGTH* to those that has GRASPED salvation through FAITH. GOD'S plan allows us to be individuals and not mindless robots. His plan gives those who love and want to be righteous the power to do so. We have the power to truly be his offspring, choosing good over evil. HIS mercy and forgiveness follows us into eternity, because all HE will see is the blood of Christ "we" applied to our lives. That blood is our justification, it allows GOD to proclaim us righteous. This HE confirms by becoming an active part of our lives. And this abiding presence, HE confirms through that wonderful FIRE and RUSH we will experience as he enters our heart.

HEY! To those that think this tremendous and unbelievable experience is not for everyone who makes this spiritual connection? I ask, "Do you really believe that the CREATOR of *ALL* THINGS, does not leave DEEP "emotional footprints" as HE takes up residency in our hearts?" HELLO—think about it.

YES! It takes effort on our part to get to that point where GOD becomes an "active" part of our lives. Not because GOD wants to make it difficult, but because of our hardness of heart, no understanding, and lack of intense desire. Like Job, this last reason is why GOD will allow us to linger in some unpleasant situations.

Let us use our imagination again. You are standing on earth reaching upward toward GOD, who is reaching downward with his outstretched Hand. Mankind can only reach 6-feet high because WE are tethered to the ground. GOD'S Hand can only reach to within 7-feet of the earth, because HE is tethered to righteousness. That leaves **1-foot** of distance **"WE"** have to go in order to connect due to the rules of righteousness "GOD has established," which will not allow HIM to. So we cry out—How do we reach you GOD? HE hollers back through preachers, teachers, and angels unawares—*It will be "emotionally painful" at first, and you most likely will cry—but it is the only way—Sever yourself from the ground through repentance— use "water baptism" to HELP pull yourself upward—use your thumb of faith and fingers of study, prayer, meditation, and trust to grip my hand, MY Word.*

This attitude of my good deeds gets me into heaven is the same as you telling GOD—I am calling the shots now—you grab "my" hand—I will do the pulling up if needed. This was the devil's attitude that got him kicked out of heaven. *[12] How art thou fallen from heaven, O Lucifer, son of the morning! how art thou cut down to the ground, which didst weaken the nations! [13] For thou hast said in thine heart, I will ascend into heaven, I will exalt my throne above the stars of God: I will sit also upon the mount of the congregation, in the sides of the north: [14] I will ascend above the heights of the clouds; I will be like the most High.* Isa. 14:12-14.

[11] (For the children being not yet born, neither having done any good or evil, that the purpose of God according to election might stand, not of works, but of him that calleth;) [13] As it is written, Jacob have I loved, but Esau have I hated. Rom. 9:11, 13. GOD is simply revealing HIS attitude in regard to the two groups. The ones who want it and the ones who do not. These two natural brothers (Esau & Jacob), parallel the two spiritual brothers (Mustard-Seed-Faith & Growing-Faith). Both were born from one seed. Both

came from faith-<u>filled</u> parents. GOD hates Esau and (Mustard-Seed-Faith), but GOD loves Jacob and (Growing-Faith). Esau & Mustard-Seed-Faith put "little value" on their inheritance, and very little effort into obtaining it. Jacob & Growing-Faith "greatly valued" their inheritance, and put <u>GREAT EFFORT</u> into obtaining it.

ROMANS 9:11&13 generated Rom. 9:14-16. *14 What shall we say then? Is there unrighteousness with God? God forbid. 15 For he saith to Moses, <u>I will have **mercy** on whom I will have **mercy**</u>, and I will have <u>compassion</u> on whom I will have <u>compassion</u>. 16 So then it is not of him that willeth, nor of him that runneth, but of God that sheweth mercy.* Rom. 9:14-16. Question—who has GOD choose to give mercy to? This mercy being, the "continual" forgiveness of our failures as we **"PROGRESS"** toward perfection. Answer—those individuals who used their GOD given power of choice to choose that mercy. Those who have applied the BLOOD of CHRIST to their lives, or should I say, those who have applied GOD'S Word to their lives. Not by are actions of doing the word, but through FAITH in GOD'S ability to fulfill his Word in us. All those actions of following GOD'S Word, such as repentance and water baptism, was to get us to place in which we could believe in GOD'S ability. Question—If the act of doing what the Word of GOD said does not make one righteous, then why do we go through the <u>actions</u> of confessing our sins and being Baptized in Water? Answer—these are spiritual tools <u>GOD choose, that has the</u> power to **pull** our FAITH **"close enough"** <u>in order to make that spiritual connection happen</u>. This is why the first two steps of salvation was placed outside the Holy Tent of Meeting in the Old Testament Tabernacle. It is GOD saying—these first two steps are ***preparing*** you to enter the Tent, where you will actually interact with GOD. And this union, once attained, will be confirmed by that uncontrollable FIRE and RUSH you will experience as the Lord becomes a part of your life.

WHOA BABY WHOA BABY   WHOA

Did you see it? No—I am not referring to the subject matter we have just discussed throughout this chapter. I am referring to one scripture recorded in this chapter. I did not see it either until now. I thought this book was finally finished. Hey! I was on my way downstairs to get a celebratory sandwich when GOD stopped me in my tracks with these words—Come with me, and I will take you inside a part of the cave that you have not been in before. Immediately my heart began to race. I could not wait to jump into this scripture GOD had for me.

The next chapter is the end of the Book. I have only recorded what I saw painted on the walls of the room within that spiritual cave.

The Exact Year Jesus Returns

2034 is the year you'll see Jesus. No, not in the flesh but thru an **unmistakable** "manifestation" of power. When GOD judges **spiritual** and **world Governments** inspired by Satan that comes against Jerusalem. REV. **19**:**12** says, *His eyes were as a flame of fire, and on his head were many crowns; <u>and he had a name written</u>, **<u>that no man knew</u>**, **<u>but he himself</u>**.* Meaning, physically as an individual he will be unidentifiable, but still <u>HE was there</u> "openly displaying" <u>HIS power</u>. And after, further revealing Himself to the world by way of His church over the next 1000-years without the devil's interference. Note! REV. "chapter" **19** means judgement and "verse" **12** or 1+2=**<u>3</u>** which is **<u>GOD</u>** passing judgement. Let us say this in another way. No one will be able to point their finger at "anyone" and say **that is <u>Jesus</u>** but all will point their finger at Jerusalem's deliverance and say **the <u>HAND of GOD</u>** did that.

The Rapture will be at least 1,335 years after (2034) when GOD separates the wheat from the weeds. This event is called "The END of TIMES" when JESUS as an individual will be physically and clearly identifiable.

Matthew 13: 24-30 says, <u>*don't separate* the **weeds** *from the* **wheat** *until harvest*</u>, which is at the end of the world. The victory at Jerusalem in (2034) users in the third ERA, a span of time **<u>without</u>** Satan's interference in mankind's relationship with the Lord.

GOD will be represented in Jerusalem by a multitude of converted Jewish believers teaching the "complete" Gospel they first rejected. These Jewish believers being represented in <u>Judges 16:29-30</u> by Samson **grabbing both pillars** (the **Old** and the **New** Testaments) and bringing the Philistine's <u>temple of "worship"</u> **down** on their heads. Samson represents those converted Jews.

The first ERA is mankind's relationship to GOD thru the Word only the <u>Old Testament</u>. The second ERA is our relationship to GOD thru the Word and Spirit the <u>New Testament</u>. And again, the third ERA is mankind's relationship to GOD thru the Word and Spirit <u>without Satan's interference</u>.

These ERAS being confirmed in <u>JOHN 1:1</u>- **#1**-*In the **beginning** was the Word,* **#2**- and *the Word was **with** GOD,* **#3**-*and the Word was GOD*. **#1**-The Old Testament, **#2**- the New Testament, **#3**- The 1000-year period ending with the RAPTURE, (the end when "JESUS will be "clearly seen" by the entire world" as the One and Only GOD Almighty).

At the start of the 3rd ERA there will be a new and more cooperative attitude "**available**" to the heart of mankind. Spiritual Truth will be "more accessible" throughout the world. Mankind will have no excuse for not connecting spiritually to GOD because <u>Satan will not be there to whisper into the ear of mankind</u>.

Why <u>2034</u>? **1967** is the starting date of the last generation which will be (**67**)-years. Israel won control of **all** Jerusalem in **1967**, something that was not in their possession in <u>1948</u>. That's why GOD acknowledged Israel as becoming a Nation in <u>1967</u> and not <u>1948</u>: 67+1967=**2034**.

Psalm 90:10 says a generation "is at least" <u>70</u>-years. <u>**67**</u>-years is the shortened generation spoken of in MATTHEW 24:22 – *And except those days should be **shortened**, there should no flesh be saved*. Watch this! MATTHEW 24:22 -2+4=**6**, 4+2=**6**, 4+2=**6**. Coincidence; **666**? Satan's judgement will be within this (67-year generation).

(**1948**) is the midnight call to the TEN-VIRGINS in Matthew 25:6. (1+9) =<u>**10**</u> (GOD'S Word) and (4+8) =<u>**12**</u> (Midnight call). By the way, 19+48=<u>**67**</u>. Another coincidence?

Besides GOD, Numbers don't lie! Every scripture has a numbered chapter and verse assigned to it and every Word within that scripture carries that same number. HE talks directly to us by connecting these Words by way of the numbers. This is why the Bible is called **The LIVING Word**. Example – GOD uses two scriptures with identical numbers to show what that last generation will see at the end of **67** years. Matthew **24:34**, *Verily I say unto you.* ***This generation*** *shall not pass, till all these things be fulfilled.* Question, what things? Answer! Luke **24:34a**, *The* **Lord is risen**, *and hath* ***APPEARED***. These are the only two scriptures in the 4 Gospels numbered 24:34. Note! 2+4= (**6**) and 3+4= (**7**). 24:34 can be **67**. Coincidence? You make the call! What generation shall witness the spectacular deliverance of Jerusalem? The **67-year-generation** that begin in **1967**!

2034 is the year you can expect to see Jesus in power only, establishing Jerusalem as the seat of spiritual authority for over the next thousand years.

Why you ask? Because 67+1967=**2034**.

Besides GOD, numbers don't lie. Much information is attached to them. They are GOD'S shorthand. (**6**), represents mankind and the devil's struggle with GOD, (**7**). (**2034**} carries these; (**2**) is the "**two Testaments**", the two witnesses; (**0**) is the completed cycle, **HE** came **HE** left **HE** returned to deliver and protect. (**3**) is Jesus fulfilling this cycle because HE rose from the grave in 3 days. (**4**) confirms the using of "Numbers" because it's (the **fourth** book). Plus, 2034 can be 27 because 20+3+4=**27** which is the number of books in the "**New Testament**." Coincidence?

Also, John said the Bible teaches to look in reverse, or, backwards to gain more understanding. Rev. 1:10a – *I was in the spirit on the Lord's-day and heard* **behind** *me a* **great** **voice**. Using this principal of looking at (**2034**) in reverse, we can see the "**Old Testament**" is represented as well, 30+2+4+**3**=**39**. Coincidence? Not when CLUES total well into the 2-digit numbers and point in the same direction. Number (**3**), **GOD is the BEGINNING and the END** (**3**), (Revelation **21:6**a).

Yes, we used <u>3</u> twice in the equation <u>3</u>0+2+4+<u>**3**</u>=39 because GOD used <u>3</u> twice. Jesus was <u>**33**</u> when crucified; One **<u>3</u>** is the Old and one **<u>3</u>** is the New Testament. GOD used **12** tribes and **12** apostles to bring us HIS Word. This number <u>12</u> can be <u>1+2</u>=**<u>3</u>**. That is why GOD took Christ's life and resurrected Him at age <u>**33**</u>. One (**3**) signals the Old Testament end and one (**3**) the beginning of the New Testament.

Even through <u>7</u> which means a completed work is mentioned more in the Bible; **<u>3</u>** is the most important number because it's "directly" linked to GOD.

<u>**1967**</u> not <u>1948</u> is when GOD acknowledged Israel as becoming a nation because that's the war when they took full control of Jerusalem, the "heart" of Israel

We get **<u>67</u>** years from adding 19+48.

See **<u>1948</u>** as 1+9=**10** mankind's responsibility to fulfill GOD'S **10** Commandments, and 4+8=**12** the **midnight call** given to the **10** virgins in <u>Matthew 25:**6**</u>. Note, 2+5=**7** and then you have (**6**): (**7**) struggling with (**6**), GOD'S midnight call. Coincidence?

You only add numbers, you don't subtract numbers because GOD'S Word comes to us in a positive progression. Nothing to some and some to more, and, from acceptable to perfect.

GOD'S "placement of Psalm" in the Bible verifies <u>1948</u> as being that **67**-year span of time leading up to the last ERA, when Satan is put in prison for "over" a **1000-years**. Psalm is the **19**th book from <u>Genesis</u> and the **48**th book from <u>Revelation</u>; 19+48=**67**. GOD thru NUMBERS brings together the two witnesses (Old and New Testaments) to show us things to come. Another coincidence?

Hey! Sarah died at (127) and Abraham at (175); **48** years between their deaths. Sarah's 127 can be seen in this manner, (**1**) and 2+7= (**9**). Put together side by side and you get (**19**). Now add **19** to **48** and you get **67**. Coincidence?

Abraham's 175 can be seen as (**67**). 1+5=**6**, and **7** which is a complete number in GOD'S eyes. Coincidence?

Read on, because Abraham's 175 will also reveal "the name thru the NUMBERS" who represented the devil, the beast; 1+7+5=**13**.

These 5 key numbers, 127-175-1948-1967-2034 must have a **seven** "openly at play" within the number if they are a part of GOD'S completed work. (12**7**) - (1**7**5) - (19+48=6**7**) - (196**7**) -(20+3+4=2**7**), which by "chance" Equals the 2**7** New Testament books. Change one number and it does not work. Coincidence, you make the call?

GOD who can't lie, said, *no man knows the* **hour or day**; but HE never said **year** because that would be a lie.

GOD gave Israel, in Daniel, the exact year Jesus would first appear, but they "IGNORED" the "NUMBERS".

Revelation **13:18**, *Here is "WISDOM," let him that hath understanding,* "***count***" *the number of the beast. For it is the number of* ***a man***; *"and" his number "is six hundred threescore and six."*

(COUNT) means to take into "consideration" the numbers. Note how the scriptures "suggest the adding of numbers" to get his name.

Revelation **13:18**, (1+3+1+8=**13**) which is Nimrod, the **13th descendent** in the line of Ham who "hated" GOD "more" than all before or after him. He built the **tower of Babel** and wicked cities such as **Nineveh**. Nimrod represents all "**individuals**" **Religions** and **Governments** "influenced" by Satan.

Abraham's age of 175 confirms - (1+5+7=**13**). Plus, 175 can be – (1+5=**6** and **7** GOD'S complete number. Another **67** coincidence?

5:13 and **5:14**-1948 are important "DATES" because at "**MIDNIGHT**" (**5:13**)-**1948** the **mandate** giving England "CONTROL" over Israel **ended**. From that moment on GOD BECAME Israel's defender; no one can pluck that nation from *HIS* hand. The next day on (**5:14**) Israel proclaim themselves a Nation. However, they did not control Jerusalem at that time, which is the HEART of that Nation. This is why **1948** represents the "**MIDNIGHT** CALL" to the TEN VIRGINS in Matthew 25:6. Note, (**5:14**), **5**+1+4=10. (**5**) is wise and the number (**14**) is the (5) foolish because (1) and (4) added together **equals** (**5**) but the (**1**) and (**4**) is **separated**. 1948 is 1+9=**10** (GOD'S call) and 4+8=**12** the (MIDNIGHT hour). This call ended at Israel's **1967** war and started the countdown to that **67**-year generation ending in **2034** when GOD'S might will deliver Israel.

The day (**5:13**) can be **5**+**13**=**18**—Note the **similarity** to Revelation **13:18**. Remember, the other number in that verse which pointed to the devil was **666** which added together equals **18**. Another Coincidence?

The (3) wars of Israel, (1948) (1956) (1967) points to the number **666**. Add the individual numbers in these 3 dates. (1+9+4+8=**22**) — (1+9+5+6="**21**") — (1+9+6+7=**23**). Now add, 22+**21**+23=**66**: Plus, the 1967 war was "LABELED" the **6**-day war: (**666**): Coincidence?

Note the number "(**21**)" and its relationship to **Daniel 10:13**. Note! 10+13= (**23**) and the war in "1967" (1+9+6+7= (**23**), *The Prince of the Kingdom of Persia resisted* me (***twenty-one*** *days)*. Gamal Nasser (who HATED Israel as much as anyone on earth) and led the coalition against Israel, was elected leader of the United Arab Republic in (1956) and reelected in (1965). Both numbers added individually equals (**21**). Note again **Daniel**

10:13! (**10**) is GOD (**13**) Satan: these two numbers added together equals (**23**) The ultimate WAR (**1967**). Coincidence?

1967, (1+9) =**10** & (6+7) =**13**): (**23**) signaled GOD'S judgement of Satan is (67)-years from 1967 which equals **2034**. Coincidence?

Remember, **1-day** can also be a 1000-years. The (**6**-day war) can represent 6000-years of "**recorded**" time of Satan's interference in mankind's affairs.

(6-6-6) is mankind's struggle with GOD (**6**), mankind's struggle with man (**6**), the devil's (**6**-day war) against GOD and mankind. The 3 together is (**666**).

Remember, (**5**) Commandments is man's (**6**) relationship to GOD, (**5**) commandments man's (**6**) relationship to others, and the total sum of the (**10**) Commandments reveals the (**6**-day war): The three together is **666**.

Here's More!

Old Testament predicted Jesus would die at age **33½** and the New Testament confirmed this **33½**: Add these two together and you get (**67**). Coincidence?

Add (33½) to **June** (the **1967** war) and you get the year **2001**. Does September 9:11 ring-a-bell? (33½) added to **2001** equals somewhere in the year (**2034**). I know; just another weird coincidence?

GOD said **to me**, *I hid four numbers of confirmation in Psalm and **only** "chapters" containing* (**14**) *verses will expose them*. (**19**) – "**27**" - (**48**) – "**148**." (**2+7=9**) which means finality. **1948** is the *final* call, or better yet, the Midnight-Call. ("27" + "148") = (**175**), Abraham's age which can be 1+5=**6** and then you have **7** GOD'S complete number, together you have (**67**). Here's what you get with these four numbers. (**1948**) is 19+48= (**67-year-generation**) starting in (**19-67**). The second 67 is Abraham's 175. Remember PSALM placement in the Bible, (**19**) from Genesis and (**48**) from Revelation; 19+48= (**67**). More coincidences?

Why me GOD? I am nobody! Some might call me a "**foolish**" choice to bring into the world information **never heard** before.

GOD'S response! *Why not you, for I choose the **foolish** to confound the wise*, 1st CORINTHIANS 1:27. Note! (**127**), Sarah's age which is a key number in this end time; Plus, 1+2+7= (**10**) of which represents "GOD'S will." **FOOLISH coincidence**; or not, you make the call?

Because of his greatness, I could not produce a legitimate argument. So, like Gideon, I asked HIM for "fleeces" to confirm this calling. I did not want to write this "CHAPTER". It's way "**above**" me. I only recorded what "**I heard** from the Spirit."

HE said, *thru the month and day of the birth of your (3) daughters I have connected you to **June** the 1967 six-day-war and the "spiritual numbers" (6) - (7) - (12) - (10). Birth of oldest **June** (6) youngest **June** (7) and number two 8th month 4th day*. Note! (**67**) and **8+4** = (**12**). Plus, I have (**10**) grandchildren. Coincidence? If you know GOD, ask HIM about this information!

GOD said, *I have also structured many key points within your family unit to help your decision in fulfilling MY call*. I have (**10**) grandkids, **1** girl and **9** boys: Note, (**19**) is judgement. Remember the important day of **5:13** when the mandate giving another nation **control** over Israel **ended** at (**midnight**). Well, this is my wife's birthday. Plus, if you applied a number from the English alphabet to each letter in **Ruth**, my wife's middle name, you get (**67**). Note! One girl and Nine boys, (**19**) and (**67**) from **RUTH**. My middle name is **Paul** which equals (**50**), which means spiritual anointing. See the coincidences I had to deal with. In addition, the three abbreviated letters of my name **G. P. G.** totals (**30**). No! I am not that spiritual, but it is another numbered connection. 30 or (**03**) is part of 2034. Coincidence?

Here's a weird fact. GOD took the (**S**) out of **Saul** and put a (**P**) in its place to make the apostle **Paul**, also, **my middle name.** If you put the (S) which is **19** next to Paul's **50**; you get **1950**, "my birth-year." Plus, I was born in the **3**rd month on the **5**th day, two important BIBLICAL numbers "at work" that you will see later in the number 13**35**. It took all these little fleeces to get me to record all this info which no one has taught as far as I know.

This is my **14**th and final addition of this book. (**TEN-years**) of "listening" to GOD as HE pulled info out of the TWO WITNESSES, the Old and the New Testaments: Matthew **7**:**7** – *Ask*, *Seek*, and *Knock*! Note **7**+**7**=**14**!

I am so slow to see things.

One fleece blew me away.

GOD asked, *what's the final **four** numbers in your phone-number that you have had since **1980**; "40-years" ago*? I answered, **2043**. Then it "dawned" on me. These are the "exact" numbers in the year "(**2034**)." BINGO, the light flashed on. WOW-WOW-WOW! Both numbers can = **27**! Coincidence?

You've been given all this information; the ball is in your court; what are you going to do with it? Will you be inspired or run further away from GOD?

What would you think or write about with all these "COINCIDENCES" to deal with?

God is so BRILLIANT in how HE uses numbers to confirm valuable information to HIS children.

Why 39 books in the Old and 27 the New?

GOD said, (**9**) means **FINALITY** and (**3**) is GOD passing judgement in **THREE-ERAS**: *Old and New Testaments plus the 1000-year after 2034*. **First ERA** ended with Christ's "DEATH" at the **9**th hour. **Second ERA** ends in (**2034**) with Satan's "DEATH" the **9**th hour. Note, the numbers in 2034 added together (2+3+4) equals (**9**). At (2034) GOD will "consider" Satan dead" which is confirmed with his imprisonment. The last ERA and **9**th hour "DEATH is **1335-years** after **2034** which added together is year **3369**, when GOD separates the WHEAT from the Weeds in the Rapture. When GOD considers all mankind and spirits that have rejected HIM "DEAD" and our Solar-System ceases to exist. Remember, *Bible said* **one-day can be 1-year or a 1000**. Note (3369), **3**+6=**9** - **3**+6=**9** and last number is **9**. Note! (39) Old Testament books is **3x9** = (**27**) which is the same number as the (**27**) New Testament books: Two ERAS ending in (**9** finality) warning mankind of the 3rd and final judgement to come. When GOD brings (**9** finality or death) to mankind. Remember, **27** is also **2**+7= (**9**) which number equals **FINALITY**! Coincidence? Don't forget, GOD is preparing an eternal home for HIS children. We will not need this Earth.

The "IMPORTANCE of number (3-369)."

Jesus (**3**) - was put on the cross at the **3**rd hour: hung there for **6** hours: **DEATH** came at the **9**th hour: 3—6—**9** represents 1—2—3 ERAS ending in **FINALITY**, number (**9**). Why, because (3) goes into (3-6-9) 1-2-3. Coincidence?

Note! Any number "connected to the Bible" containing (**33**) is extremely important: 1**33**5 and **33**69 means these are GOD'S NUMBERS where HE has hide vital information.

Daniel **12:12** which can also be (**3:3**) gives us the number **1(33)5**.

What is Time -Times - and ½ Times found in Daniel **7**:25? Note! 2+5=**7**; you have **7:7**; "the Old-testament ERA and the New Testament ERA. Note! **3**+3+6+9 = (**21**), and this number represented Satan. Plus, **21** is the sum of **3x7**. Three SEVENS equals (3 works or 3 ERAS completed) and all ending with (**9**): **FINALITY**. Coincidence?

Time -Times – and ½ Times is (**3**) (**3**) (**3**) added together equals (**9**) **FINALITY**; Three ERAS "JUDGED" by GOD.

The LAST ERA spoken of is "GENESIS **6:3**," *And the Lord said, my spirit "shall not" always strive with man*. Note! **6**+**3** = **9** (**FINALITY**). First two NINES, the two Testaments, equals (**18**) and the third (**9**) is (½) of (**18**). The two Testaments is "linked-together" because both had Satan to contend with. Note! 3x6=**18**, Satan. The third ERA, or (**9**), had no such interference. (½) 0f mankind's problem was removed until GOD "HURLS" Satan to the Earth a few years before the rapture.

Coincidence coming at you again by the numbers! (**39** Old Testament Books) or (**3x9**) = (**27**) = (**27** New Testament Books) and **2+7**= (**9**) plus **2+7**= (**9**) = two ERAS warning mankind of the coming (**3ᴿᴰ ERA**) which ends with (**9**), FINALITY. A clever use of NUMBERS to confirm; what BRILLIANCE!

Again, (3369), (3+6=**9**) (3+6=**9**) which equals two Testaments. The single (**9**) left is the last ERA when *GOD ceases to strive with mankind*: GENESIS **6:3** confirms, (**6**) is two ERAS (time-times) and (**3**) is (½ times): Plus, 6+3=**9** which equals **FINALITY**. Coincidence?

GOD asked me? *What is the **last number** before the end of a (**1000**-year period)?* My answer, **999**. Coincidence?

Thirty-Three in the number 1**33**5 is the first two ERAS which had one thing in common, Satan's interference. Note, in the number (1335) **3**+**3**= (**6**) and the numbers (**1**) (**5**) that is "(**separated**) and (**left**)" added together equals (**6**); 6+6= GOD'S struggle with "mankind" and "Satan" which added total is (12); and 1+2= (**3**) -- GENESIS **6:3** (equals **9**) which is the sum total of **3+3+3**, or (**THREE ERAS**). *HE will not always "strive with man*." The last **3** is ½ **of times** because ½ of the 1335 equation had to be added to the two Threes. ½ of Times is the ERA that had only GOD to deal with. ½ the problem was removed for mankind's benefit. Coincidence? In (**1335**) - number (**1**) is GOD and (**33**) the two Testaments warning the (5 foolish) of the coming catastrophic consequences of rejection.

OUCH! Coincidence kicked me again in the shin! **Revelation** 21:6 (2+1=**3**:6) -- *He is the **beginning** and the **end*** connects by the numbers to **Genesis** 6:3: Both equations equal (9) finality; the basic subject matter of each scripture.

My best FRIEND (GOD) is BRILLIANT in the handling of NUMBERS.

The numbers (1290 **days**) and (1335 **days**) in Daniel 12:11-12 can also represent **years**.

Isaiah 14:12, *How art thou **fallen**, O Lucifer, son of the morning! How art thou **cut down*** *to the ground, which didst weaken the nations.* NOTE the numbers 14:12 can be (5:3) or reversed (**35**) the last two numbers in (13**35**). Old mister Coincidence is kicking my hind end.

Fallen is when GOD "first" placed Satan in the Garden hoping he would repent; but he didn't.

Cut Down is when GOD at the "last" **hurls** Satan for a short time to earth in anger for mankind's "**FINAL**" REJECTION.

In other words: You love him and his ways? You can have him "along with the judgement due him."

Daniel 12:11-12 says from (1290 days) to (1335 days); a total of (**45**-days) which can also be (**years**). Why, because GOD said thru **scriptures** *one day* can also be *a year*.

Wither or not it's **45-days** or **45-years**; you don't want to be around at that time without GOD.

Satan and all his angels will be released **a short time** to wreak havoc on the earth because they know their times up. Though it's the worst time ever on earth, GOD still protects those few believers left.

By the way, **45** can be 4+5= (**9**) which equals **FINALITY**. Come on! How many "coincidences" does it take to generate YOUR interest?

The RAPTURE will be (**19** generations) from (**2034**). Why? Because **70** (a complete generation) goes into 1335 (**19** times) with (**5**) left-over. (**19**) represents judgement and "the left-over (**5**)" the **foolish** who rejected GOD'S offer. DO THE MATH. Coincidence?

GOD wants HIS children to have this additional information at this particular "**juncture**" because many will lose faith when the Rapture doesn't happen in their generation.

People will say, 2nd Peter 3:4, *Where is the "promise" of his coming*. NOTE! **2**ND+ **3** + **4** = (**9**), **finality**? GOD is so clever!

I am NO spiritual-guru. I am 100% disabled Vietnam Vet who's as normal as they come, well, almost? I am no writer. Every time I thought I had finished and issued this book, GOD had me "recall it" and "ADD' in something else" until we reached the end, and I do mean; the END.

Another fleece "**GOD**" structured into my life. I was born (**3**rd-month) (**5**th-day) and have "direct connection" to (**13**), (**3**) daughters and (**10**) grand-children. Look at "my" connection to number (**1335**). A number referring to the END of which I am writing about. Look at **my life numbers** in reverse: (**13**)-(**3**)-(**5**) (**1335**): (**3**) daughters "PLUS" (**10**) grandchildren and I was born 3rd day 5th month, 3+10=**13+3+5** (**1335**). Coincidence? Come on now!

Coincidence coming at you! 1+3+3+5 = (**12**): OR, 13+3+5 = (**21**): BINGO! Two KEY "biblical" numbers!

TRUTH corresponds to fact or reality; **TRUTH** is consistent or in agreement with something else; **TRUTH** is similar and equivalent to something; **TRUTH** is **conscientious** in its "support" of somebody or something!

Are you, like Israel, going to ignore this information? At least **50 coincidences** that corresponds to **TRUTH -TRUTH-TRUTH -TRUTH**? Really!

Then I haft to ask; **who's the "foolish one**?" The one who wrote what he heard or the one who "ignored" what HE or SHE read?

A coincidence you got to love from the most popular scripture in the Bible. PSALM 23:4- *Yea, though I walk through the "**valley**" of the "**shadow**" of "**DEATH**," (I will fear no evil): (for thou art with me): (thy rod and thy staff comfort me).* Note! **Valley** *first ERA,* **Shadow** *second ERA,* **Death** *Third and final ERA.*

NOTE! 23:4, (2+3+4) = (**9**) which equals DEATH (**FINALITY**): Plus, **same** numbers in the year **2034**, Just "include" the **zero**; **HE** came **HE** left **HE** returned.

"Truth" is similar and equivalent to something and conscientious in its support of something. Psalm's numbers **2-3-4** are in the year-**2034** in the same specific order; (2-3-4). Coincidence?

Here is more **TRUTH** that is consistent and in agreement.

JUDGES 16:24-30 tells how GOD through Samson brought DEATH (**FINALITY**) to the Philistines government and religion. NOTE the NUMBERS 16:24-30: 1+6= (**7**) which is a completed work and 24-30 or 2+4+3= (**9**) which number is DEATH, *finality*. Plus, look at the similarity between the year (**2034**) and the start and finish of the (**7**) verses (**24-30**) in Judges chapter 16 which brings us to the "**end**" of the Philistines **false** worship. The "NUMBERS" **are the same**. Coincidence?

<u>Verse 24</u> started the sequence – *And when <u>they saw him</u>, they **praised** their god: for they said, "<u>our god</u>" <u>hath delivered into our hands our enemy</u>, and the destroyer of our country, which slew many of us.* **NOTE their FALSE WORSHIP**.

<u>Verse 30</u> ended the sequence – *And Samson said, let me die with the Philistines. And he bowed himself with all his might; and the house fell upon the lords, and all the people that were therein. So the dead which he slew at his **DEATH** were more than they which he slew in his life.* **FALSE WORSHIP JUDGED**.

<u>Judges 16:24-30</u>, (1+6=**7**) a finished work and **24-30** (2+3+4 =**9**), **DEATH** is the **FINAL** work. Coincidence?

Year **2034** is when Religions and Governments inspired by Satan will be judged.

How many times does the numbers (2-3-4) that totals (**9**) which is connected to <u>death</u> (FINALITY) have to make an appearance before it sparks your curiosity?

Note the (year-**2034**) confirmed in the (last **four**) in my phone-number (**2043**)! Huh, what do you think?

COINCIDENCE? Come on, you don't really believe that! -- DO YOU?

"GOD loves his children" and wants **us** to have a **heads-up** on "what is to come."

Matthew 13:30, *Let both grow together until harvest: and in the time of harvest I will say to the reapers, Gather ye together "**first**" the **tares**, and bind them in bundles to burn them: but **gather** the **wheat** into my barn.*

The **TARES** gathered in bundles to <u>later burn</u> happens in year (**2034**) when GOD imprisons Satan for over one thousand years. The **GATHER** of **WHEAT** into <u>my barn</u> is the 3rd ERA of harvest starting in (**year-2034**) when GOD'S Word will not be distorted by Satan. There are (**3**) ERAS of Harvest, (Time-Times) — (1/2 Times), (Old Testament-New Testament) — (1000 "plus" years after).

Matthew Chapter **13**:1-58 is about Satan's interference. Note! **13**+1+5+8=**27** and 2+7=**9 death (finality)**. Coincidence? Or GOD just being HIS Old "clever" SELF. The 58th verse can also be 5+8=**13**. Satan's number "**begins** and **ends**" this chapter. Scriptures that clearly speaks of Satan's interference being removed for a time confirmed by the number (**27**). The (**7** verse) parable (**24—30**) within (chapter **13**) clearly reveals this removal. Note! The "**first** and **last**" numbers in the (**7**) verse parables (**24—30**) in JUDGES and MATTHEW are the same numbers in the year (**2034**). Coincidence? This year (**2034**) is confirmed in **(1) VERSE**, Matthew **24:30**, *And then shall appear the sign of the Son of man in heaven: and then shall the tribes mourn, and shall see the Son of man coming in the **clouds** of heaven with power and great glory*. The power and glory will be easily identifiable as GOD; but because of the "covering clouds" the person of Jesus will not be identifiable until the rapture at the last day near (3369). The nations (*or tribes*) will mourn because their "errant ways" of worshipping GOD will be exposed in year (**2034**).

This equation GOD saved for the END (blew me away).

Matthew **24:34** — (2+4:3+4) is (6:7) - when added equals (**13**). This number (**13**) placed in front of the very "NEXT" **verse** 24:(**35**) *Heaven and earth* "**shall pass away**" but *my words shall never pass away* "**BECOMES**" (**1335**). Coincidence, or GOD being **very creative**? *Heaven* is spirits and *earth* mankind that rejected GOD; *my words* is GOD'S children; we are children of the Word. 1335+2034 equals (**year 3369**) when GOD separates the WHEAT from the Weeds. The approximate time the "Lord fulfills" *my spirit* "**shall not**" always "**strive**" *with man* **GENESIS 6:3**, 6+3=**9** which number equals **FINALITY**. Note! Wheat and Weeds are the Earth's **natural** fruit which is (**mankind**). Year (**2034**) is the beginning of the 3rd and last ERA. Note the "NUMBERS" in the "equation" **Genesis 6+3 = 9** is the "SAME NUMBERS" in "YEAR" (**3369**) and what JESUS experienced on the CROSS (**3 – 6 – 9**): Coincidence?

Look at the numbers (3) (12) (21).

(3) or 12 which is 1+2=**3** is ONE-GOD struggling with TWO opponents, the spiritual and the natural 1st Corinthians 15:44b. (**12 tribes** 1+2=**3**) and (**12 apostles** 1+2=**3**) brought us GOD'S Word (**Old &New** Testaments). (21) represents this (2) front battle migrating into a (1) front battle. This is the 3rd ERA starting in (**year 2034**) when the TARES in Matthew 13:30 will be bundled up for over 1000-years to burn latter; fallen angels will not be able to interfere. It will be one-on-one. Note! The (2) migrates to (1) in the number 21. (2) is (**Time-Times**) and (1) is (½ **Times**) spoken of in Daniel 7:25: The (3) ERAS GOD **gathers wheat**.

The Prince of the Kingdom of Persia resisted me 21 days, Daniel **10:13**; GOD (10) at "**war**" with Satan (13); when added together = (23) the 1967 war (1+9+6+7) the FINAL CALL of the MIDNIGHT HOUR. **Judgement** of RELIGIONS and GOVERNMENTS inspired by Satan have been cast from (**1967**) and will arrive in (**2034**). Gamal Nasser "led" the nations that was a part of the old Persian Empire against Israel in (**two WARS**), (1956 & 1967). Gamal represents Prince (Satan) who **resisted** GOD (**21** days) in Daniel 10:13 because he was elected leader of the UNITED-ARAB-REPUBLIC in **1956** and **1965**. Both numbers added individually equals (**21**), the number of the Prince of Persia. The (**two WARS**) he led in 1956 and 1967 represents "TWO ERAS" of **Satan's** INTERFERENCE (**time-times**) in **DANIEL 7:25**. The (½ times) in Daniel starts around the year (**2034**) and ends (**1335**) years later. Gamal died at age (52); **5+2=7**, a number representing the judgement of GOD; an ERA completed. Coincidence?

An even stranger "coincidence" you get when looking in reverse at equation **5+2=7** is, you get **Daniel 7:25.** Come on now! You got to be kidding me!

Another "eerie" coincidence connected to the "**numbers**" in **year** (2)(0)(3)(4): (2+3=**5**) (2+4=**6**), Placed **Side** by **Side** you get **56** or reversed **65**. Gamal Nasser who represented Satan and led the Arabs in TWO WARS against Israel was elected and reelected LEADER of the UNITED Arab Republic in 19**56** and 19**65**: Both numbers added individually equals (**21**): Let us give another WHO-RAH to MR. Coincidence!

Gamal Abdul Nasser who represented Satan DIED **9**-2**9**-70. His DEATH was announced by vice president Anwar Sadat at (1 minute before **MIDNIGHT**), and he was **declared** to be **more "IMMORTAL"** than **all words**. We know what words they were talking about, (Bible Words). Note the **two NINES** in his DEATH. The END of Two ERAS of Satan's interference. YAWSERS, it's MR. COINCIDENCE again!

Another BIG coincidence jumping on your back!

Gamal's three abbreviated letters of his name (G.A.N. 7+1+14=**22**) which equals the 1948 war (1+9+4+8=**22** the midnight call). He was only a soldier in the 1948 war and became a **hero** when his small group he led **held the Israelites "at bay"** for 2 months. It was Egypt's only success in that war. 1948 = **22** and G.A.N. = **22**. Coincidence. He is **CONNECTED** to all THREE wars (1948-1956-1967). Remember, "he led" **TWO** wars.

Is your vehicle "full" of coincidences? If so, exchange them for one word; **TRUTH**! It will lighten your load!

The next paragraph starting with September 9:11 which date is first mention in the previous chapter, titled, (Now You're Ready to Solve the Confusion), is what inspired me to holler at the "end" of that chapter: WHOA BABY WHOA BABY WHOA and to ask: **Did you see it**? It's what jumped-started my END of TIMES study.

September **9-11** referenced in Revelation **9:11** is HALFWAY from June (1967) to year (2034). These "TWO" names **Abaddon** and **Apollyon** found together side by side in this one and only verse means destruction and represents the twin towers brought down on **9:11**. OUCH, another "KICK" in the "Butt" by mister coincidence!

Don't be scared of **2034** because afterwards it's going be a great time to live in. There will be more cooperation between all mankind than ever before because Isaiah 11:9b said, *Earth will be "__FULL__ of the knowledge of the Lord."* No Satan to cause additional problems for over 1000 years.

I don't think it wise to pass this information off as "**foolishness**" because the evidence is compelling. *But the **natural man** <u>receives not the things of the</u> <u>Spirit of God</u>: for they are **FOOLISNESS** unto him: neither can he know them, because they are <u>spiritually discerned</u>*, 1st Corinthians 2:14.

Many things in the Bible are easily understood by simple deduction: Meaning, knowledge of word definitions customs of the day attitude and history of the individual or country in question. But many trails of thought must be opened by spiritual influence such as GOD PERSONALLY SPEAKING OR POINTING OUT SOME DETAIL IN THE "MIND" OF THE "BELIEVER". **1ST Corinthians 2:9-10** said this about the natural man: <u>*Eye hath not seen nor Ear heard*</u>: *but <u>God hath **revealed** them unto us by His spirit</u>*. **1st Kings 19:9** said GOD whispered these WORDS in the mind of Elijah when fleeing for his life from Jezebel; <u>*WHAT DOEST thou HERE Elijah*</u>. By the way, look at the two NINES in 1st Kings 1**9:9** and ponder over these equations. <u>1</u>+<u>9</u>=**10** and <u>1</u>+<u>9</u>=**10** GOD'S Word (Old and New Testaments). GOD IS NUMBER (1) bringing the END (**finality** number **9**) to Elijah's situation.

GOD'S Word is the **FIRST** and "**NUMBERS**" is the second most important commodity in updating both spiritual and natural positions. GOD set the "UNIVERSE" to operate by the Numbers. They give me my location not only in the Universe but on Earth - (3rd planet from the sun and you will find me at latitude **36 degrees north** and longitude **95 south**): They help in our food preparation (**1** cup sugar **2** sticks of butter **3** cups of flour): They regulate our purchases (socks 10 dollars shirt 50 dollars jeans 100 dollars): They update our children's progress (my son took **1** step yesterday **2** steps today and I bet **3** steps tomorrow). Question? Why is it hard to accept GOD using numbers to reveal or CONFIRM the hidden?

This is why quiet meditation of scriptures is "extremely" important accompanied by 100% faith in GOD Giving **you** the answer: *Or if he ask a fish, will he give him a serpent,* **Matthew 7:10**. Without this faith you'll be stuck in the "corridor" of other men's influence and opinions and unable to go into; *My thoughts not yours,* **Isaiah 55:8a**. Through we our limited beings, some of our thoughts fall in line with GOD. HE is infinitely Intelligent, thus HIS thoughts infinitely higher. Human thought has a beginning. Yet, GOD is the **beginning** and the **end**. Like where HE used the **first** and **last** of **SEVEN** verses **24—30** in the 16th and 13th chapters of Judges and Matthew to CONFIRM the year (2034). Bottom line, GOD needs space and time in our lives to insert thoughts in order to reveal the hidden. He confirms information through the numbers attached to the WORD.

Do **You** want to go where others "have not" gone before? Then **You** connect "spiritually" with GOD. Do **You** want "delightful" and personal conversations with the LORD? -- **You** can! ----- **You** do know this don't **You**?

YOU need not that any man "teach" YOU, 1ST **John 2:27b**. This does not mean **You** will not learn from others. It simply means the SPIRIT of GOD will put **You** within ear-shot of beneficial information to further **Your** relationship with HIM, and HE will use this information to reveal the hidden during quiet meditation.

Example of a **private conversation** (with a-touch of **humor**) between myself and GOD. HE said, *I AM going to give you personalized confirmation in PSALM of the three-ERAS that only you can appreciate*. God said, *add the numbers in the alphabet that apply to you and your wife's middle name of Paul and Ruth*. The total sum of 50+67=**117**. GOD asked, *what is the "SHORTEST chapter in the Bible and what does it say*. PSALM 117:1-2, *"Praise" the Lord all ye nations: "Praise" him all ye people.*

2ND - For his merciful kindness is great toward us: and the truth of the Lord endureth forever, "Praise" ye the Lord. The **TWO Praises** in verse one is TWO ERAS (**time-times**) and the **SINGLE Praise** in verse two is the third ERA. Plus, chapter 117 added 1+1+7=**9**, **death** (finality). Verses (1) and (2) added equals (**3**). This chapter and two verses gave us the NUMBERS (**9**) and (**3**). Check this out, (**39**) is (**3**) ERAS THAT GOD brings (**9** FINALITY). I have got a word to give you; ***BIG DADDY*** COINCIDENCE!

The funny part of our conversation is where GOD asked, *what is the "SHORTEST" chapter*. This hinted toward my **4**-foot **11**-inch wife whose number is (**67**), the "SHORTEST" in the family and the "SHORTEST" person I know. Our grandchildren tease their GRANDMOTHER about her shortness. She is the most thoughtful respected and loved one among family and friends; but she's the "SHORTEST."

Note in Psalm 117:1, **nations** comes first and (**all**) **people** comes second. (**Nations** judged in **2034**) and ("**all**" **People** judged **1335** years later).

See how GOD used the word "SHORTEST" to get **MY** attention.

Quiet meditation of the Word is the corridor to a private conversation with GOD.

Bottom line: hold the Word of GOD in that HEAD of yours and then.

SHUT-UP -- WATCH -- LISTEN!

(Subjects to consider)!

Daniel's 70 weeks has been completed: GOD waited on a certain number of Jews to fully accept both gospels: That number was completed in year **1967**, the **end** of the **midnight call**. From this date JUDGEMENT of RELIONS and GOVERNMENTS inspired by Satan was sent forth and will arrive in (**2034**).

Paul completed Jesus missing 3½ years ministry. Remember the **three-plus- years** in Arabia (Galatians 1:18) when he was taught by the Lord. God said he is a chosen vessel and is responsible for (**14**) books. P.S. **2x7** = 14 which hints toward the Old and NEW Testaments (two completed works).

Two witnesses in Revelation slain in the streets of Jerusalem is John the Baptist and Jesus Christ whose DEATHS came very close together. The resurrection of those two witnesses is Jesus Christ coming back to life. HE is both Testaments, (BOTH WITNESSES).

The **MARK of the BEAST** is what <u>**ALL mankind**</u> is born with that must be removed: It is not the implanting of numbers in the hands and forehead: It is the "works of our hands" and "thoughts coming from that forehead" <u>that has to be changed</u>.

Quickly, let us talk about Apostle Paul representing those 3½ years of Jesus Christ's ministry. GOD linked Paul and Samson together for a reason. **Both** thought they were doing GOD'S will by killing the unbelievers. **Both** lost their SIGHT during their ministries. **Both** <u>took in hand</u> the two Testaments and exposed false worship; the **two PILLARS** Samson put his hands on and the <u>14</u> books Paul was responsible for represented the two Testaments.

But the question remains, what proof comes from linking Samson and Paul together confirms those 3½-years? <u>Well, the proof is in the **numbers**</u>.

Christ ministry started at age (**30**) and should have lasted (**7**) years but it was cut in-half according to (**Daniel 9:27**). Jesus should have been (**37**) when he ascended up to heaven. P.S. (**9**:2+7 = **9**): TWO ERAS; (number **27** can be associated with both Testaments), 39 Old Testament books or 3x9= 27 = 27 New Testament books. Coincidence?

Question is; can the number (**37**) be found as a part of the Samson story, because <u>Samson</u> "**Jesus**" and <u>Paul</u> used the two pillars (Old and New Testaments) to bring down false worship? "Jesus" being both. Note "Jesus" positioned between Samson and Paul; the **LINK** between the Old and New Testaments.

Judges 16:30 says Samson brought the house down after his hands touched those two pillars. Note! (1+6=**7**) and (**7**+**30**) = (**37**). Numbers don't lie!

NUMBERS ARE ATTACHED to EVERY WORD IN THE BIBLE *for a reason*.

I am going to leave you with this last coincidence which actually was the very **first**. It came the very next day after I asked GOD about this year (**2034**) he introduced me to. My middle daughter who whose birthday 8th month 4th day represented the MIDNIGHT-CALL has a complicated schedule with her three children. She posted on Face-Book; I don't know when I will ever be able to take a day to sit down and relax; I guess not until (**2034**). P.S. - I did not mention this date to anyone including my wife until after I read her post on Face-Book!

COINCIDENCE!

I hope this book blesses you.

THE END

Coming shortly? Wow! TIME flies!

Hey! Sing with me—oh happy day—oh happy day—oh happy day.

BECAUSE

The end is just the beginning for GOD'S redeemed.

Tables and Drawings

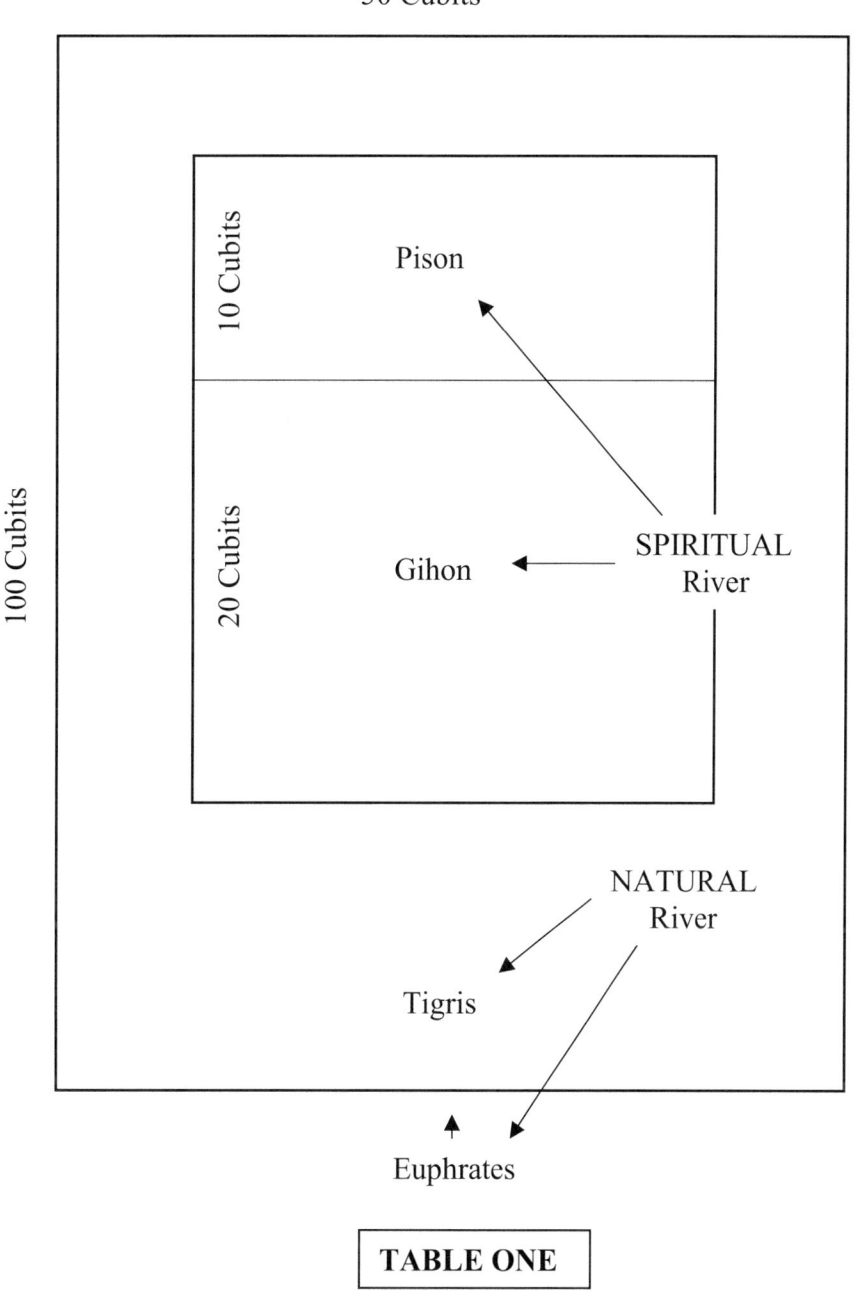

50 Cubits

100 Cubits

10 Cubits

20 Cubits

Pison

Gihon ← SPIRITUAL River

NATURAL River

Tigris

Euphrates

TABLE ONE

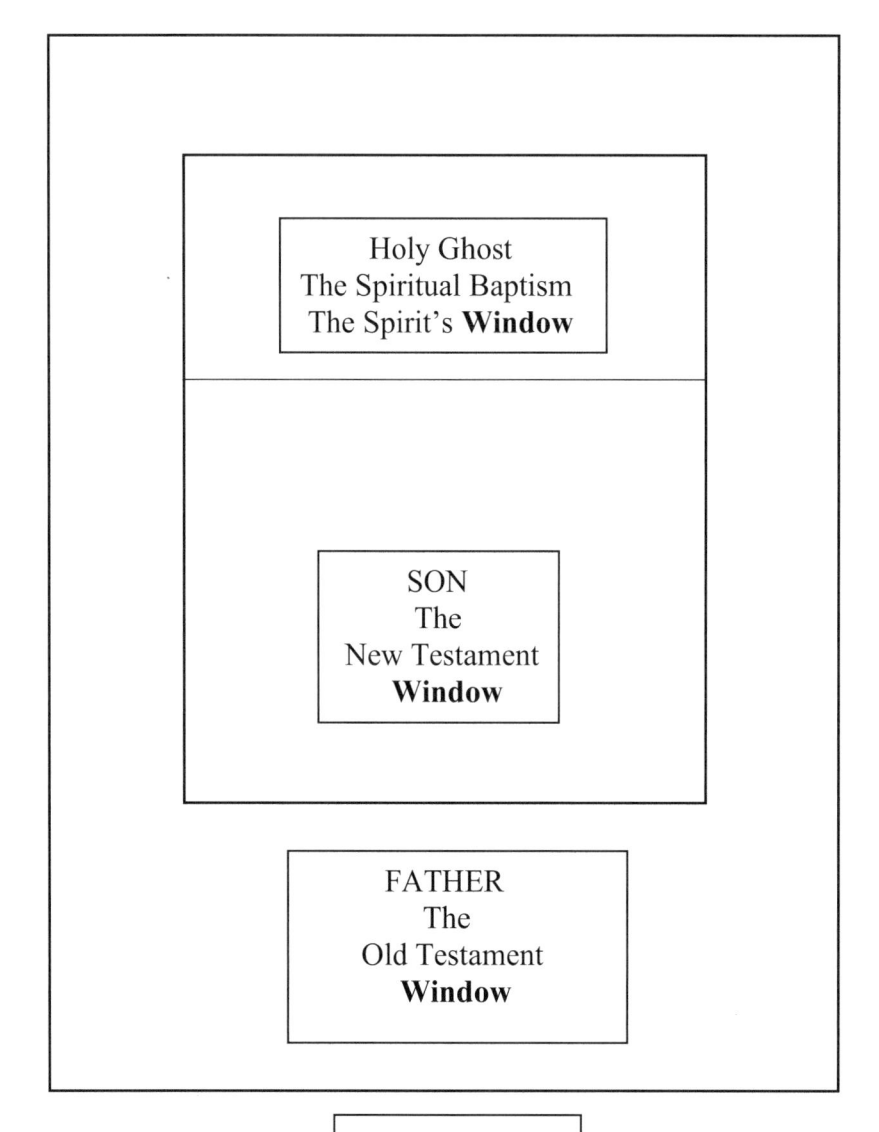

```
┌─────────────────────────────────────┐
│                                     │
│      ┌───────────────────────┐      │
│      │  ┌─────────────────┐  │      │
│      │  │   Holy Ghost    │  │      │
│      │  │ The Spiritual Baptism │ │      │
│      │  │ The Spirit's **Window** │ │      │
│      │  └─────────────────┘  │      │
│      │                       │      │
│      │                       │      │
│      │   ┌─────────────┐     │      │
│      │   │    SON      │     │      │
│      │   │    The      │     │      │
│      │   │ New Testament│    │      │
│      │   │  **Window**  │    │      │
│      │   └─────────────┘     │      │
│      └───────────────────────┘      │
│                                     │
│       ┌───────────────────┐         │
│       │     FATHER        │         │
│       │      The          │         │
│       │  Old Testament    │         │
│       │    **Window**     │         │
│       └───────────────────┘         │
│                                     │
└─────────────────────────────────────┘

                **TABLE TWO**
```

NUMBERS

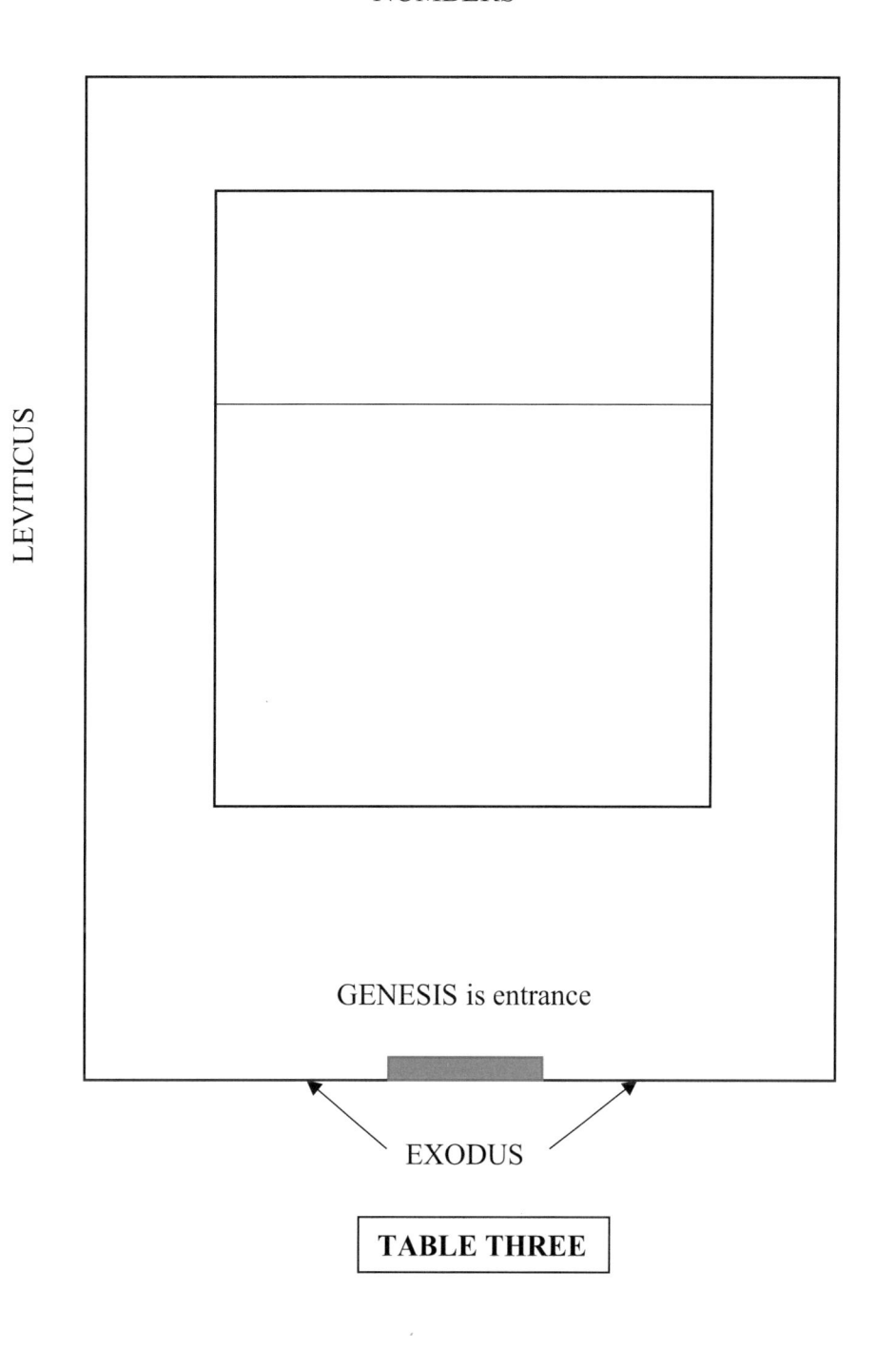

LEVITICUS

DEUTERONOMY

GENESIS is entrance

EXODUS

TABLE THREE

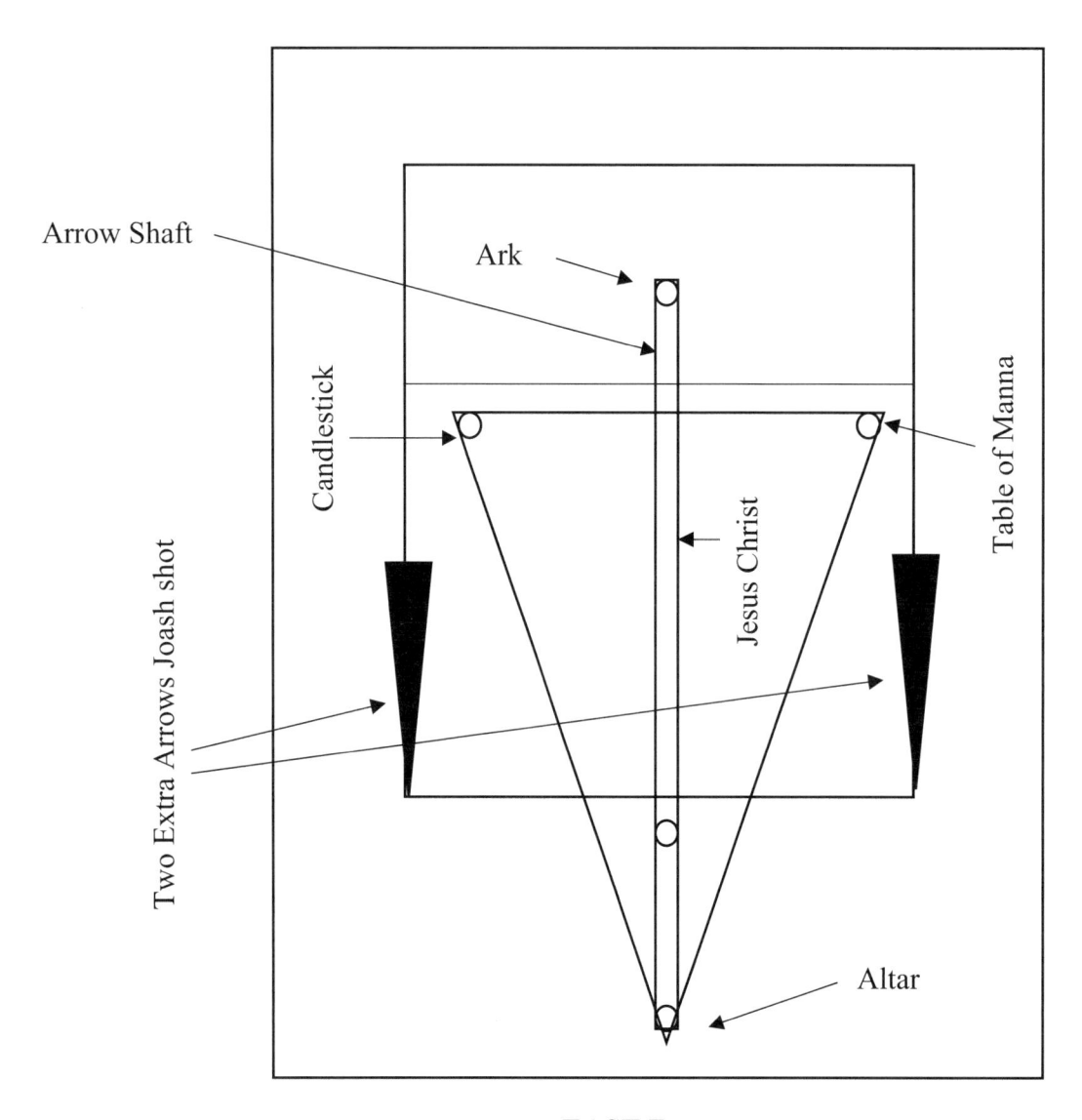

TABLE FOUR

We look through the Spirit's Window

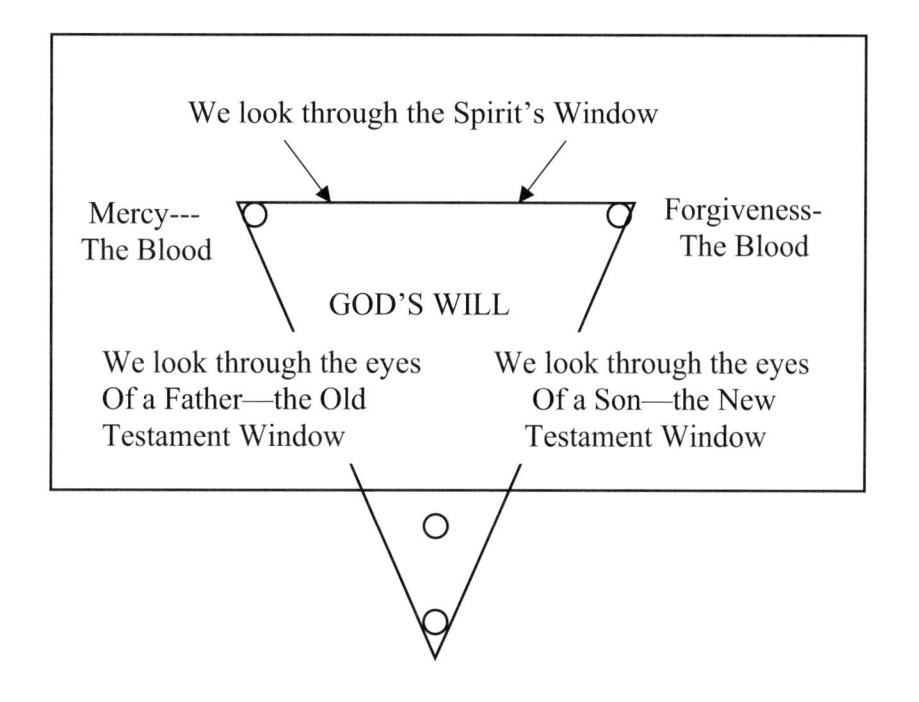

Mercy---
The Blood

Forgiveness-
The Blood

GOD'S WILL

We look through the eyes
Of a Father—the Old
Testament Window

We look through the eyes
Of a Son—the New
Testament Window

TABLE FIVE

GOD'S Spiritual Baptism

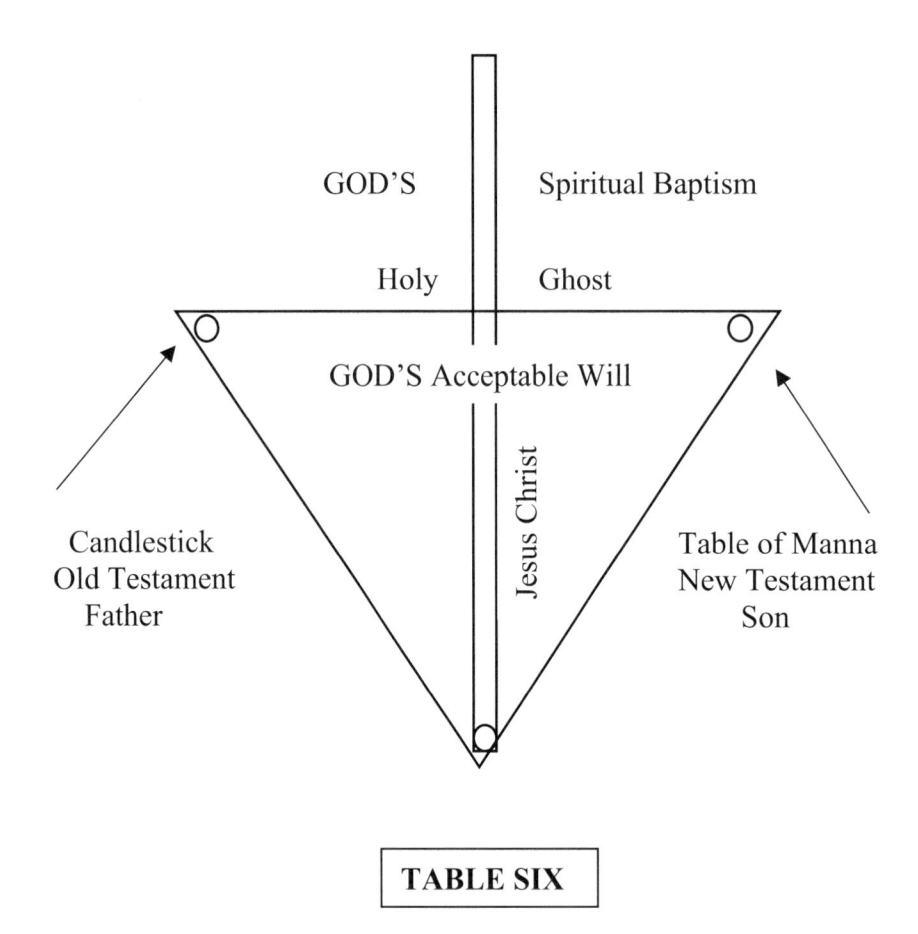

Holy Ghost

GOD'S Acceptable Will

Candlestick
Old Testament
Father

Jesus Christ

Table of Manna
New Testament
Son

TABLE SIX

Deeper Still and In Between the Lines · 333

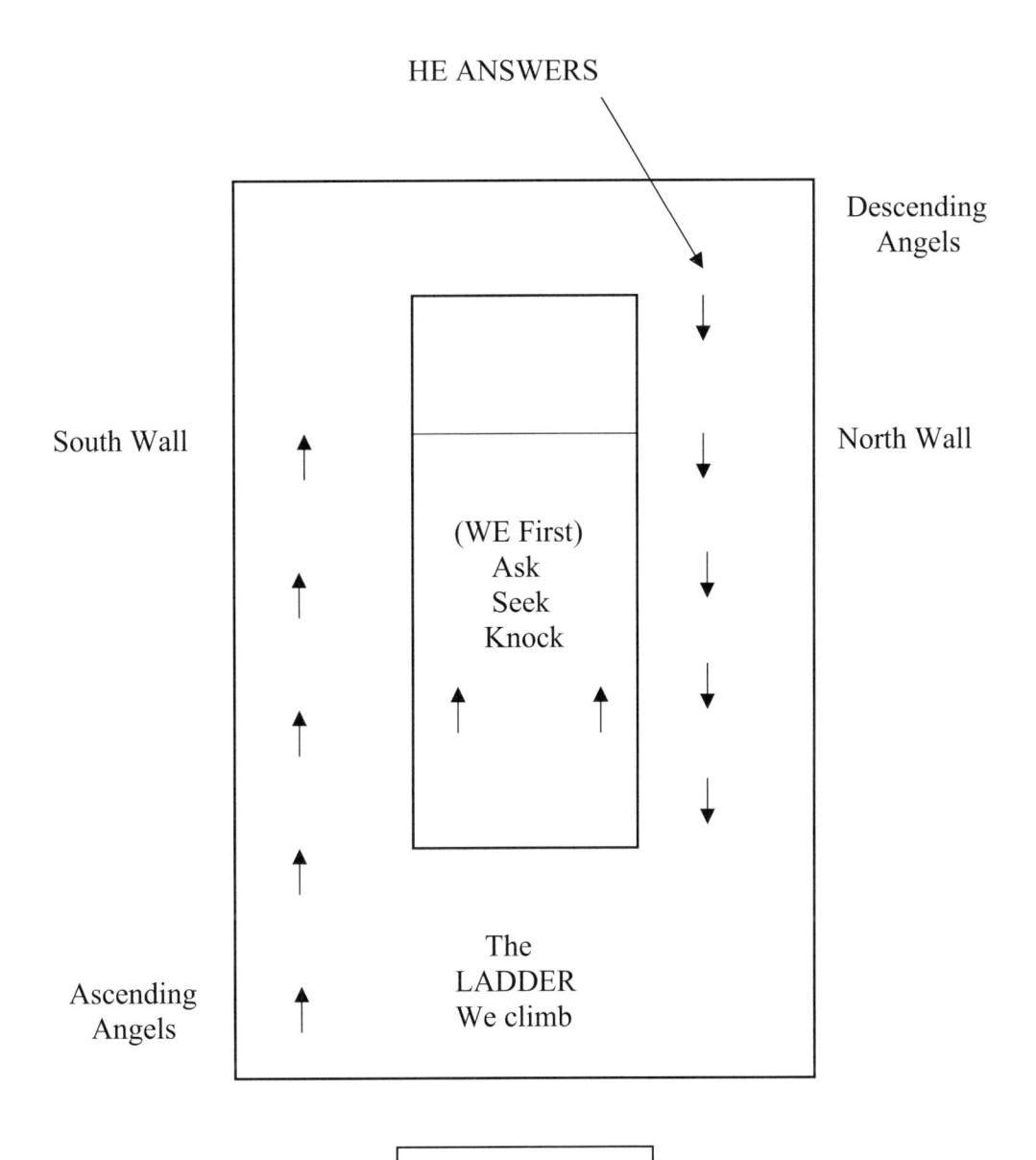

HE ANSWERS

Descending Angels

South Wall

North Wall

(WE First)
Ask
Seek
Knock

The
LADDER
We climb

Ascending
Angels

TABLE SEVEN

Luke

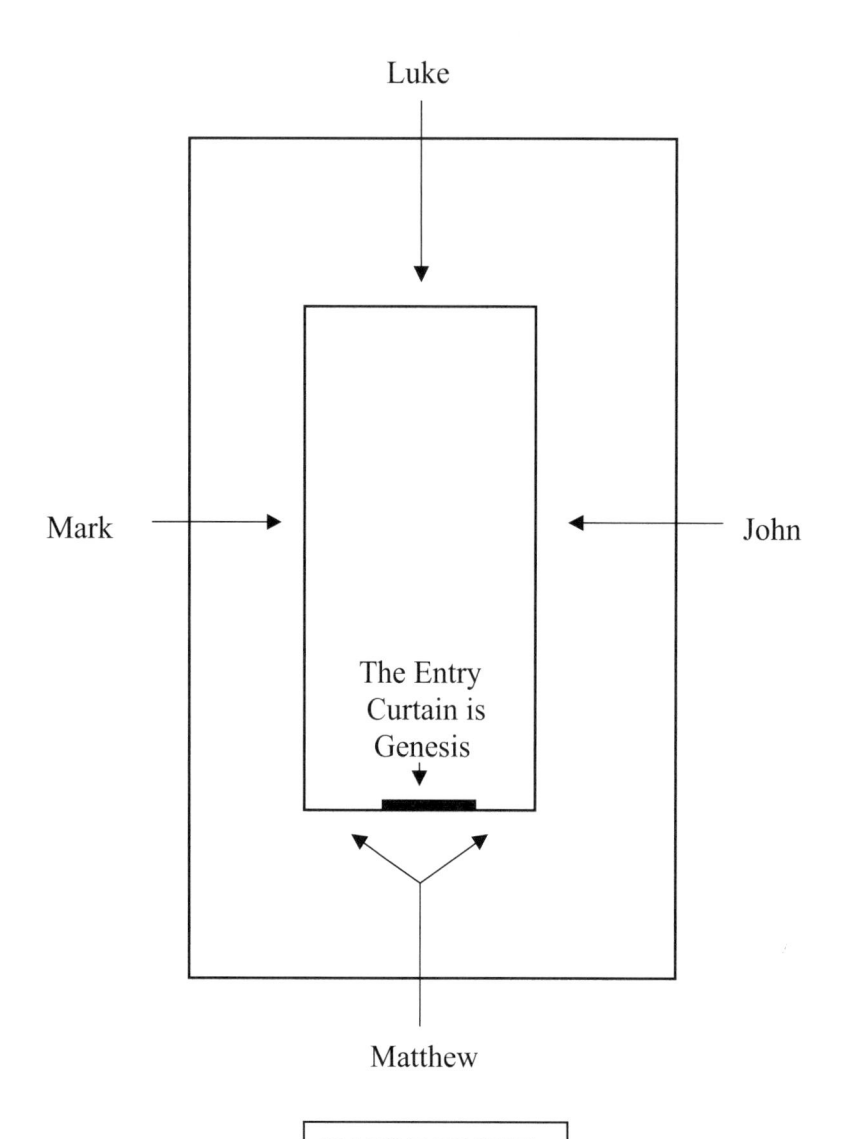

Mark →   ← John

The Entry
Curtain is
Genesis

Matthew

TABLE EIGHT

Made in the USA
Columbia, SC
06 February 2024